SECRET INGREDIENTS

SECRET INGREDIENTS
THE BRAVE NEW WORLD OF INDUSTRIAL FARMING

STUART LAIDLAW

M&S

National Library of Canada Cataloguing in Publication

Laidlaw, Stuart
 Secret ingredients : the brave new world of industrial farming / Stuart
Laidlaw.

Includes index.
ISBN 0-7710-4595-6

 1. Farm corporations – Canada. 2. Livestock factories – Canada. I. Title.

HD1785.L33 2003   338.1'0971   C2002-905905-4

We acknowledge the financial support of the Government of Canada
through the Book Publishing Industry Development Program and that
of the Government of Ontario through the Ontario Media Development
Corporation's Ontario Book Initiative. We further acknowledge the support
of the Canada Council for the Arts and the Ontario Arts Council for our
publishing program.

Typeset in Janson by M&S, Toronto
Printed and bound in Canada

McClelland & Stewart Ltd.
The Canadian Publishers
481 University Avenue
Toronto, Ontario
M5G 2E9
www.mcclelland.com

1 2 3 4 5   07 06 05 04 03

Eating is an agricultural act.

– Wendell Berry

For Fiona, Maggie, and Noah

CONTENTS

ACKNOWLEDGEMENTS

The first people who need to be acknowledged are my family: my wife, Fiona, and our children, Maggie and Noah. These are the people I share meals with every day, and who have had to eat some meals without me as I worked on this book, or have had to endure lectures from me on what we were eating or other aspects of this book when we did sit down together. My meals with them, my enjoyment of them, and my hope for more, fill every page of this book in one way or other. Without their support and belief in me, this book would not have been possible.

My brother, Blair, deserves some credit, too. From an early age, he taught me to be unafraid of thinking differently from others, and to enjoy food. Like our mother, he helped me to realize that the best food is simple food. He also read an early version of this book, which helped a great deal.

At the *Toronto Star*, there are many people to acknowledge, beginning with publisher John Honderich, who encouraged business editor Ken Kidd to let me pursue a summer-long project on food in Canada. The research for that project fed this book. When it came time to write the book, I moved to the editorial board of the paper, where the support and indulgence of Carol Goar, one of the best editors I've ever had, was invaluable. Co-workers who have written books, including Tom Walkom, Bill Schiller, Scott Simmie, Dan Smith, and Geoff Pevere, offered their unrestricted and welcome advice on getting through the process. Dan and Tom also read early versions of the book. Other co-workers such as Sue Pigg and Dana Flavelle helped by listening politely whenever I went off on a tangent about some aspect of the book that might or might not ever make it to the page. Their indulgence, like Carol's, was noticed and appreciated.

From the beginning, Dean Cooke, my agent, and Dinah Forbes, my editor, have believed strongly in the possibilities of the book's subject matter and my ability to write about it.

Food has been a hot topic lately for writers. Each effort to capture the debate in newspapers, magazines, or books enlightens the next. I appreciate the efforts of those before me who have helped inform this book – they are listed in the bibliography – and hope this book can help some future author in the same way.

Finally, I must acknowledge the contribution of the hundreds of farmers I have met over the years, though only a handful appear in this book by name. Rest assured, they are all here. They have all – even those I did not agree with – informed my understanding of Canada's food system and strengthened my belief in Canada's rural roots. I feel privileged as a reporter to have had the chance to meet them and tell their stories. They were under no obligation to talk to me, and yet they did.

Some hae meat and canna eat,
and some wad eat that want it,
but we hae meat and we can eat,
and sae the Lord be thankit.

"The Selkirk Grace"
Robbie Burns

THE NIGHT THE COWS ESCAPED

I grew up in the last house on the last street in Kingston, Ontario. In front of our suburban bungalow lay one of the oldest cities in Canada. Behind lay farm fields where cows and horses roamed. There were also ponds and swamps and train tracks – all irresistible temptations to the children in the neighbourhood. We spent our summers exploring those fields and our winters on the frozen ponds and swamps. When we were done, we returned to our homes, secure in the knowledge that the animals remained behind the fences.

One night, all that changed. A call went through the neighbourhood: the cows had escaped. The fences were not in good shape. One had come down at some point near the road and a cow had ventured through in search of fresh grass. Then another. Then another. Being herd animals, they all walked through eventually and ended up wandering our neighbourhood. Every kid on the block was out looking for them. We hopped backyard fences as we had the farm fences. We were, every one of us, excited beyond imagination.

And just a little scared. The farm had come into the city. We weren't quite sure what we were going to do if we found a cow. We had seen them many times. Chased them, even. But that was in the fields, where the cows were supposed to be. These cows were on our turf, in our streets. We never found the cows, and I'm not even sure they ever really escaped. The whole thing could have been started by an older brother trying to be funny.

But the excitement of that night, the search, and the uneasiness of us kids at the thought of farm animals strolling on our side of the fence were real. I've thought about that night several times in writing this book. The realities of farm life rarely reach those of us who live in cities. We have been cut off from the places where our food is grown and know little about what's involved in keeping us fed and healthy. Most movies, books, and television shows portray only the stereotype of the family farm, with chickens in the yard, pigs in the mud, and cows in the fields. In fact, such farms rarely exist today, and farming practices have changed drastically since city people stopped paying attention.

With this book, I hope to bring the farmers and their struggles to the attention of urban Canadians. I will do that by serving up a simple meal of chicken, french fries, mixed vegetables, a slice of bread, and a glass of milk and using each of these ingredients as a conduit to discuss an aspect of how modern farming delivers food to our tables.

The meal we'll use as our map through this journey is one of many I've shared with farmers from across Canada over the years. I chose this particular meal, though, for two reasons. First, I had this meal on a trip through New York State and Pennsylvania in March of 2000 when I was there with a number of Ontario dairy farmers. We were there to look at what dairy farming was like in the United States, where farmers do not have a milk marketing board looking out for their interests. What we found were farms forty-six times larger than is typical in Canada, with huge sewage lagoons behind the barns and trailers full of poor Mexican migrant workers. One farm even had its own rabbi to certify that the eggs were kosher. The trip left the farmers I went with worried about what the future might hold for them.

I could just as easily have picked a meal I shared with John Lugtigheid, a vegetable farmer in Ontario, as we discussed free trade and contract farming, or the breakfast Nettie Godenir cooked as her husband, George, and I discussed farm subsidies. Or it could have been the lunch I shared with the Pfenning family and their hired hands in the farmhouse kitchen as we talked about the fast growth of the organic food sector and the challenges that brought. But as the Canadian food industry is, as ever, following the lead set by the United States, it seemed appropriate to pick a meal eaten in the United States with Canadian farmers on a wary journey to look at what they feared would be their future.

It is all too easy to criticize this or that aspect of a food system that has brought us cheap and plentiful food. Canadians are healthier today than any society that has come before, and the ready availability of affordable food has a lot to do with that. This is why critics are often dismissed by the food industry as spoiled brats holding up progress that might help feed the world's hungry. It is worth taking a look, then, at why 800 million people around the world go hungry, and why despite two World Food summits in five years, their situation isn't getting any better. Hunger is used to justify all the innovations that critics find distasteful about modern agriculture, but will the solutions being offered by the industrial food economy really help?

Many people and competing issues and priorities brought me that meal I shared with the Ontario dairy farmers, the same issues and priorities that bring you your dinner each night. My hope is that, after reading this book, you will look down at your plate and think about where everything came from, and what had to happen to bring it to you.

The American writer Wendell Berry says that "eating is an agricultural act." That is his answer whenever he's asked what city people could do to help preserve rural communities and ensure a better food supply. The act of eating a meal, he is saying, is one stage in a long process of food production. But it is not the last stage, as one might think. By choosing to eat certain things, we are not at the end of the agricultural process, but at the beginning. It is our demand for food that sets the process in motion. The secret ingredients in this book, then, are of our own making – added over the years by companies claiming they were just meeting consumer demand. As consumers, we have a responsibility to know what is being done in our name. This book is part of finding that out.

Peter Stent's veterinary bills for Cow 133

"He is a proud farmer is Peter. He likes to see his cattle looking good. Indeed, they do look good. He is not a greedy farmer. He likes to make a good income, but he is not out to maximize every penny."

David Bee,
British veterinarian

CHAPTER ONE

PITSHAM FARM SYNDROME

Three days before Christmas 1984, British veterinarian David Bee got a call at his practice in Petersfield, Hampshire. Peter Stent, owner of Pitsham Farm near Midhurst in West Sussex, needed a hand. One of his three hundred dairy cattle had been acting strangely, and Stent needed Bee to take a look at her. The cow, known only as Cow 133, had been losing weight, Stent said. Her back was arched and she was staggering about the field. Bee had been to Pitsham farm many times during his nine years of practice. He knew Stent was a good farmer, who took care of his animals and never hesitated to call Bee if there was a problem. "He is a proud farmer is Peter," Bee later told a government inquiry. "He likes to see his cattle looking good. Indeed, they do look good. He is not a greedy farmer. He likes to make a good income, but he is not out to maximize every penny."

Neither man, however, had ever seen anything like what was afflicting Cow 133. Her temperament had changed, Stent said. Bee had no idea what the problem was and gave the cow a shot of antibiotics for a suspected kidney infection – thinking that perhaps toxins had got into the feed. It didn't work. In the following days, she grew worse, developing head tremors and increasing uncoordination – symptoms that would soon become familiar to farmers and consumers, first in Britain and then around the world. Bee returned to the farm six days later, after the Christmas holiday, and again four days into the New Year. The cow just kept getting worse. Her fourth stomach, the abomasum, had become displaced. Bee treated her for that, made note of the tremors and lack of coordination, and consulted veterinarians from the Ministry of Agriculture to figure out what was wrong. He called in his partner, Michael Teale, for a second opinion on February 8, 1985.

So many symptoms were pointing to so many possible ailments that Bee's real job was to eliminate possibilities, drawing on his own knowledge and experience, his partners', and the government vets'. When Stent told Bee, on his third visit, that he had mistakenly applied mercury to his corn seeds before planting, Bee tested to see if the cow had been accidentally poisoned. Head tremors had been linked to poisons in feed before. By this time, three other cows on the farm had died. Other cows were also sick and acting very strangely. One, unable to get up, chased Stent across the barn on her knees.

The test for mercury poisoning came back negative. It had to be something else. Bee and the ministry kept their focus on toxins on the feed. Stent had a small brickworks on the farm, and Bee speculated that lead, used to make bricks, might have made its way into the feed. The tests were negative. He conducted more tests for mercury. Still nothing. The discovery of a dead magpie on the farm made them suspect deliberate poisoning, but again the tests were negative. They noticed fungus in the feed and wondered if the cows had simply been given rotten food, but the tests came back negative, just like the rest.

On February 11, Cow 133 died, seven weeks after Bee's first visit. There was still no diagnosis. A post-mortem showed internal bleeding. Segments of nematode parasites, or worms, were found in the kidney, seemingly confirming that the cow had been suffering some sort of kidney problems, possibly due to toxic poisoning. Bee's focus in the coming months shifted to two other animals, cows 142 and 139, the only two showing the same strange symptoms that were still alive; by the end of April six others had died. They too were tested for toxic poisoning, liver and kidney problems, and parasites. Nothing. Cow 133 was sent for slaughter, and samples of her organs were given to the Ministry of Agriculture for testing. The most important sample, however, proved unusable. "The brain was of no diagnostic value as the animal had been shot twice [in the head]," Bee told the British government's BSE inquiry.

On September 2, 1985, an unusually sunny day in southern England, Cow 142, the last surviving animal showing the bizarre symptoms that had by then killed nine cows at Pitsham Farm, was slaughtered and sent to the ministry labs for testing. After ten months and still no answers, Stent was willing to sacrifice the cow to find out what was going on at his farm. This time, the brain was kept intact. A week later, Carol Richardson, a vet at the ministry's Central Veterinary Laboratory in Weybridge, Surrey, looked at a section of Cow 142's brain under a microscope and saw something no vet had ever believed possible – tiny holes like those caused by scrapie, a common disease among British sheep for more than two hundred years. "What was exciting was that this was in a cow," she told the BBC years later. "This was the first time I had seen these lesions in a cow."

The task became one of figuring out what had caused the holes. The instincts of the vets were right – they blamed the feed. But they were wrong, as it turned out, thinking that toxins were the problem, with Richardson suggesting bacterial infections of the feed. "I recall my disbelief at this statement at the time. I believed the problem had been associated with fungal contamination of feed and mycotoxin production," Bee wrote later for the inquiry that followed. A month after sending Cow 142 away for testing, Bee received a positive toxin test from Stent's farm. His earlier suspicions seemed to have been confirmed, and he closed the case. "By this time, new cases had ceased to be developed. I imagined that the problem had run its course," he told the inquiry.

Back in Weybridge, Richardson went on maternity leave. While she was gone, one of her colleagues at the lab, senior neuropathologist Dr. Gerald Wells, began to come across similar cases. He had seen a few cases before Richardson made her discovery, and he saw more afterwards. Like her, he believed Cow 142 had suffered some form of toxic infection that caused holes to develop in her brain. Two years later, however, on Halloween Day, 1987, Wells made history by publishing an article in the *Veterinary Record* about "a novel spongiform encephalopathy in cattle" he had found in a cow from Kent County, miles from Pitsham Farm. He dubbed the new disease bovine spongiform encephalopathy, or BSE. The press called it mad cow disease and told stories of a new "incurable disease wiping out dairy cows."

Richardson approached Wells at a Christmas party and reminded him of Cow 142 and the nine others at Pitsham Farm. Like vets across the country, the two began to wonder about other cases they had previously blamed on toxins or infections and speculated whether they had confronted mad cow disease before without realizing it. It had been three years since Bee's trip to Pitsham Farm to see Cow 133, and the disease that he thought had run its course was showing up again, two counties over. The mad cow crisis had begun, and modern agriculture would never be the same.

Mad cow disease is not a result of nature gone wild. Instead, it is a direct, if unintended, result of an attempt to make modern farming more efficient. Faced with squeezed margins and increased demands, well-intentioned farmers like Peter Stent turned to the tools offered them to keep their farms profitable. One of them was high protein cattle feed. Few who have studied the situation have found fault with the farmers themselves. "Farmers could not have assumed that something was wrong with the feed, for no farmer in the world would be so stupid to feed a product to their animals knowing that it would jeopardize not only their health, but finally their living as well, with no compensation whatsoever," wrote Kerstin Dressel, a German researcher whose examinations of the mad cow crisis remain among the most penetrating and compelling.

Only about 58 per cent of a slaughtered cow makes it to the human food chain. The rest ends up in rendering plants, where it is converted into ingredients used in prepared foods, cosmetics, medi-cines, glue, and animal feed. In Canada, about 1.7 million tonnes of inedible animal materials pass through rendering plants each year. Jeffery Allmond, one of the scientists who looked into how mad cow disease developed and spread for the British government, summed it up nicely for the *Atlantic Monthly*: "Every bit of the carcass is used – it's all valuable, isn't it? . . . They cut off what they can; then they use solvents and sprays to get off the last bits to make the mince and paté, gravies and sauces. And they put the bones – including the ver-tebrae – into gelatin. It's a messy business, hard to control." It is a wonder of recycling, really, that we have found ways to use virtually every part of a cow.

Throughout history, we have used cattle to feed, clothe, and even house ourselves. Collagen is used to make the glue in wall-paper, bandages, emery boards, and drywall, and it is also used in sausage casing. The fats, once used almost exclusively to make soap, are now also used in creams, crayons, floor wax, cosmetics, per-fumes, and insecticides. The hoofs and horns are used for combs and imitation ivory. The hide, of course, is made into shoes, luggage, and a number of other leather goods. Modern medicine also relies on the rendering plant's recycling efforts, getting insulin from the beef pancreas, blood plasma to treat hemophilia and anemia, sutures from beef intestines, and cartilage for use in plastic surgery. Parts of the cow are even sometimes used as binders in road paving and as industrial lubricants.

A rendering plant takes all the parts of an animal that are not used as food and crushes and cooks them down. Renderers refer to themselves as recyclers, performing a valuable community service by taking the 42 per cent of a cow that would otherwise be waste. They also take pigs, chickens, horses, and other farm animals; meat scraps from supermarkets, restaurants, and butcher shops; and used cooking oil from restaurants. The fat is mechanically separated from the bones, feathers, blood, and other sources of protein and is sent on to a separate production line. Giant grinders chop up the raw materials before they are put into huge cookers that further separate fats from proteins. A press and a spinner draw off the liquids from the solids before a series of dryers and milling machines turn what's left into ground bone meal and dried protein pellets. They are then stored in tanks until they can be transported to the companies that use them to make everything from lipstick and candy to animal feed.

The first references to using animal by-products in feed for livestock dates to the 1860s in England, when small-scale knackers acted as sort of neighbourhood rendering plants and soap factories. About a hundred years ago, the Swift Company of Chicago took the process to the industrial level when it began using rendered cattle to make animal feed. In 1914, pigs fed Swift's mixture took first prize at the International Livestock Show in Chicago, showcasing the potential of the new high-protein feed. By the 1920s, the practice had become well established, with legislation in most countries governing the use of animal proteins in feed.

The practice really took off in the 1940s during the Second World War. With everything in short supply because of the war effort, the British government required that animal feed contain at least 5 per cent meat and bone meal, or MBM. This jump-started the move to feeding animal proteins to livestock. Farmers in North America, facing similar shortages of protein to feed their animals, also began increasing their use of animal proteins. At this point, animal proteins were still just an alternative to traditional foods such as soy or canola, though that would soon change.

After the war, farmers were reluctant to cut back on their use of feed made from animals. Researchers had noticed that cattle were more efficient at digesting protein from other animals than from plants. That increased efficiency translated into greater milk and meat production, and farmers were encouraged to keep feeding animal proteins to their cattle, especially in Britain where there was limited land available to grow feed crops.

Farmers soon found, however, that they could not feed their cows any more than about 5 per cent ground-up animal parts before their cattle started to reject the feed as unpalatable. But despite the cows' evident instinct to remain vegetarian, it seemed like a good idea at the time to boost their production by turning them into carnivores, even cannibals.

The timing was perfect. Demand for milk and beef was booming with the post-war prosperity. In North America, a roast on Sunday and barbecues in the backyard became symbols of the new, suburban lifestyle being embraced by the burgeoning middle class. Within a decade, the hamburger was a staple of the North American diet, led by the rapid expansion of the fast-food industry. The steak had become the middle-class trophy meal. Milk was marketed more aggressively than ever before as a healthy drink for children and adults alike. With the advent of affordable refrigerators in the post-war period, families bought more milk than they ever had before. The baby boom was on, and mothers were not breastfeeding as much as they had in the past, instead feeding their babies cow's milk or milk-based formulas.

The necessities of the war, which had forced farmers to look for new ways to feed their animals, became the imperatives of the consumer-driven post-war boom. It was no longer enough for farmers just to keep up with past production levels, as they had struggled to do during the war. Now they had to keep expanding production to meet the exploding demand. People had more money in their pockets, and they were spending it on more food, more meat, more milk, more of everything.

Using animal proteins to boost production seemed like an ideal solution. It was certainly simpler than increasing the number of cows – especially as booming cities took over their surrounding farmlands to build suburbs. It also made business sense down on the farm. Indeed, a farmer would have been foolish to pass up a chance to get more milk or meat from the same sized herd by just switching feeds.

But inside the cows, bigger changes were taking place that would have devastating health implications for both the animals and humans. Cows have four stomachs. The first, the rumen, is the largest. It is also what joins cows to a broader group of mammals called ruminants, or animals with rumen stomachs, including sheep, deer, and elk. The rumen is a sort of storage tank for the cow, where she holds feed that has been chewed once before regurgitating it, chewing it more, and passing it to her other three stomachs. While the feed is in the rumen, micro-organisms extract protein from the cow's traditional vegetarian diet, in a manner that non-ruminants – such as pigs, poultry, or humans – cannot. This is why cattle and sheep, for thousands of years, have been sent out into hills and marginal farmland to forage for their own food and thrive where other beasts have starved.

The rumen, however, cannot extract animal protein. Enzymes in the gastric juices of the fourth stomach, the abomasum, digest them. The British BSE inquiry heard that generations of cows eating animal proteins had begun to alter their evolution. Unless fed animal proteins, a cow's milk production would drop off dramatically, and she might even have trouble reproducing. She had, in short, become dependent on meat. She had become a carnivore.

Spongiform diseases occur naturally in all animals, including humans. As horrifying as these cases are, however, they are rare and remain isolated. Isolated, that is, until cannibalism allows the disease to spread. In their groundbreaking study in the 1950s and 1960s of a disease among the Fore people of New Guinea, Dr. Carleton Gajdusek and Vincent Zigas found that the Fore practice of eating the brains of their dead after the funeral was causing a disease known as kuru (after the Fore word for trembling or shivering) to spread throughout the population. The practice has since been stopped, and new cases that cropped up in the years after the ban were believed to illustrate the long incubation period of spongiform diseases.

The same sort of thing is believed to have happened in cattle. Constant feeding and refeeding of ground-up animal parts to cattle, including the brains of infected cattle, meant that mad cow disease soon built up in the cattle herds of Great Britain, where scrapie was first diagnosed in sheep in 1732. Back then, scrapie was called rubbers, "from their seeming to rub themselves to death, by which some very capital flocks, in the vicinity of Bury, have lost several hundred," one observer wrote at the time.

While Britain's large sheep herds have been infected with scrapie for more than two hundred years, the disease was never considered a big problem since it could not be passed to humans, and only the brains – the least marketable part of a lamb – were infected. Bee summed up the prevailing attitude when he told the British BSE inquiry that scrapie was considered more of a nuisance than anything else, with the animals often not even worth the cost of taking to slaughterhouses. "As far as I recall, it was thought just to be a problem for those flocks which had scrapie in them. And it was purely thought to be an economic problem, a loss of income to the farmer, rather than anything more sinister than that."

Bee, like most vets, farmers, and health officials at the time, never made any connection to scrapie in the mystery disease on Pitsham Farm. Other vets gave similar testimony and told the inquiry that dead animals – both sheep and cattle – would be picked up by renderers or sold to hunting kennels. If an animal was considered too sick to keep, but not yet dead, it would likely be driven to a slaughterhouse and put directly into the human food chain. Few, if any, would be buried on the farm, since, as one vet said, the farmer could at least earn some money if the animal was sold to a renderer.

Under such conditions, the disease was able to build and spread. Farmers saw no reason to stop their feeding practices, and their vets did not know enough about the disease to tell them otherwise. Simply put, no one knew any better. All they knew and understood was that using animal proteins boosted production. The practice had continued for decades, seemingly without adverse consequences, so was presumed to not suddenly have become a problem.

What had once been an assumption – that feeding animals to animals posed no threat – had become common knowledge. Even once connections were made between farm practices and mad cow disease, and the British government banned feeding animal-based proteins to cows, farmers kept up the same practices as long as they could – continuing to feed animal proteins to their cattle until their own supplies ran out. The ban, after all, had been put forward by the British government as no more than a precautionary measure, set in place to address the concerns of consumers and foreign buyers of British beef.

Despite imposing the ban, the government continued to deny there was any evidence proving that feeding cows to cows had caused the disease to spread, or that there was any evidence the disease could spread to humans. This gave the renderers, the farmers, and the food and animal feed industries the signal that the precautionary measures need not be followed, and the lack of rigorous enforcement by the government only encouraged the view. They assumed that if the government were serious about the ban, it would do more to enforce it.

Canada has not had to face the horrors that Britain and the rest of Europe have had to deal with. The only known case of mad cow disease in this country was a cow imported from Britain. She and all her herd mates were destroyed. The only known case of vCJD, variant Creutzfeldt-Jakob disease, the human form of mad cow disease, was a Saskatchewan man who most likely contracted the disease during an extended stay in England during its mad cow crisis. Measures taken by Canada – including a feed ban in 1997, nine years after Britain's, and a ban on imports of British beef in 1990 – should keep the disease out of Canada. "This [disease] has been found in Europe. It's a European disease, and that's about it. . . . We're free of this disease. We don't have it and we're trying to keep it out," said Dr. Claude Lavigne, deputy director of animal health at the Canadian Food Inspection Agency. It is his job to make sure mad cow disease stays out of Canada.

That statement seems dangerously complacent. On the one hand, he says that the disease is a high priority, and that the government of Canada is doing everything in its powers to keep it out of

Canada. On the other, he says it's a "European" disease, so we need not worry. He is sending out the same, dangerously mixed messages that Margaret Thatcher's government in Britain had, with deadly results. Just as in Britain, Canada's rules have a disconcerting hint of public relations about them, put in place to placate the public without imposing too much hardship on the industry.

Canada's feed ban, for instance, does not go as far as Britain's. While we ban feeding cows to cows, we don't ban feeding cows to pigs or chickens, or pigs and chickens to cows. Given mad cow's well-documented ability to jump the species barrier – it is, after all, classified as a *transmissible* spongiform encephalopathy, or TSE – it seems like folly to keep feeding any farm animals to any other farm animals. And yet we do. All it would take is for pigs or chickens to do what was once thought impossible – develop their own form of spongiform encephalopathy – and we would have a situation on our hands as bad as Britain's in the early 1980s, when constant feeding and refeeding of TSE-infected animals to cattle set off the mad cow crisis. Both mad cow disease and variant Creutzfeldt-Jakob disease (vCJD) have long incubation periods. Though it is not known with any scientific accuracy just how long, scientists believe the disease can incubate for a decade or more before any outward signs are apparent.

Mad cow disease is not like botulism or salmonella, which can make you sick within hours, making it relatively easy to detect what made you ill. BSE can take years to show itself, slowly eating away at the brains of our animals and our loved ones before we realize there is a problem. "By the time people get sick, it's too late to do anything," says Mike McBane of the Canadian Health Coalition. Britain now bans all feeding of animals to animals and has virtually eradicated BSE. If a ban is that effective at getting rid of the disease, it would be a great way to stop the disease from taking hold in the first place.

In the summer of 2001, mad cow disease broke out in Japan, a country that also once considered itself BSE free. Before the outbreak, the Japanese government assured the country that England was too far away for it to worry about a European disease. After the outbreak – like the British before it – the government tried again to reassure the public, with Agriculture Minister Tsutomu Takebe making a very public show of eating a beef dinner. *Time* magazine observed: "If there's one thing Japanese have learned: when government big shots go before the cameras during a crisis to say that everything is *daijobu* (okay), it may be time to head for the hills." The beef industry collapsed.

Japan was not alone. Italy offered its citizens similar assurances, and to prove that the meat was safe began to actually test the country's beef. It found that the disease, despite precautions, had made its way to Italy. And a year after Japan made its startling discovery, Israel announced that it had discovered its first case, in a cow born in that country. Chile was forced in 2002 to make a similar admission. Despite this, Lavigne stuck to the argument during a September 2002 interview that mad cow disease was "mostly" a European disease. "Israel is almost a European country," he said. But the lesson of the Japanese, Italian, Israeli, and Chilean experiences is that BSE can pop up without warning.

Both the United Nations Food and Agriculture Organization and the World Health Organization have advised all countries to consider mad cow disease a worldwide concern, not a disease confined to any one region, and warned them not to become complacent about their preventive strategies. "All countries that imported cattle or meat and bone meal from Western Europe, especially the U.K., during and since the 1980s, can be considered to be at risk from the disease," the FAO said. That would include Canada.

David Bee dubbed the strange ailment running through Peter Stent's herd Pitsham Farm Syndrome. He chose to name it after the farm, he told the BSE inquiry, because he had seen no other cases among the many other farms he visited, and the problem showed no signs of spreading. "This problem had exercised our mind for nine months, and . . . it was specific to Pitsham Farm – we deal with about forty biggish dairy clients in our practice – and not one other farm had any cases of disease of this type. So it was Pitsham Farm. It was not a problem that was occurring throughout the practice, it was purely on this farm, hence the name," he told the inquiry. His bill for the Christmas 1984 visit to Pitsham Farm was small, his examination of Cow 133 short. Bee charged the standard £10 for the visit itself, another £7.70 to examine the cow, and £12 for injecting her with 100 cc of Duphacycline, an antibiotic – for a total of £29.70, about $70 Canadian.

In the following years, the bill would become much higher. As *The Observer* in London put it, when Bee examined Cow 133 that Christmas, "[he] was staring into the eyes of a disaster." It was a disaster that would grow to monstrous proportions before the British government would acknowledge, twelve years later, that the disease posed a threat to humans. Throughout those dozen years and beyond, both government and industry officials dismissed the public's concerns as "scientifically" unfounded and argued that there was no "scientific proof" that modern farm practices posed any threat to animals or human health. Critics were dismissed as "Luddites" using BSE to raise money for left-wing causes.

The U.K.'s premier organic group, the Soil Association, argued as early as 1979, five years before Bee's visit to Pitsham Farm, that it was wrong to make cows into cannibals. A British royal commission on environmental pollution around the same time warned that pathogens could be spread among animals "and thence to humans" through the use of animal proteins in feed. The practices that gave birth to mad cow disease continued, however, and were justified by government and industry as necessary to help farmers survive. Consumers were blamed for continually demanding cheap, plentiful food.

These themes and arguments have been used ever since, as the world has confronted such issues as genetic engineering and animal welfare. The penchant for forging ahead despite growing warning signs that something might be wrong is the true nature of Pitsham Farm Syndrome – a disease that infected not just Peter Stent's cows, but the people who were supposed to help him and protect us. The tendency by industry, government, and their scientists to dismiss the precautionary approach of their critics – saying that only "sound science" could determine the safety of a given farm practice – is what made Pitsham Farm Syndrome infectious.

This Pitsham Farm Syndrome is a disease of complacency by government, arrogance of science, and greed by the companies that control the food industry. And it infects every item on our plate.

Stuart Laidlaw

Turkeys being delivered to slaughter,
Winnipeg, Manitoba, July 2001

*"We farmers have been told for decades to
specialize. Specialize, specialize, specialize. And
what do these big companies do? They diversify.
And, folks, they're wiping us out."*

Bill Heffernan,
rural sociologist

CHAPTER TWO

THE LIVESTOCK REVOLUTION

M odern farming was born in the spring of 1936 in the Arkansas countryside, when John Tyson, a trucker, picked up a load of five hundred chickens and drove them a thousand kilometres north to Chicago for slaughter. He made $235 for his efforts – a hefty sum in the middle of the Depression. He kept $15 to pay his expenses back to Springdale, Arkansas, for another load of chickens and wired the rest home. The money was used to pay off his debts, buy more chickens, and get them ready for another trip to Chicago. Tyson's decision to bypass the slaughterhouses in St. Louis and Kansas City and make the much longer trip to Chicago began a revolution that would transform the poultry industry in not only the United States, but the world – and is now spreading into the pork and beef industries. "Although no one knew it at the time, he was laying the foundation for the modern-day poultry business and Tyson Foods," the company factbook boasts.

Tyson's drive to Chicago broke the bond between local farmers and slaughterhouses. He showed that poultry could be transported long distances to a slaughterhouse, if the price was right. He also proved – more ominously for family farmers – that slaughterhouses could look far beyond the immediate area to find the cheapest birds. Price became the dominant factor in deciding which farmers could sell their poultry and which could not. For farmers, who had always had to keep their costs as low as possible, the stakes were now much higher. They were no longer just competing with their neighbours – people they went to church with and whose children their kids went to school with – but with every farmer in the country. They were competing with strangers.

An impersonality was introduced that would change the nature of farming. Tyson had started his company in 1935 to serve the needs of local farmers, driving their chickens to the slaughterhouse for them. He soon turned that relationship around and demanded that the farmers serve him. Within a generation, he had industrialized poultry farming and turned the farmers supplying him into little more than employees of his company.

At the heart of our modern economy is the assembly line. It is a simple model of production that breaks each stage of the production process into simple tasks, each performed by a different worker. No one task is particularly difficult, but put together they can produce great things.

Henry Ford's assembly line, which transformed cars from hand-built luxury items into products of mass production and affordability, was a classic application of Adam Smith's economic theories. The Scottish economist opened his 1776 classic *The Wealth of Nations* by detailing how each stage in the manufacture of a straight pin could be broken down into smaller and smaller steps. "One man draws out the wire, another straights it, a third cuts it, a fourth points it, and a fifth grinds it at the top for receiving the head." Each step, individually, required a very specialized, but easy to learn, skill. Over time, the workers would become increasingly proficient at their tasks, further boosting the productivity of the company. In the pin example, Smith described a factory in which ten workers made 48,000 pins a day, far more than they would have been able to make working individually. The net effect was a jump in production and, despite the factory owner having to hire more workers, a drop in the cost per pin.

Since the end of the Second World War, the agriculture industry has applied this model to farming. One influential think-tank in Washington has dubbed it the "Livestock Revolution," and it is transforming how meat makes its way to our plates. "A revolution is taking place in global agriculture that has profound implications for our health, livelihoods and environment," a team of researchers at the Washington-based International Food Policy Research Institute wrote in a 2000 study.

The industrial structure of Tyson's company and the entire poultry industry was established in 1947, just in time for the post-war boom. Poultry had been excluded from wartime rationing in North America, so it soon became a popular dinner choice. The federal government in Canada encouraged the birth of the modern poultry industry at this time by subsidizing the cost of building chicken barns. As well, grocery stores were cashing in on the popularity of chickens by offering in-store specials. On October 7, 1947, Tyson incorporated his company as a supplier of baby chicks and feed for farmers who would raise the chicks to adulthood so they could be taken to a Tyson slaughterhouse. The strategy was financially brilliant. Tyson took control of the most profitable parts of poultry production, while leaving farmers to assume all the risks for the most volatile part of the business – raising the birds.

By the turn of the century, Tyson Foods controlled about one-quarter of the U.S. chicken industry, processing 42 million chickens a week at fifty-six slaughterhouses. It owns the chickens from the day they are hatched to the day they are killed. The farmers it hires under contract feed the birds Tyson's brand of feed, formulated to maximize the growth rate of company-bred birds. Farmers under contract to Tyson are required to follow exacting standards for production and agree to regular inspections by the company. At the end of the six-week lifespan of the birds, Tyson picks up the birds and takes them to one of its plants for slaughter.

It is called "vertical integration," and it gives Tyson complete control of the process from fertilized egg to the grocery store shelf. Unlike in Canada, American farmers under contract to Tyson don't own the birds in their barns, but are responsible for raising them. The cost of any harm to the Tyson-owned chickens – caused by disease or weather – comes out of the pocket of the farmer, who is paid about five cents a pound for raising the chickens. "I never own the chicken until it dies," Bob Lakey, an Arkansas chicken farmer, told the 1993 meeting of the Chicken Farmers of Ontario. He was producing 600,000 chickens a year, about three times as many as anyone in the audience.

The industrialization of the poultry industry has progressed much further in the United States than in Canada, where supply management has stemmed the growth of factory farms. Under supply management, farmers buy and sell production quotas dictating how many chickens or turkeys they can produce. The birds are then sold to a slaughterhouse at prices negotiated through marketing boards on an industry-wide basis. Superficially, the Canadian industry resembles the structure of the U.S. industry – with processors supplying the chicks and feed, and then buying the fully grown birds – except for one key difference: Canadian farmers negotiate their prices and production levels as a group, not individually, and their marketing boards distribute the production quotas among the farmers. It's called supply management, and it gives farmers a stronger voice in the industry.

Under the U.S. system, production is also tightly managed, but by the companies at the top of the food chain. Tyson decides how many chickens it wants and distributes the production rights among its contract growers, dictating to each the price that will be paid. Lakey told the Ontario farmers he receives a call telling him when a load of chickens will be dropped off, along with the feed and medication he is to give them. He never knows how many chicks he will be getting or how much he will be paid, but is responsible for raising them and disposing of any that do not survive. Vertical integration has become corporate-run supply management with large food companies holding all the cards – a system that rewards only those at the top.

At the time of Lakey's visit, the United States was making its first moves against supply management, arguing at the Uruguay round of world trade talks that the quota system was an unfair restriction on trade. Lakey came to the meeting to warn Ontario chicken farmers what life would be like without supply management. "We have no say whatever in these contracts," Lakey told the meeting. He urged them not to give up a system that worked so well for them, saying his poverty-level wages of $12,000 a year ensured that Canada would be overrun with American birds if supply management ever ended. "We can produce chickens a lot cheaper than you can," he said.

Lakey was in Canada at the invitation of Roy Maxwell, head of communications at the Chicken Farmers of Ontario. Maxwell had toured dozens of American chicken farms in the U.S. southeast – where Tyson got its start and where the bulk of the American industry is still located – in the fall of 1992. It was a depressing sight. "It was just chicken barn after chicken barn," he says. Farms there were two or three times the size of the average Canadian farm, and yet the farmers made less money. Farmers cut corners wherever they could, often cleaning their barns only once a year. The Canadian standard is to clean and disinfect barns five or six times a year, after each flock of chickens has passed through.

Don Timmins, a Texas farmer, told Maxwell that the company he raised chickens for required that he continually upgrade his barns if he wanted to keep his contract. Each upgrade, however, just put him further into debt. And that debt, he said, kept him tied to the company to service his loans. "When the integrator comes along and tells you to do $30,000 worth of stuff, you've got no choice. If you don't go along with things, they'll cut you off your supply of chicks," he said. "They want to keep you at a point where you are just barely hanging on, where you don't have any leeway to lash out at them." The result, he said, was that farmers had no power to bargain for a better deal. "My farm grossed $29,000 last year. Out of that, I paid utilities and made repairs. When it was all said and done, my return on 175,000 birds was $500," he told Maxwell. In an investigation of the U.S. poultry industry in 1999, the *Baltimore Sun* said of American farmers: "They became the land-owning serfs in an agricultural feudal system."

When Maxwell visited, farmers put together an invitation-only meeting. They gathered in secret, fearing the companies they worked for would find out and cancel their contracts. Lakey was one of those farmers. Standing in a Toronto hotel ballroom months later, speaking to a room full of farmers, he was amazed that such a meeting could take place in the open, with representatives of the industry present. "This could just never happen back home," he said.

Few outsiders ever get a chance to peek inside the inner workings of the poultry industry. Rules about hygiene keep most visitors out, and fear of unfavourable stories in urban papers makes farms and slaughterhouses off limits for most reporters. But in September 2000, I managed to visit a Manitoba turkey operation.

There turkeys are hatched in a dark chamber on a plastic tray about the size of an oven rack. There were more than 140 eggs on that tray, and thousands more on the trays above and below it, all carefully bred to hatch at about the same time. "Once they start hatching, it's just like popcorn popping," said Shane Saunders, manager of Charison's Turkey Hatchery Ltd., who took me on my tour. At just a few hours old, the baby turkeys are put on an assembly line, where their beaks and nails are clipped so they won't damage each other, and they are given their first antibiotic injection. About a hundred at a time are then stuffed into boxes about the size of a roasting pan, loaded onto a truck, and driven to another farm, where they are put into windowless, climate-controlled barns to be raised to young adulthood.

The degree of specialization has become so intense that it takes upwards of ten different barns to bring a turkey to market. The process starts with the bird's great-grandparents, called pure lines in the industry. These pure-line birds each display the best of just one feature desired by the industry, such as a big breast, big drumsticks, or fast growth. Four pairs of these pure-line birds are inbred in four different barns. Their offspring, your turkey dinner's grandparents, are then taken to two more barns for breeding. That's six barns so far, and the turkey going to market has not even been hatched yet. The next stage is the parent barn, where the eggs that will eventually become turkey dinners are laid.

The parent barns are to turkeys what assembly plants are to cars. Just as an assembly plant uses car parts from other factories to make a car, the parent farm assembles the desirable genetic traits developed on other farms to make an egg. From the parent barn, the eggs are shipped within hours to a farm specializing in hatching. From there, the chicks, called poults, are shipped to a poult farm, where they spend the next five weeks growing. The birds are then sent to a grower barn, where they are fattened up for six weeks before going to a slaughterhouse. While some farms combine different stages of production under one corporate banner, they maintain this division of tasks. Charison's, for instance, has a hatchery, a poult barn, and a grower barn. Saunders's cousin runs a parent barn nearby.

This is classic assembly-line production. Each stage in a turkey's life has been broken down into a different job performed in a different barn by a different set of workers performing very specific and low-skilled tasks. The women who clip beaks and nails, for instance, know nothing about feeding and caring for a poult, and they don't need to. Like auto workers, they have one task and they do it quickly and efficiently. They do not need to be taught or paid to do anything else. Even the act of reproduction, the most basic instinct of all living things, has been replaced by assembly-line production through artificial insemination.

An insemination crew of four men was at Charison's the day I visited. One took the semen from the male birds, called toms. Another collected the hens and stuffed them onto a covered conveyor belt. The belt is covered because the birds, upset at having been corralled and stuffed onto the belt, will calm down in the darkness. At the end of the belt, a man grabbed the hens and handed them to a fourth man sitting next to him, who placed a plastic straw filled with turkey semen into a gun and inserted the gun into the hen, impregnating her. He then tossed her to the barn floor and reached for another hen.

The crew inseminated turkeys at a rate of about one hen every thirty seconds, a speed that comes from performing the same task over and over again. The men wore face masks to protect their lungs from the dust tossed up as the turkeys scurried about the sesame seed shells spread on the floor, and from the smell of ammonia. "If you're in here all day, the dust gets to you," Saunders said as we watched the crew work.

Craig Eros, who runs the parent barn that supplies Charison's, said the hens are inseminated artificially to ensure that the desired genetic traits were passed along. As well, artificial insemination means that all the hens are impregnated on the same day and so will start laying eggs on the same day, leading to greater efficiency when it comes time to collect the eggs. Impregnating hens is a specialized task, with freelance crews touring farms to inseminate turkeys as need be. "They're the specialists. They can do it much more efficiently," said Saunders, expressing the mantra that defines modern industrial agriculture.

Such efficiencies, both Eros and Saunders were fast to point out, are why consumers got such cheap, plentiful meat at the grocery store. Besides, said Eros, it wouldn't be safe to let the seventy-pound male turkeys mate with the thirty-pound hens. "The toms are so big they would injure the hens," he said.

It all makes for cheap meat, but at a price. For one thing, the small family poultry farm no longer exists in the United States where this industrial model started – and is under threat wherever else the model has been adopted. Small farms cannot give the poultry companies the cheap, uniform-sized birds they demand. In order to keep its slaughterhouses operating at peak efficiency, Tyson and other big poultry companies require all the birds to be within a very tight range of shape and weight. This allows its automated slaughtering systems to kill and dismember the birds without having to adjust for variations in size.

A tour of any chicken processing plant reveals the importance of such uniformity. At the Maple Lodge chicken plant just outside of Toronto, workers disassemble birds speeding past them on a conveyor belt at a rate of thirty-five a minute, or one every 1.7 seconds. Each worker has an assigned cut to make. One skins the birds, another removes a leg, another the other leg. A fourth cuts the meat from the breast, and so on down the line until the bird's skeleton is taken from the line for rendering at a specialized plant. Each worker's hand, wielding a sharp knife, moves in perfect precision, each cut exactly the same as the last. The workers chat as they cut, barely looking at the chickens that never stop moving past. In the evisceration room, veterinarians and government inspectors scrutinize the birds as they are whisked past their stations. Thanks to the uniformity of the birds, any slight difference is easy for a trained eye to spot, and the bird is removed from the line.

This uniformity starts with the breeding of the chickens. By controlling reproduction, poultry companies ensure that the birds start out in life about the same. By controlling what they are fed and how they are raised, the company can count on birds remaining virtually identical until they reach the slaughterhouse. Automated feeding and water systems feed the birds at regular intervals, which maximizes their growth and minimizes labour costs. Such systems do not come cheap – it can cost upwards of $1 million to build a modern poultry barn – and in the United States small farmers are forced to become big if they wish to keep selling to the companies that control the industry.

In July 2002, three East Texas farmers sued Pilgrim's Pride, the third largest chicken company in the United States, alleging unfair contracts. "Throughout the duration of these contractual relationships, Pilgrim's has engaged in conduct that can be described as manipulative, coercive, fraudulent, overreaching, deceptive and unfair," the suit claimed. The farmers said they provided half the capital costs involved in raising the chickens, but had no control over how their farms operated. Pilgrim's Pride responded by saying the contracts were within industry standards – with the company providing farmers with hundreds of thousands of chicks and feed, and farmers providing the barns, utilities, and water.

Selective breeding has cut the time needed to grow a chicken to market weight from eighteen weeks in the 1920s to six weeks today. Similar advances have been made in other animals, as well. Cattle, for instance, reach a market weight of 1,200 pounds in about a year. Fifty years ago, it took two or three years. In both the chicken and turkey industries, faster growth was achieved by breeding only a narrow range of white birds, but the practice has led to a thinning of the genetic lines on which the poultry industry is based. The breeding stock of just three companies, for instance, dominates turkey production, and half a dozen Holstein bulls have each fathered more than 1 million cows around the world through artificial insemination. Sixty per cent of Canada's 1.2 million dairy cows are descended from just four breeding lines. A 1998 study in the *Journal of Dairy Science* found that inbreeding in the dairy industry could cause milk production to drop and hurt the fertility of cows – essential for producing milk. Dairy cows have also become more high-strung and tougher to handle as their gene pool has shallowed.

At the 2002 VIV Canada trade show in Toronto for chicken and pig farmers, several of the industry magazines and journals being handed out warned of the danger of thin genetic lines in their industries. "Birds are being bred to perform closer to the edge of the physiological limits," *Ontario Poultry Farmer* magazine cautioned. The article recommended farmers spend more time in barns to watch for problems – even though the point of barn automation was to allow farmers to spend less time tending to their flocks.

The emphasis on white skin, large breasts, meaty drumsticks, and fast growth in the poultry industry has put great stress on the birds' bodies. Their hearts and lungs have trouble keeping up with the fast muscle growth. Their bones are also not able to develop as fast as the meat that hangs from them and have broken under the weight. Birds laying eggs for hatcheries also develop brittle bones as calcium needed to keep bones strong instead goes to produce more eggs. A century ago, hens laid about 80 eggs a year. By 1960, they were laying an average of 193 eggs, and today, thanks to improved breeding and better feed and housing, which extends their laying season, they lay an average of 272 eggs each year.

Ronald Slavnik, sales manager with Hybrid Turkeys in Kitchener, the only commercial turkey breeding company in Canada, says his company has been working to fix growth problems – referred to as "durability" in the industry. "That's been the learning curve for the breeding companies the last twenty years," he said. "The key is to keep it all in balance."

Canada's largest poultry company, Maple Leaf Foods, used the Tyson model as the company built its Prime Naturally brand of chicken and Medallion Naturally pork. "We could not have developed Maple Leaf Prime Naturally as quickly and successfully as we did were it not for our vertical co-ordination approach to the protein value chain – farm, feed, processing and rendering," the company said in its 2001 annual report. "They are tightly co-ordinated to deliver superior performance at intersection points."

Supply management, however, has prevented industrialization from reaching the same level as it has in the United States. We have factory farms in Canada, to be sure, but they are smaller and better run. "If you didn't have the marketing board, the industry here would be the same as in the U.S.," says Maxwell. The average Canadian farm has about 29,500 birds at any one time and raises about 192,000 birds a year; the average U.S. farm has 41,000 birds and raises about 268,000 chickens. The Canadian farms produce birds just as efficiently as the American farms, but on a smaller scale and at a sustainable income for the farmers.

Supply management gives Canadian farmers a measure of independence U.S. growers no longer have, since under the rules of supply management, only farmers can own chickens. That means companies pursuing vertical integration, or vertical coordination as Maple Leaf prefers to call it, in Canada must sell baby chicks to farmers and then buy back the fully grown birds at prices negotiated between the provincial marketing boards and the slaughterhouses. By owning the birds at one stage of their production, and using the quota system to control how many birds will be raised, Canadian farmers are able to exert some power in their industry that American farmers cannot. "I don't want to sound like a traitor," one farmer told Maxwell during his tour of southern U.S. chicken farms, "but free enterprise down here means that I get poorer and the integrators get richer."

John Youngman, chair of the animal welfare committee of the Winnipeg Humane Society, says that the people he talks to are usually shocked when they realize how far industrialization has taken farms away from the picturesque image of a few dozen birds scratching about the barnyard, wandering in and out of their coops at will. "The farmers are not the bad guys. They are dealing with a system that has told them to produce cheap food since the Second World War," Youngman says. That system requires that farmers, to stay profitable, cram as many birds as they can into a barn and fatten them up as quickly as possible.

In the barns, the chickens and turkeys are unable to move without touching another bird, which leads to fighting, known in the industry as "cannibalism." The birds literally peck each other to death. In the Charison barn I visited, several turkeys in the eight-thousand-bird barn had bare spots or cuts from past fights, and a few had to be penned separately while their wounds healed. This is why the tips of the birds' beaks and nails are cut off when they are a few hours old. "It's definitely for their own good. Otherwise, they'd be a mess," Saunders says.

A dead pig in a mailbox. Slashed tires. Death threats, and threats of rape. These are some of the incidents that have marked the bitter fights against industrial hog farms across Canada. Pork has only recently adopted the industrial model set by poultry decades ago, and its transition has sparked more animosity than poultry's industrialization ever did. Maybe it's the stink of pig manure. Maybe it's because by the time industrialization hit pork, the industry was already dominated by family farms specializing in hogs. Before industrialization, turkeys and chickens were raised on most farms only as a sideline operation, so industrializing poultry did not displace a large group of farmers whose livelihood depended on the birds.

The trend to big hog barns began in North Carolina in the early 1990s. Barns containing thousands of hogs – standing on slotted cement floors built over pools of manure – provided pork cheap enough to bring down prices across the continent. Free trade forced Canadian farmers to adopt similar models on their farms. The industrial model was first adopted in Quebec, then in Ontario and Manitoba. In each province, hog farmers had to take on huge debts to convert to factory farming if they wanted to get a contract with the big slaughterhouses and compete on price. From 1990 to 2000, the number of animals on Canadian hog farms increased by more than two and a half times.

In each province, neighbours objected to living next to hog operations because of the smell. Five thousand sows produce as much liquid manure as a city of forty thousand people, but hog farms have none of the sewage treatment systems required of municipalities. Instead, the manure is stored in holding tanks under the barns and periodically flushed into massive open-air lagoons. In every jurisdiction that has played host to these barns, the lagoons have leaked, polluting local fields, drinking water, rivers, streams, lakes,

and beaches – killing fish and wildlife and making the water undrink-
able and unsafe for swimming. The smell coming off the lagoons is
strong, seeping into people's homes and clinging to their clothes.
Before long, the pastoral life many cherished is ruined. "You go to
town or work in the morning, and the smell comes with you," says
Bryan Welsh, who fought a 2,500-sow barn planned for his rural
Ontario community on the banks of the Trent River.

Federal studies obtained by the *Ottawa Citizen* in September
2002 found that large hog farms were to blame for a litany of health
and environmental problems. "There is new evidence . . . that the
substances that give rise to odours can also affect human health,
causing nausea, headaches, sleep disturbances, upset stomach, loss of
appetite and depression," one study found. Workers in hog barns
were prone to bronchitis and asthma. The studies found that dust
particles could carry the stench over long distances and that particu-
lates blowing in from the farms were able to "bypass the normal
defences of the respiratory system."

I met two hog farm workers in southeastern Saskatchewan in the
fall of 2001. Both were former wheat farmers with a thousand acres
each. They had been driven out of farming by mounting debts and
low grain prices. Work in the hog barns was dirty, and they stank
when they went home to their families at night. But the work was
steady and the regular paycheque did more to keep their families
going than farming their own land ever had. The previous June, they
had both sold off their farm equipment, making official their transition from independent farmer to waged farm worker. "My daughter
said she's never going to marry a farmer," said one.

In B.C.'s Fraser Valley, the chemical soup from the area's hog
barns is sometimes so thick that a haze can be seen rising off it, and
70 per cent of the airborne particles in the summer air came from
hog barns, the documents obtained by the *Ottawa Citizen* showed.
The land surrounding the barns could not absorb all the manure
spread on it, and the excess ran off into the water supply, polluting
it. Despite these studies, the federal agriculture ministry continues

to promote large hog operations, the documents showed. The objective of one ministerial communications strategy is "to reduce public resistance to hog operations." The strategy document claims that manure doesn't pollute, but instead is "contributing nutrients to the ecosystem." In November 2002, the federal government announced $202,000 in funding for the pork industry to improve pig breeding systems.

As with Tyson's industrialization of poultry, the needs of the slaughterhouses drove the transformation of hog production. In Brandon, Manitoba, Maple Leaf Foods built a $112-million plant it boasted would forever change the meat packing industry in this country. In his address to the company's 2001 annual meeting, Maple Leaf chief executive Michael McCain said the company was on a "mission" that went beyond making a lot of money – which he also promised to do – to change the way food was produced in Canada.

Comparing Maple Leaf's ambition to former U.S. president John Kennedy's mission to put a man on the moon, McCain called upon the faithful to stay with him as he restructured the industry, invoking images of self-sacrifice for the corporate good and welcoming the "burden" of fixing what he saw as a broken industry. "As with most every great vision, we must be prepared to bear the burdens of making it successful. Our goals have come with a price tag. In the past five years, we have made the largest down payment on this price tag – fixing industry problems, addressing company ills, being pioneers in new areas, and committing significant financial resources."

The problems that needed to be fixed, going by Maple Leaf's subsequent actions, were the small family hog farms, which have since been wiped out, and workers' wages, which have been kept barely above the poverty line. He continued: "We have a commitment, an unwavering commitment, backed not just by our passion, our words or our time – but with our *own* money as well."

But Maple Leaf isn't operating with entirely its own money. Brandon needed the pork packing plant and welcomed it with an

$8.5-million contribution toward water and waste facilities. The Manitoba government pitched in another $11 million.

The company's move to Brandon followed the pattern set by the industrialization of U.S. farming. A study by the United States Department of Agriculture found that livestock companies tend to set up shop in communities in rapid decline. Tyson, for instance, industrialized the poultry industry in the depressed southern United States. The industrialization of hog farming began in North Carolina just as that state's once-rich tobacco industry fell into decline. In both cases, according to the study, the new face of farming was welcomed as an economic saviour. In Brandon, Maple Leaf set up shop just as the wheat industry that had powered the local economy was waning. Within a few years, the company was killing 43,000 hogs a week at its plant in Brandon at a rate of 1,250 an hour and making plans to add a second shift. Through its fast-growing Elite Swine contract program, a Tyson-styled vertical coordination of the pork industry, Maple Leaf is a part owner in about three hundred hog farms, typically with a 40 per cent stake that gives farmers the capital to build bigger barns. In 2001, 93,000 hogs were raised under Elite contracts across Canada, a 33 per cent jump from the year before.

Since Maple Leaf came to town, Brandon has seen a rapid increase in both its population – as a 60 per cent turnover rate at the plant leads Maple Leaf to bring in workers from as far away as the Maritimes and Mexico – and its crime rate. Crime in Brandon in 1999 was up 14 per cent over the year before, after declining from 1996 to 1998, and the police say that they seem to be kept especially busy by slaughterhouse workers. Maple Leaf workers I talked to were not surprised by the crime rate, saying that work in the plant was brutal. They talked about their work in low voices, with occasional flashes of anger. The plant workers could not expect anything better in their lives, it angered them, and when they blew off steam, they got into trouble. The city's only murder and traffic fatality victims in 1999 were Maple Leaf workers.

Brandon was still in the early days of playing home to a major packing plant when I visited in 2001. The city needed only to look at Brooks, Alberta, to see what to expect. Brooks is home to Lakeside Packers, and local residents were feeling the effects of turning so much of their local economy over to a branch plant of American giant Iowa Beef Processors, the world's largest red-meat processor. "It was a rather dramatic change and it happened virtually over-night," Mayor Don Weisbeck says. IBP was founded in Denison, Iowa, in 1960 with a $300,000 U.S. government loan. It immediately set about changing the beef industry, just as Tyson had changed poultry. In 2001, Tyson bought IBP.

IBP's founding marked the beginning of Chicago's decline as the centre of beef packing in the United States. It built a highly mecha-nized slaughterhouse in rural Iowa that did not rely on skilled labour, and its fierce anti-union stance helped it keep costs down. "Until 1989, there had never been a negotiation settled without a strike and the company became skilled in the use of replacement workers and other tactics designed to break strikes," wrote Ian MacLachlan, an associate professor at the University of Lethbridge in his 2001 study of the beef industry, *Kill and Chill*. To help keep costs down, the company broke with the industry's past practice of locating in big cities near its main markets, preferring small towns with a limited economic base where labour and land could be had cheap.

Brooks in 1994 fit the bill. An agricultural town of nine thousand in one of the driest parts of the country, Brooks welcomed IBP with open arms. By this time, IBP had gone public and was looking to expand beyond its Iowa base. It bought Lakeside Packers of Brooks, which had been a locally owned feed supplier, beef feedlot, and small slaughterhouse on the edge of town for twenty-eight years. IBP soon set about expanding both the plant and the feedlot, and speeding up the kill rate inside the plant. Within five years, 28,000 cattle were being killed at the plant each week, two and a half times the number when IBP came to town and ten times the number killed a decade earlier. The plant slaughters about 1 million cattle a year, enough to supply 30 per cent of the Canadian market, and has the capacity to kill 1.2 million. The feedlot was expanded as well, to become the largest in Canada with 75,000 head of cattle – up from 40,000 when IBP came to Brooks. It is also the only feedlot in Canada that is integrated with a slaughterhouse.

Driving through Brooks in the summer of 2001, the first thing I noticed was not the packing plant. It was the fast-food restaurants, economy hotels, and big-box discount stores. There seemed to be too many for a town Brooks's size, and they all looked new. The second thing I noticed was the large number of visible minorities. Living in Toronto, I am used to seeing people of many races on the streets. During two weeks of driving through the Prairies, however, the only non-white faces I had seen were those of natives. In Brooks, the variety was back.

The town's population grew to 11,584 by April 2000, an increase of almost 30 per cent in the six years since IBP bought Lakeside. Much of that increase was made up of people from Asia, Africa, and Central and South America lured to Brooks by the prospect of a job. Just over a thousand people, or 9 per cent of the town's population, were born outside of Canada. The transformation of the town reflects the changes in the meat packing industry. Once dominated by middle-aged white men in strong unions, the industry's workforce is increasingly made up of unskilled young men and women earning low wages, with either no union or a weak one. The employee turnover rate in a modern plant is typically 100 per cent a year. For IBP, which employs 2,500 people in Brooks, that meant hiring forty to fifty people a week to replace workers quitting the plant. The company had a billboard posted at its plant advertising "100 jobs to be filled immediately."

But finding 2,500 workers a year in a town of just 11,000 is a tall order, so the company looked elsewhere to find people willing to work in its plants – first across Alberta, then across the Prairies, then across the country, to find them. "It's a problem across the industry," Kevin Grier, an analyst at the George Morris Centre, a think-tank in

Guelph funded by the food industry, told Canadian Press. "Packers in Alberta are looking all across the Prairies and Canada for labour."

Ten per cent of the Brooks population comes from the Atlantic provinces, where a slow economy has traditionally provided the west with a cheap pool of labour. The company finally had to look around the world to find workers, pulling people out of impoverished nations with the prospect of higher wages in a Canadian meat plant. "Workers from Somalia and southeast Asia are conspicuous by their presence in packing plants in small Alberta towns that until recently were notable for their lack of visible minorities," MacLachlan wrote in *Kill and Chill*. More than seventy languages are spoken among the immigrants at the Lakeside plant, as many as are spoken in some Toronto schools.

It's a depressingly familiar pattern, as if today's meat packing executives read Upton Sinclair's novel *The Jungle* as an instruction book instead of a cautionary tale. "The people had come in hordes; and old Durham had squeezed them tighter and tighter, speeding up and grinding them to pieces, and sending for new ones. The Poles, who had come by tens of thousands, had been driven to the wall by the Lithuanians, and now the Lithuanians were giving way to the Slovaks. Who there was poorer and more miserable than the Slovaks, Grandmother Majauszkiene had no idea, but the packers would find them, never fear. It was easy to bring them, for wages were really much higher, and it was only when it was too late that the poor people found that everything else was higher too."

The wages in modern packing plants are low by Canadian standards – between $8 and $11 an hour, or $16,000 to $23,000 a year – but high enough to draw in people from the poorest parts of the globe. As in *The Jungle*, however, the workers arrive to find that not only are their wages higher than they could have expected at home, but so is everything else. Flooding any small town, for whatever reason, with waves of newcomers every year drives up demand for housing, making it tougher for everyone to make ends meet. "There's really nothing inexpensive in Brooks. It's really high-priced

living here," Betty Berg, manager of the local Salvation Army, told
The Western Producer newspaper. Accommodation is so tight and so
expensive that it is not uncommon to find half a dozen workers
sharing a two-bedroom apartment, and every day seven hundred
workers commute from Medicine Hat, an hour away. "We have a
negative vacancy rate," Weisbeck says. "Every apartment building
has a waiting list."

Lakeside built a dormitory-style trailer park next to the plant,
where 168 workers pay the company between $5 and $7.50 a night
for a place to stay. To attract workers, the company even offers to let
them stay in the trailers for up to two months free. Each worker gets
a single bed, a writing table, a wardrobe, and linen. They can eat in a
company cafeteria. Meal tickets are handed out to those workers who
have no other source of money while they wait for their first paycheque. "To me, it's like going back to nineteenth-century England,"
Professor Michael Broadway told *The Western Producer*. Broadway
teaches geography at Northern Michigan University and has studied
the effect of meat packing plants on small towns.

The company also wanted to build a 272-unit trailer park near
the centre of town, but was turned down by the town council when
local residents complained. Weisbeck says plans for a slightly smaller
trailer park on the edge of town stood a better chance of going ahead,
since it was farther from established residential areas. "Our biggest
challenge is housing," he says. There were four trailer parks in the
town already, and they all expanded after IBP arrived. Trailer parks
also popped up on the outskirts of town, where Newell County
Councillor Cory Baksa said the IBP expansion was good for the area:
"I hope we get another mall and more big name stores," she says.
"This isn't the sixties. We either go forward or backwards. I hope we
get to thirty thousand population soon." Baksa owns a fifty-unit
trailer park on the edge of Brooks. Half her tenants work at Lakeside.

The biggest impact packing plants have on a town's workforce
is not within the plant itself – but in the service sector, with stores
and fast-food restaurants opening to serve plant workers and their

families. These operations pay minimum wage and employ primarily part-time staff, making it tough for workers to make ends meet. For small-town boosters, however, such businesses are proof that their community is thriving: "Look at this town. It's booming. To me that's great. Hey, we have a Wendy's and a McDonald's. How many towns can say that?" Jon Nesbit, manager of the local paper (the *Brooks Bulletin*) and past chair of the Chamber of Commerce, boasted to *The Western Producer*. That McDonald's used to be owned by Weisbeck, who says many local businesses owe their livelihood to the increased traffic the plant's expansion brought to Brooks. The day I visited, my family had a long debate about which fast-food restaurant to eat at. They were all busy. "The McDonald's in Brooks is one of the highest volume restaurants in Alberta," Weisbeck says.

Weisbeck also helped found one of the town's two food banks, which struggle to keep up with demand. A survey in 2000 found that 70 per cent of the food banks' clients worked at Lakeside, and another 12 per cent had worked at the plant and quit. Demand doubled in the first two years after IBP began expanding the plant and bringing more workers to town. Bill Peterson, who manages Brooks Food Bank Foundation, said the rapid growth of the low-paying service sector would mean more people coming to the food bank for help. Weisbeck said such problems were to be expected when a town grows as quickly as Brooks did. "Southern Alberta is booming," he said. "You always end up with people falling through the cracks. People come to places like Brooks looking for work, and if things don't work out they end up on social assistance."

Social services agencies in town saw a big jump in demand after IBP bought Lakeside. Two hundred people signed up for an English-as-a-second-language course set up to accommodate just eighty; an emergency shelter was established to deal with homelessness in a town that never before had such a problem; transitional welfare payments jumped by almost ten times in the three years after the plant expanded; and the local school board set up a breakfast program for hungry children and struggled to establish before- and after-school care for students whose parents worked. Law enforcement also became a challenge. In 1996, before the expansion, three hundred people spent a night in the local jail. In 1999, a thousand people were taken in to custody – almost a 300 per cent jump during a period when the city's population increased by 30 per cent. Arrests were up on both assault and theft charges.

Brandon, which has seen much the same pattern emerge, couldn't say it wasn't warned. Like Brooks, the city welcomed a big meat packer to town. Richard Rounds, a local development consultant who studied Maple Leaf's impact on Brandon for the city, says, "That Maple Leaf came here was fortuitous. School enrolments were dropping. We couldn't keep our young people."

At the time of Maple Leaf's arrival, grain prices were heading into a tailspin as the Crow Rate came to an end. "The Crow" was set up in 1897 as an incentive for the Canadian Pacific Railway to build a second pass through the mountains of British Columbia, through the Crowsnest Pass, by subsidizing the cost of shipping grain to market. The cheap freight rates, in turn, encouraged farmers to grow wheat for the export market. By the 1970s, the fee charged by the rail companies and paid by the farmers covered only 30 per cent of the cost, with the government paying the rest. Ottawa cancelled the Crow Rate in 1995, blaming World Trade Organization rules against subsidies for farmers. The move had the expected effect of boosting the western livestock industry as farmers either turned to livestock or switched to growing crops for animal feed that could be sold locally. The result has been a 40 per cent jump in hog production in the west, according to *Pig International* magazine, with the Prairie provinces now home to almost half the 1.4 million hogs raised annually in Canada. In Manitoba, the jump in pork production also brought Canada's largest hog slaughtering plant to Brandon.

On December 18, 2000, Brandon city officials and politicians were handed a study by Rounds and Associates, a local consulting firm, saying the plant would have a massive impact on Brandon and the entire Manitoba economy. "Owing to the scale of the Maple Leaf

Pork operation, the social, demographic and economic effects will be far reaching," Rounds wrote. Using demographic models taken from other communities, the report said the population of Brandon would jump by 11,290 as the plant moved into a second shift, a 29 per cent increase. According to the report, however, only 3,232 of the new residents would work at the plant; the rest would work in the service sector. That meant that the major effect the plant would have on the city would be a big hike in low-paying, notoriously insecure fast-food and retail jobs. Local residents who welcomed the plant with visions of high-paying factory jobs instead found the local job market increasingly dominated by minimum-wage, part-time jobs. "It's a service community, basically," says Rounds.

Many of those jobs were filled by newcomers arriving in Brandon hoping to get high-paying jobs, but instead finding themselves flipping burgers or stocking shelves at minimum wage. Such uprooting of a family – the Rounds Report projected that 70 per cent of these "secondary workers" would have children – for minimal return adds great stress to home life, especially for those who find themselves far from friends and family. The result, the report predicted, would be an increase in domestic violence, social service costs, and crime. "Both violent and property crimes increase noticeably when the major population increase expected with the two shifts of operation occurs."

There would be two to three additional violent crimes a year, and one hundred additional property crimes attributable to Maple Leaf coming to town, the report said. This would force the city and surrounding municipalities to hire more police and social workers to deal with the fallout. Local taxpayers would also have to find money to pay for more schools since the newcomers' children would fill a hundred new classrooms, and to cover increased infrastructure costs for extended water and sewage lines. As well, since most of the new jobs in town would be low-paying, the city would have to find space for trailer parks – the only form of housing the Rounds Report expected the new workers would be able to afford. It projected that the city would have 452 mobile homes by 2003, and another 200 the following year. "Housing has been a big issue," Rounds says. "We have an extremely tight rental market." He estimates that the vacancy rate has been about 0.5 per cent since Maple Leaf came to town.

Rounds's 2000 report proved prophetic. In 2002, Brandon commissioned a study into homelessness in the city that found the Maple Leaf plant's coming to town had left Brandon short of affordable housing and with a growing homeless problem. It expected the vacancy rate to drop further when the plant started a second shift. "The incidence of homelessness will increase over the short term," the report said. Rounds estimates that there were between seventeen and fifty people with nowhere to go at night, and more who had no place of their own but had managed to find a friend with a spare couch or patch of floor on which to sleep. "There's a fair bit of couch-surfing that goes on," he says. The homelessness report called for more emergency shelter beds and public housing in Brandon, as well as money to help landlords reopen apartments that had been taken off the market because of building or fire code violations.

Brandon's experience is consistent with that of other communities that are home to massive new slaughterhouses. The report reflected much of what had already happened in Brooks, a thousand kilometres to the west. In an interview, however, Rounds says that Brandon was better able to absorb the plant into the community because it was bigger. "Brooks was too small to handle that expansion," he says. "The town grew so fast it wasn't really well planned."

The experience in small U.S. towns bears that out. In Lexington, Nebraska, for instance, the number of serious crimes doubled after IBP came to town in 1990, and the town became a major centre for illegal drugs. This small town of seven thousand had the state's highest number of gang members and drive-by shootings. When IBP arrived, it promised stable jobs. It didn't work out that way, and most of the town's long-time white residents moved out, replaced by Mexican and Guatemalan immigrants working at bad jobs in the slaughterhouse or the new fast-food restaurants and discount retailers. *Meat and Poultry* magazine – an industry publication in the United States – estimated in 2002 that 25 per cent of the workers in the American meat packing industry are illegal immigrants, mostly from Central America.

Despite its size Brandon soon saw the trends associated with welcoming such a new player to town being played out in its streets. Rounds estimates that $40 million was poured into the city through workers' wages alone. "That much money is going to have an impact," he says. When I visited in the summer of 2001, my aunt and uncle boasted about all the new restaurants and stores in town. My uncle took me on a drive, and the city reminded me in many ways of Brooks, with its strip of fast-food restaurants and big new Wal-Mart on the highway out of town. Success was measured by having one of the largest Canadian Tire outlets in the country.

From my family there, I had heard many times about Brandon's struggles to keep the town economically viable so that its young people would want to stay. I can understand why people in the city welcomed the plant so eagerly. After years of decline, the city was growing again, no mean feat in a part of the country more noted for its economic troubles than its successes. Along with the new stores and restaurants, however, there were also low-rent housing units being built within a few metres of the railroad tracks running through the middle of town and a proliferation of trailer parks – just as the Rounds Report predicted.

As in Brooks, turnover at the Brandon plant is a big problem, and Maple Leaf followed IBP's lead by recruiting in the Maritimes. The move was not a complete success. Only one in ten of the Maritime recruits lasted more than a year on the job. Next, the company began recruiting in Mexico, and the first twenty-one workers arrived early in 2002 on two-year work visas. The company, however, did not see any connection between low pay and trouble recruiting people to work in its plants. "Our wages, fully loaded in, are actually very competitive as far as the local market goes," Steve

Leblanc, human resources manager at the Brandon plant, told Canadian Press.

With the local market increasingly dominated by the service sector, that's not much to be proud of and did not bode well for the prospects of improving working conditions at the plant. But while Maple Leaf apparently did not have trouble with an admitted annual turnover rate of 60 per cent (the union at the plant pegged it at more than 100 per cent) thanks to low wages, the investment community was starting to question the strategy. "Perhaps the strategy of paying relatively low wages is not so good or not so smart given today's low unemployment levels," Shawn Allen, an independent industry analyst with investment-picks.com, wrote in a report posted on the firm's Web site.

Even within the industry, commentators were calling on the big meat companies to rethink their low-wage, high-turnover strategy. John Luter III, chairman of Smithfield, the world's largest pork company, told the annual meeting of the U.S. National Meat Association in 2002 that "absolutely, no question, we need to pay our people more," saying that the hourly wage "hasn't changed in twenty years, and that hasn't done a damn bit of good. It hasn't helped us become more profitable, our markets haven't changed." Asked if he would be first to raise wages, he said no. With competitive pressures keeping wages low, he advocated an industry-wide move by all companies at once.

Commenting on this speech, Steve Bjerkie, editor of industry magazine *Meat Processing*, condemned Luter for identifying a problem but lacking the leadership to fix it. Better pay, he said, would serve many purposes. "The communities in which these plants are located suffer instability in its many forms: lack of cohesiveness, poor schools, and troubled relationships between temporary residents and police, all of which have been well documented." Luter told the conference: "A lot of communities no longer want meat plants to be built in them or near them."

In Canada, an effort has been made to ease foreign recruits into their new communities. In Brandon, Maple Leaf and the city hosted welcoming parties for the Mexicans when they arrived, and volunteer groups were formed to help them adjust to their new home. The community had done much the same when a wave of Vietnamese refugees came to town decades earlier. In Brooks, local shops began to cater to the newcomers by stocking the food that is typically in their cuisine, as the community adjusted to its new multicultural makeup. "The culture shock wasn't just for those coming over. It was for long-term residents, as well," Weisbeck says. "The town had been mostly Caucasian."

You might expect that, given the problems arising from the Tyson model of meat production, the industry might rethink its strategy. But it's not. Instead, it is forging ahead as if nothing were the matter. Forces in both the retail sector of the food industry and cost pressures on the production side are likely to continue pushing the industrialization of farming in Canada.

One of the fastest-growing sectors of the grocery industry is the home meal replacement sector, a $923-million industry in Canada. The term "home meal replacement" was first used to describe the barbecued chickens and meat pies available in supermarket deli sections, but has since expanded to include frozen lasagnes and other entrees, as well as already cooked roasts now making their way into the meat section. Sales of refrigerated entrees were up 44 per cent in 2000 over the year before, and frozen and refrigerated pizzas 41 per cent. Prepackaged salads sales were up 23 per cent.

Grocery store managers love home replacement meals. The profits are higher than for the rest of the store, where margins are notoriously thin, and shopkeepers can cross-merchandise the barbecued chicken with prepared side dishes such as pasta, potato salad, or bread. Some supermarkets even sell wine in a barely separated store. More importantly, perhaps, retailers can build customer loyalty by selling meals under the store's own brand name, such as Loblaw's

popular President's Choice brand. "Consumers will become loyal to
a specific store offering the fully prepared meal category and will not
easily accept another store's same product offering," Kevin Grier
wrote in his assessment of the industry, *An Update on the Canadian
Home Meal Replacement Market* in November 2001.

He estimates that prepared meal sections expanded by about 30
per cent in the late 1990s, with many retailers operating stand-alone
meal replacement departments within their stores. Prepared meals
were first developed as a way for grocery stores to fight the trend of
people eating in restaurants or buying takeout dinners. The strategy
seemed to work, with the average number of restaurant meals dropping by between 3 and 4 per cent between 1999 and 2000 as people
increasingly opted for home-cooked meals. "But they are not
cooking so much as heating up an array of frozen pizzas, entrees and
meat products," Grier wrote.

The biggest challenge Grier saw for the new category was the
need to provide a consistent offering. Customer loyalty was based on
more than just the convenience prepared meals offered; it was based
on the expectation that each meal would be the same as the last. "It is
the challenge for chains to manage the consistency of the offering."

Companies filling the meat case face the same challenge. Where
once cuts of meat were slapped with generic labels listing only the
weight and price of the meat, the meat case now offers branded cuts
such as Maple Leaf's Prime Naturally chicken and Cargill's Sterling
Silver Beef. These so-called case-ready meats, packaged at faraway
factories, are rapidly replacing the in-store butcher's cuts. Case-ready
meats are not fully prepared meals, though some of them have been
seasoned. Each, however, seeks to gain consumer loyalty by offering a
consistent product. We can expect to see more brands in the meat case
since, as with home meal replacements, the profit margin is higher.
"We've found that consumers will pay more for branded products.
There's a consistent quality. They know what they are getting," says
Randy Johnston, Ontario sales supervisor for Maple Leaf Poultry. And
that consistency is helping to propel industrial agriculture.

"Success and cost-effectiveness requires rigorous planning and disciplined execution. One key element of a successful brand is consistency," Maple Leaf wrote in its 2001 annual report. But consistency is tough to achieve when a food company buys animals from hundreds, or even thousands, of small farmers – each with his or her own preference for the types of animals they want to raise. So companies contract with farmers to grow only certain types of animals or birds. And in the case of poultry, to make sure that farmers grow only the birds wanted by the company, the company even supplies the baby chicks.

At its $3.5-million hatching barn in New Hamburg, Ontario, Maple Leaf hatches more than 1 million chicks a week to supply farmers who later sell the fully grown birds to Maple Leaf's slaughter-houses. In the meantime, the farmers buy Maple Leaf's Shur-Gain feed, which has been especially formulated to the needs of the company's chicks. In a conference call in June 2001 with Bay Street decision makers, Michael McCain of Maple Leaf said the Prime Naturally brand was "made possible by our approach to vertical coordination."

Farmers got the same message. In a pamphlet used by the company to entice farmers into joining the industrial model, Maple Leaf outlined how vertical integration and branding went hand in hand: "Maple Leaf chicks, on a Shur-Gain nutrition program will result in Maple Leaf Prime Chicken . . . Canada's leading brand of fresh chicken for today's consumer!" Maple Leaf's sales of branded products grew from $30 million a year in 1996 to $200 million in 2000. Maple Leaf then introduced branding to pork, with its Medallion Naturally brand.

Expanding brands, however, meant recruiting ever more farmers to the fold. Every summer, the *Ontario Farmer* newspaper features full- and half-page ads for open houses sponsored by Maple Leaf to show off the latest factory farm it has signed up. Pamphlets handed out at the open houses boast about the higher prices consumers would pay for branded products, with one quoting a company study that found 61 per cent of shoppers would pay more for an "all natural" chicken product such as Maple Leaf's Prime Naturally. At the open houses, the company hands out doughnuts, coffee, and chicken sandwiches, and has feed and breeding experts on hand to explain to the curious how the new operation would work, and to entice them into making the $1-million investment needed to become a big chicken farmer.

The new barns have computerized feeding and watering machines to give the birds exactly the amount of food the company has determined – based on the genetics it has built into the birds – the chickens need. Watering systems in place make sure the birds stay hydrated and get their antibiotics. "The filtration system keeps the nipple valves clean and ensures drinking water with less impurities. Medication is easily distributed through the medicator manifold," reads a pamphlet from Illinois-based Cumberland, a company selling automated watering systems to factory farms. The heat in the 60- by 360-foot barn is regulated by computers, which can be programmed to call the farmer at home or on a cellular phone if there is a problem. "You wouldn't want to spend more than two and a half to three hours in a facility like this – picking up the odd dead bird and checking the equipment," Roger Hubble, a former hog farmer now building big chicken and pig barns for other farmers, said at one open house.

Barns holding 28,000 birds cost about $250,000, plus another $200,000 for the equipment to run it. That's almost half a million dollars before a single bird is bought. Buying the chickens and paying for the quota pushes the total to more than $1 million. Farmers making such a huge investment bet their livelihoods on the poultry industry and their relationship with the company selling them their chicks and their feed and buying back their birds.

As the big food companies move to producing home meal replacements and branded meats, they buy more and more of their livestock from factory farms that can better guarantee them the consistent quality of animal than can a larger number of small farms with their own preferences for bird breeds and types of feed. Maple Leaf encouraged this evolution by collecting the production quota needed to participate in Canada's supply-managed poultry sector and distributing it to the farmers it chose to deal with. In 2001, 1.8 million chicken quota units changed hands in Ontario "without premises," according to the Chicken Farmers of Ontario, more than twice the rate just four years earlier. Without-premises transfers occur when quota is collected from one farm, but not immediately transferred to another.

While they forced changes to the livestock industry that pushed farmers into high-stakes gambles on specialization, the companies themselves diversified. Maple Leaf, for instance, is not only Canada's largest poultry company, but also operates the country's largest hog-slaughtering plant in Brandon. It also has a bakery division, the Shur-Gain animal feed division, and the Rothsay chain of rendering plants to dispose of the waste from its slaughterhouses. This helps the company weather any troubles in one sector with better fortunes in another – just as farmers once did.

The strategy worked for Maple Leaf: "In 2000, our pork operations suffered due to high hog costs, and processed meat margins were pressed for similar reasons. However, our poultry business continued to march forward with sales of branded Prime poultry reaching $197 million. The Agribusiness Group experienced continued steady improvement. And, our Bakery Group has been an excellent turnaround and development story, both in Canada and the United States," Michael McCain told the company's 2001 annual general meeting.

Tyson, the company that developed the industrial agriculture model, expanded beyond its poultry base with its purchase of IBP, the company that owns the Brooks cattle-slaughtering plant. With IBP, Tyson became the largest U.S. meat company, controlling one-quarter of the chicken market, one-fifth of the pork market, and almost one-third of the beef market. Its production of 42 million chickens a week is larger than the entire Canadian industry.

This integration of the red and white meat industries should protect Tyson from any downturn in either beef or poultry sales. After half a century of telling farmers it was inefficient to have both cattle and chickens on the same farm, Tyson, Maple Leaf, and the other corporations controlling our food supply evidently decided such rules didn't apply to them. "We farmers have been told for decades to specialize," Bill Heffernan, a rural sociologist from the University of Missouri, told a gathering of Ontario farmers in November 2000. "Specialize, specialize, specialize. And what do these big companies do? They diversify. And folks, they're wiping us out."

Soccer pitch at Englewood School, Crapaud, P.E.I., 2002

"That spray's pretty safe, but it's not good for fish."

Barry Cudmore,
potato farmer

CHAPTER THREE

THE RIVERS RUN RED

Englewood School sits among the rolling hills of red soil that made Prince Edward Island famous. Down the road, Annie's Country Kitchen coaxes tourists inside for home-cooked meals and doughnuts, and there is an Irving service station should they stop for gas. White frame houses dominate the streets, and big trees cast long shadows the evening in July 2002 when children and parents gathered for the opening night of the summer soccer league. The entire village of Crapaud, one of the oldest communities on the island, had pitched in to make the new goals being used for the first time that night. There had been golf tournaments, yard sales, and raffles. A local farmer volunteered to weld the goal frames together, and townsfolk used donated junipers to build the playground equipment that sits alongside the soccer pitches.

Built in 1962 as a high school, Englewood had nothing for the school children to climb or swing on when it was converted to a 230-student elementary school in the late 1990s. A $35,000 building program organized by the home and school association fixed the problem with new climbers, swings, slides, a sandbox, teeter-totters, and soccer fields. A day camp opened at the school, ensuring the halls and fields are filled with children's laughter and play all year round. Monday night soccer brings them back in the evening.

Along with most of P.E.I., the hills around Crapaud succumbed to the potato boom in the 1990s. Each spring, the hills are carefully carved into straight lines that run up the slopes. All around the school, potatoes grow, their broad leaves swaying in the gentle breeze off the Northumberland Strait just a few kilometres away.

The people of P.E.I., many descended from Irish immigrants, hold a deep affection for the potato. It's been the subject of story and song, and in O'Leary, near the western shore, a museum is dedicated to the potato. The long mounds of soil distinctive to potato fields are as much a symbol of the island as the red beaches and sandstone cliffs along its northern shores. The province's 2002 tourist guide contains half a dozen photos of potato fields.

The potato is big business. A $75-million Cavendish Farms french fry plant opened in 1996, a year after the accounting giant Deloitte and Touche told the provincial government that agriculture and food production offered the island the greatest opportunities for economic growth. Combined, the two industries generated about $750 million in business in 1996 – $300 million for farming and the rest for processing. That's three times the amount 1 million tourists brought to the island.

The processing industry was able to take full advantage of a crisis that hit one of the three pillars of the potato industry on the island – seed potatoes. In the early 1990s, about 30 per cent of the industry was dedicated to seed potatoes, 25 to 30 per cent to french fries, and the rest to table potatoes. "Until then, we had a kind of balance in the industry," said Marie Burge of the Cooper Institute, a Charlottetown think-tank. But in the early 1990s, a virus called PVYn hit the island. It didn't hurt the potatoes themselves but could damage tobacco, green peppers, and tomatoes. Borders were closed to the island's seed potatoes by Agriculture Canada in hopes of quarantining the virus. The move eradicated the disease, but left one-third of P.E.I.'s farmers suddenly without a market. They couldn't move into table potatoes, since that required that they have bagging equipment and spend more money on pesticides and other chemicals to ensure their produce would look good for consumers. "The line of least resistance was moving to processing potatoes," said Burge. "It was convenient for the processing industry. They profited from it. They got lots of potatoes, and their businesses flourished."

Within two years of the Cavendish plant being built, 110,000 acres of island farmland were dedicated to potatoes, up from just 68,000 in 1989. Half the 2.8 billion pounds of potatoes dug from the soil each year went to the Cavendish plant, which employed about seven hundred people; the smaller McCain's french fry plant nearby, with 160 workers; and a handful of other processors such as the Small Fry chip plant in Summerside.

A 1998 study by the Canadian Institute for Research on Regional Development warned the province that the rapid jump in potato production could cause environmental problems: "The balance has never been as tilted towards potato production as it is now," said the report. "The increased acreage devoted to potatoes . . . has had side-effects. These include a greater use of chemical fertilizers and anti-fungal sprays, the reclamation for agriculture of land once surrendered to forest, as well as the soil-risking use of steeply sloped land for potatoes." All this, the report said, represented a threat to "the quality of water downstream."

The expansion of potato farming also meant increasing the size of existing fields, inching them closer to residential areas and schools. Englewood's new soccer nets are placed about ten metres from the edge of a potato field that gently slopes toward the schoolyard. A few trees, and little else, separate the soccer field from the potato field. On opening night of the soccer league, the six- to eight-year-olds playing twice kicked the ball into the potatoes and ran in to retrieve it. Earlier that day, I had gone into that field. White residue on the leaves and fresh tractor marks in the dirt revealed that the field had been sprayed with fungicide that morning. Fungicides typically carry warnings to not enter a field for twenty-four to forty-eight hours after a spraying. There was no such warning posted for the children that day, however, and within hours of the spraying, children were running in and out of the field.

Neila Auld, head of the home and school association, was optimistic that the farmer would have held off spraying if he had known that children would be playing soccer. "He's a pretty reasonable fellow," she said. "He's got kids at the school." The opening of the soccer season had been advertised all over the village in store-window posters and a sign at the school.

Despite her optimism, Auld was still concerned about all the potatoes being grown around the school. "The school is surrounded by potato fields. Just surrounded," she said. She had some leftover lumber from the playground building project and thought she might build a fence to keep soccer balls and kids from going into the potato field. Her bigger concern, however, was on the other side of the school, where school property was being rented out to another potato farmer – and nothing separated the farm field from a second soccer pitch, this one running lengthwise along the field. "We want the school to tell him he can't grow potatoes any more," she said. Asked why, she replied, "Well, the chemicals."

Englewood is not the only school feeling the effects of potato fields. In September 1997, Natalie Hunt, a Grade 3 student at Gulf Shore School in North Rustico, was outside for recess when she smelled sulphur in the air. She knew the smell. Her house in nearby Millvale was across the road from a potato farm, and for the past year her parents had been battling the farmer over his use of pesticides. "We used to live near potato fields, so I recognized the smell. It was really gross," Natalie said, the experience still fresh in her mind five years later. "My throat started to tighten, and my head hurt. Me and my friends went into a doorway of the school. It was the only place we couldn't smell it."

Her parents, Nancy and John, complained to the school principal. So did a number of other parents and teachers, and the farmer was eventually fined $200 for improper use of a pesticide. Nancy and John took Natalie to a doctor after the incident. She had been having breathing problems and feeling weak since the farmer across the road began spraying pesticides. She was tested for asthma, multiple sclerosis, and other ailments, all negative. John was worried that the doctors were not taking his concerns about pesticides seriously. "You tell them you think it's pesticides, and they don't even write it down," he said. "And then they claim there's no documented proof pesticides are a problem," Nancy added.

Eventually, the family moved away from the potato fields of Millvale to a more wooded part of the island, and Natalie switched schools. Her health problems diminished but did not disappear. The Hunts talked about growing their own food to avoid pesticides altogether but recognized that doing so would not be a solution to pesticide problems on the island – only an escape for the family. The real solution, they became convinced, was to cut out pesticide use altogether and the Green Revolution monoculture that made them necessary. "This sort of thing is happening all over the world," Nancy said. "This place is not unique. We just have more of it."

About 20 per cent of children on P.E.I. have asthma, compared with 13 per cent across Canada. Children with asthma get out of breath after even a little physical exertion, so they are unable to take part in normal playtime activities. At soccer games across the island, kids come off the fields and run to their parents for a puff from their inhalers.

In 1997, Queen Elizabeth Hospital in Charlottetown opened an asthma education centre in response to the huge number of cases it was seeing. "Each year, there are 900 emergency room visits [at QE alone] related to asthma," Health Minister Mildred Dover said at the time. The centre was set up with money from the federal and provincial governments, and Glaxo Wellcome and Astra Pharma drug companies.

The spina bifida rate is also higher in P.E.I. – 16.6 cases per 10,000 births, compared with 7.8 for all of Canada. Spina bifida is marked by a failure of the spine to close properly during pregnancy. In the worst cases, the child is born with a portion of its spine protruding through its back. An operation soon after birth can often correct the problem but leaves the child crippled. The disorder is often accompanied by hydrocephalus, an accumulation of fluid in the brain that can cause learning disabilities. And repeated use of shunts to drain a buildup of cerebrospinal fluid can lead to development of a latex allergy.

A November 2002 article in the *International Journal of Occupational and Environmental Health* found that women under fifty-five who grew up on a farm were nine times more likely to develop breast cancer in later life than women who did not grow up on a farm. "We don't know from our study if it's pesticides or not," said study author James Brophy, executive director of the Occupational Health Clinic in Sarnia, Ontario, and a lecturer at the University of Windsor. "There is good evidence for conjecture that [pesticides] would certainly be the primary substances of investigation."

Environmentalist Sharon Labchuk draws a straight line between such ailments and potato fields like the ones surrounding Englewood and other schools. Labchuk began fighting chemical use on her native P.E.I. after returning to the island with her two children in 1988, handing out pamphlets at farmers' markets and to tourists coming for vacations on the island's beaches. "People thought I was trying to ruin the tourist industry, but visitors have a right to know what they are getting into," she says. Several tourists have written her to say they suffered sore throats and watery eyes when driving through the countryside. "Those people are not coming back," she says.

That will most likely be true for my family. About halfway through a two-week stay on the island, both my children started complaining about sore throats, headaches, and nausea. Potato fields surrounded the campgrounds where we stayed, and our tent trailer offered little protection. The children felt best when we went to the beach, where the breeze was coming off the ocean. But whenever we ventured inland to see a show in Charlottetown or visit a museum, their symptoms returned. By the time we reached Fundy National Park after leaving the island, the symptoms were gone. They have not returned.

Labchuk's most recent project, three years in the making, looked at the proximity of schoolyards to potato fields sprayed with chemicals, and the effect of those chemicals on people. She visited every school on the island, and what she found was astounding. In Canada's most densely populated province, 85 per cent of rural schoolyards were within five hundred metres of a potato field. Sixty-four per cent – including Englewood – had potato fields immediately adjacent. "We've got a real serious problem here," Labchuk says as she sorts through a fifteen-centimetre-high stack of dog-eared studies, surveys, and articles marked with Post-it notes in an attempt to keep things organized. Putting schools and farm fields so close together was dangerous to the health of the children, she says.

Across P.E.I., the boom in potato production brought spuds to fields that never grew them before, along roadsides and beside schools. In some communities – such as Stratford, a suburb of Charlottetown – potato production is even allowed within town limits. The 1998 report by the Canadian Institute for Research on Regional Development said that other forms of agriculture were being squeezed off the island by the heavy emphasis on potatoes. The number of dairy farms dropped from 585 to 335 over the previous decade and hog operations from 220 to 100 – outpacing reductions in the number of farms across Canada. "Tobacco used to be an important crop in the eastern part of the island, but none is grown now," the report says.

Within a couple of years of the Cavendish plant's opening, potatoes were being grown on almost 30 per cent of P.E.I.'s farmland, up from 16 per cent twenty years before. Such concentration allowed the pests that thrive in potato fields to flourish. That's led to a dramatic increase in pesticides to kill the Colorado potato beetle, other chemicals to kill weeds, and especially fungicide to kill blight – the scourge of any potato farmer. From 1982 to 2000, there was a 632 per cent increase in the use of pesticides on the island, according to provincial government tallies. This happened at the same time as potato fields were edging closer to towns, villages, and schools to feed the expanded french fry plants.

Few crops are sprayed with as many chemicals as potatoes, which receive up to twenty dousings a season to fight bugs, blight, and weeds. "The ugly truth is the P.E.I. landscape is dominated by industrial agriculture and Islanders are among the most pesticide-exposed people in North America," Labchuk wrote in her study of schools and potato fields. In 2000, 17.7 pounds of active pesticide (not including the material carrying it) were used per person in P.E.I., compared with four pounds across Canada. Eighty-two per cent of island spraying is fungicide to control blight. In fields in the rest of Canada, fungicide accounts for only about 7 per cent of the active pesticide used. In the United States, the national average was 3.1 pounds per person, peaking at 6.5 pounds in California.

The most popular fungicides on P.E.I. are mancozeb, chlorothalonil, and thiophanate-methyl. All are believed to cause cancer. They work by coating the leaves of the potato and killing any blight spores that land. The constant breezes of P.E.I. blow the blight spores from field to field. But fungicides wash off, or break down in sunlight after a few days. The P.E.I. Ministry of Agriculture recommends that farmers spray as frequently as every four days in late summer to keep blight out, a gruelling schedule that farmers do their best to uphold. "You have to keep your spraying schedule up. Once [the blight's] in there, there's nothing you can do," says Robert MacDonald, who farms on the eastern tip of the island.

Blight is devastating. It can wipe out an entire potato crop in a matter of days. Because no chemical can kill blight without also killing the plant, all a farmer can do is spray to prevent it. Blight holds a particular terror for potato farmers. It was blight that caused the Irish Potato Famine of 1845, turning that island's crop into a putrid mess. It was blight that left millions to starve and millions more to flee Ireland in search of a better life, including to P.E.I. They brought their tales of blight's devastation with them, instilling them in their children, who passed them down through the generations.

On P.E.I., blight's cruel power has never been forgotten. "It's wicked. It'll cut down a field in a week to nothing but garbage,"

MacDonald says. Vowing never to lose another crop to blight, farmers spray fungicide at least once a week when the weather permits, and every week and a half when it doesn't. Over the hundred-day lifespan of a potato, that can mean fifteen fungicide sprays. Add to that sprays for beetles and weeds, and potato fields can receive as many as twenty chemical sprays a year.

Labchuk says that potato farmers learned the wrong lessons from the Irish famine. The real culprit was not the blight, but the monoculture that let it spread. The solution is not to spray chemicals to fight the blight, but to grow other crops, which would slow its spread. "We've got to get away from this potato mentality," she says. That mentality led to a 25 per cent jump in weed-killer sales on P.E.I. from 1982 to 2000. Insecticides, mostly to kill the Colorado potato beetle, account for only about 6 per cent of pesticide sales in P.E.I.

Most of that is one product: Bayer's Admire, which has dominated the market since its introduction in 1999. It is sprayed on the soil once a year and taken up by the roots of the potato plant as it grows. The pesticides it has replaced had to be sprayed several times a year. Admire has led to a cut in insecticide use, but, as Labchuk was quick to point out, it can stay in the soil as long as two years. "Overall risk to human health and the environment has not changed," she wrote in her schools study. The refusal by both Cavendish and McCain to buy genetically modified potatoes engineered to kill beetles means that GM potatoes were never able to capture any more than about 5 per cent of the market before they were taken off the market.

Pesticides are spread with thirty-metre boom sprayers dragged behind tractors. The booms stretch over the rows of potatoes like the wings of a giant bird and leave behind a fog of chemicals. MacDonald has two boom sprayers so he can keep up his schedule across eight hundred acres. During my visit, one of the sprayers is working a field only a few metres from a neighbour's home. "That guy up there, he's from away. He doesn't understand the realities of potato farming," MacDonald says. Most of the criticism of chemicals, he says, came from people moving to the countryside who have never lived on farms. Up the road, MacDonald notices that another neighbour has set up a tent trailer next to another of his fields and guesses that there might be visitors who would complain about his spraying. "It's a good thing we got in there yesterday. We sure couldn't spray there now," he says. "I just hope they're gone next week."

MacDonald has good reason to worry. In her study, Labchuk cites Environment Canada studies that have found that less than 1 per cent of the pesticide sprayed on a field actually reaches the pest, and that only 60 to 80 per cent lands on the crop or on the ground. The rest – as much as 40 per cent – blows away. The difference in the figures is caused by factors such as wind speed and attachments like the one on MacDonald's boom that sprays the pesticide down harder, reducing drift. The attachment also cut his costs, since he was better able to get the chemical to go where he wanted. Not all farmers follow MacDonald's example, however. "Even on the calmest day, some pesticide will always drift," Labchuk wrote. The island has banned spraying when the wind speed exceeds twenty-four kilometres per hour, but Labchuk says the ban is useless. Few farmers would spray on such a windy day anyway – it would be too costly to see their chemicals carried away on the wind. "Only now, citizens cannot complain about spray drift because pesticide sprayers are protected by law."

Labchuk used the federal Access to Information Act to obtain a federal study of air quality in Summerside, P.E.I.'s second-largest city. The study, based on air samples taken in the summers of 1998 and 1999, found that a mix of chemicals sprayed on potato fields including chlorothalonil, a fungicide used to fight blight, were borne into the city on the wind. Traces of chlorothalonil were even found in a test sample taken at the end of a wharf in a village where potatoes were not grown. The federal researchers had taken this sample expecting that it would be clean air they could use as a standard against which to compare the others. Chlorothalonil is classified as a carcinogen by the U.S. government and can cause eye and skin irritation. Insecticides and weed killers were also detected in the sample. In the fall of 2002, pesticides from a large strawberry farm were found in four private wells in western P.E.I.

Ivan Noonan of the P.E.I. Potato Board said he was more worried about an import ban the United States had imposed over fears of warts on P.E.I. potatoes than he was about chemicals in the air. "I breathe the same air as Sharon Labchuk breathes, and I'm not worried," he told reporters. "The problem she is raising is very minor in people's lives. On a scale of one to ten, it's a negative."

P.E.I.'s farms are laid out in long, thin strips fanning out from streams and rivers. This gives each farm access to fresh water. Farmers plough up the hills away from the water, since it is more efficient to plough a field lengthwise, reducing the number of times the tractor must be turned around. Two or three times a year, the farmer ploughs the soil up around the base of the plants. This keeps the potatoes from being exposed to the sunlight, which would ruin them. The result is foot-high mounds of soil about three feet apart, running up and down the fields – the distinctive sign of a potato field. Between those mounds are trenches that on rainy days act like ditches carrying rainwater and pesticides washed from the plants into one of the island's 263 waterways. "You see it all over the island, steep hills with trenches running straight down into the water," Labchuk says.

The province has tried to persuade farmers to plough across their hills instead of up and down, but with limited success. Most still plough deep trenches that run straight to a waterway. In many fields, divided by twisting streams and rivers, trenches still lead directly to water, no matter how the fields are ploughed. I began to wonder how the province's dictum against ploughing up and down hills could possibly be enforced.

Chemical use on P.E.I. first made national headlines after a torrential rain in the summer of 1999 washed away tonnes of the island's distinctive ruby-coloured soil. "The rivers ran red for days," said

Labchuk. Dead fish soon washed up on the banks of streams and rivers. Islanders and tourists started asking what had gone wrong, and farmers went on the defensive. The province took immediate action, laying charges against several farmers for improper use of chemicals and appointing an inquiry. A few months later, the inquiry concluded that the kills were a fluke, echoing the explanation offered by farmers from the start, the result of abnormally heavy rains at a time when the leaves on the potato plants were wilted and unable to catch the rainwater. Measures taken since then, the province said, such as crop rotations and the creation of buffer zones along the banks of rivers and streams, would help farmers cut back on chemical use. The public furor died down, the next year's planting got underway, and farmers looked forward to a record crop under ideal growing conditions.

Then more fish died. Another heavy rain in August 2000 flushed bug killers and fungicides into three island rivers, killing almost three thousand more fish, mostly trout. In the Indian River, near the popular tourist destination of Cavendish and the Gulf Shore School, dead fish washed up along a two-kilometre stretch. More charges were laid, and the province talked about taking tough action. But the timing couldn't have been worse, coming at the height of the summer tourist season and just days after the charges laid after the fish kill of the previous year were dropped.

Hayden Produce Inc. had been charged under P.E.I.'s Fisheries Act for its part in the 1999 fish kill. Runoff from three of its potato fields washed into the Valleyfield River, killing more than 2,500 fish. The charges were dropped when the farm paid $10,000 to help revitalize the river and promised to abide by environmental laws. For Labchuk, that deal is proof that the province does not take the issue seriously, and that the farmers are not moving fast enough to fix the problem. "How much of a penalty is it to be made to say you'll abide by the law?" she asks. "It's a joke."

In the wake of the fish kills, the province pushed farmers to cut back on chemical use. "We encourage farmers to develop environmental farm plans and action plans to implement them," says Teresa

Mellish, a planning officer with the province's ministry of agriculture. Farmers are eligible for provincial grants to help wean them off chemicals if they move to crop rotation, leave buffer zones around streams and rivers, and replace trees and hedgerows removed a generation earlier to make way for big potato fields. Hedges help stop topsoil from blowing away, reducing the need for fertilizers to replenish the soil, and prevent pesticides from blowing off the field. Crop rotations break the life cycle of bugs, reducing the need for chemicals. The province wanted farmers to plant potatoes in the same field only once every three years. And buffer zones – ten-metre strips along waterways that are not planted – help filter out chemicals before they reach the water and kill fish. All these measures were meant to get farmers to use more natural methods to grow their crops – in short, to take a step back from the Green Revolution.

Many of these measures were later made mandatory. All farmers must now have ten-metre buffers along waterways, and potatoes and other row crops have been banned from steep hills where runoff is worst.

The moves proved a tough sell. Grocers and processors demand perfect produce from farmers, the manager of Eric C. Robinson Inc., one of the island's largest farms, told me, echoing the operating principle of farmers across the country. "That's the reality of it. We haven't identified a market yet for rotted potatoes," said Steve Watts. At best, a disease or bug-infested crop can be sold for animal feed, at a price less than the cost of production. At worst, it cannot be sold at all. Growing perfect potatoes means that farmers must not allow any bug or disease to eat into their returns. And that takes chemicals, sometimes a lot of chemicals. "We spray because we have to. No other reason," said Watts.

Still, ask any farmer, and he'll tell you he wished he could cut down on chemicals, if only to lessen operating costs or reduce his family's exposure to them. Watts took me past some test plots Robinson had set up with the World Wildlife Fund to find ways to cut chemical use. It was part of the WWF's Field to Table program in which fields are scouted intensely to make sure only needed chemicals are sprayed. Other methods the WWF promotes include crop rotation and spraying only crops on the edges of fields to keep pests from getting in. These techniques are more labour intensive and more costly than a quick run over the fields with a boom sprayer, so the WWF promises to help the farmers sell their produce as a premium product commanding a higher price. "If we can get more money for our crop, it makes the extra effort worth while," said Watts.

Such efforts were expanded island-wide in 2002 with the launch of Foodtrust PEI, a provincially sponsored effort to brand P.E.I. food as more wholesome and higher quality than other food. To start, farmers selling through Foodtrust have to do little more than live up to existing environmental rules, though eventually they will be expected to exceed them. As compensation, their food will be sold under the Foodtrust brand at premium prices. They hope to profit from taking a step back from the Green Revolution.

The Green Revolution was born in Mexico during the Second World War when Henry Wallace went there shortly after he was elected vice-president of the United States on Franklin Roosevelt's ticket. Some fifteen years earlier, Wallace had invented hybrid corn, which boosted production, and founded the Pioneer Hi-Bred seed company. At the time Mexico was not able to feed itself, and its staple crop of corn was yielding far less food than Wallace's invention was producing for American farmers. When he got back to the United States, Wallace tried to convince Congress to help the Mexicans, but got nowhere. He turned, then, to the Rockefeller Foundation, which had begun funding public health programs around the world. "I said I thought it would be a fine thing if they went to Mexico," he said later.

The foundation followed the vice-president's advice and within a few years was paying American crop breeders to go to Mexico to teach intensive farming techniques and to develop better-yielding crops. One of those scientists was Norman Borlaug, who won the

1970 Nobel Peace Prize for his work to improve wheat yields and was later dubbed the father of the Green Revolution. Borlaug and the others made fast progress in Mexico. By 1948, the country was able to feed itself for the first time since the 1910 revolution, thanks to higher corn, wheat, and potato yields.

During this period, wartime chemicals were being converted to civilian use on farms. Defoliants used to clear the jungles and insecticides used to stop the spread of malaria during the campaign in the South Pacific were repackaged for use on farms. For the first time in history, farmers had effective tools to control insects and weeds. Around the same time, nitrate explosives developed during the First World War were converted into nitrogen-based fertilizers that give an artificial boost to the soil, helping crops grow. After the Second World War, synthetic ammonias were also made into chemical fertilizers.

These innovations, along with improvements in the crops themselves, boosted yields by 3 per cent a year – enough to double grain production by the 1980s. In Mexico, Borlaug was able to help farmers triple their production. In the late 1920s, farmers there were getting about seven hundred kilograms of wheat from every hectare of land. By the time Borlaug left in the 1960s, a hectare was producing about 2,400 kilograms. From Mexico, Borlaug went to India and Pakistan, convinced that his new wheat could help alleviate starvation. It was for this later work that Borlaug won the Nobel Peace Prize. William Daud of the U.S. Agency for International Development coined the phrase "Green Revolution" to describe Borlaug's work in Asia. Since then, the moniker has come to take in the work Borlaug did in Mexico, as well as the chemical revolution that came to farming at the same time and the widespread use of irrigation that made Borlaug's intensive farming methods possible and on which his strains of wheat depended.

Borlaug's main contribution was to develop dwarf strains of wheat that were more responsive to fertilizers than traditional strains. In a field of grain, the tallest plants capture the most sunlight

and rainwater. Shorter plants wither, unable to get the needed sunlight or water. This gives evolutionary preference to tall grains. Such
plants, however, dedicate much of their energy to growing long
stalks and little to developing kernels, which in a farmer's field means
a small yield. Borlaug figured that if he could get all the grain to grow
at the same height, the plants would not compete for sunlight or
water and all could thrive. As well, if the stalks could be kept short,
the plants would dedicate more energy to developing kernels –
boosting yield. Tall plants also tend to fall down at harvest time, or
"lodge," under the weight of their maturing kernels. Mechanical
threshers and combines cannot harvest a field that has lodged. The
dwarf strains are stiffer and so better able to support the weight of
the new strains' heavier stalks of grain.

Borlaug's plan worked. In 1950, 692 million tons of grain were
grown worldwide on 1.7 billion acres of farmland. In 1992, 1.9
billion tons were grown on 1.73 billion acres. With only a 1 per cent
increase in the amount of land under cultivation, production had
been boosted 170 per cent. Borlaug took his dwarf wheat to the
Asian subcontinent in 1965 just as India and Pakistan were facing
widespread famine and population experts were doubting that the
two countries could ever feed themselves. By 1968, Pakistan was
self-sufficient in wheat. Production jumped from 3.4 million tons a
year in the mid-1960s to 18 million in the late 1990s. India became
self-sufficient in cereals for the first time in 1974 and on occasion
since has even managed to export wheat. India grows about 60
million tons of wheat a year – five and a half times what it grew when
Borlaug arrived.

By the late 1980s, however, the limits of crop breeding were
being reached, and yields began to stagnate and even fall. The tools
of the Green Revolution – new improved strains, chemicals, irrigation, and the machinery needed to put them to use – were expensive.
As long as yields kept growing faster than the costs, all seemed fine.
But once yield growth slowed, the juggling act became harder to
maintain. Rising fuel prices added to farmers' costs in an industry

that relied on fossil fuels both to produce and to spread the chemicals of the Green Revolution.

Slowing growth in crop yields in Canada and elsewhere led to a crisis in agriculture as farmers were squeezed out of the industry. More and more farmers went into bankruptcy, and their land and machinery were seized and sold off to the highest bidder. I was working in Owen Sound, Ontario, at the time, where just south of the city a group called Canadian Farmers' Survival Association had tried to revive a tactic from the Great Depression – the penny auction – to protest banks foreclosing and selling off a farmer's livelihood. Group leader Allen Wilford was arrested after organizing a penny auction at which a neighbour's equipment and cattle, worth $200,000, sold for $19.81 (including 6 cents for 170 cattle). It was all given back to the farmer the next day. Wilford then went on an eight-day hunger strike at the Stratford jail until the House of Commons passed second reading on a bill restricting the actions of receivers and giving farmers access to the courts to settle debt problems before their farms were auctioned off. The Farmers' Creditors Arrangements Act was eventually allowed to die on the order paper.

While stunts like Wilford's captured headlines, they couldn't stem the tide of bankruptcies sweeping through farm country. Farms and their equipment were sold off piece by piece, with neighbouring farmers picking up a few bits of equipment cheap in hopes of gaining a few more years on the land. At the auction of his land in 1987, Wilford got into a shouting match with a neighbour who said he needed the land if he was to keep his farm viable. The livelihoods of farmers were not the only thing lost at those auctions, nor just the small farms that once made up a rural community. Lost also was the bond that held them together. What emerged from the crisis were large farms run by men and women who had learned a hard lesson in economics and who began to see themselves as business people, calling themselves "producers" instead of "farmers."

In India, Green Revolution debts pushed more than twenty thousand farmers to suicide in the late 1990s and early years of this century as the cost of production jumped more than six times from 1974 to 1997, from 2,894.33 rupees ($95 Canadian) per hectare to 17,966.85 rupees, according to Indian Ministry of Agriculture figures. The cost of fertilizer jumped from 387.67 rupees per hectare to 1,724.63 rupees in the same period, while the price of insecticides increased from 0.31 to 825.04 rupees per hectare. As costs increased, so did debt. In the Punjab region, one group of farmers even offered themselves for sale, along with their farms and equipment, to the highest bidder in hopes of paying off debts of up to 75,000 rupees each. "Commodification of food is leading to a commodification of life, and we're in only the early stages of this transformation of agriculture," says Vandana Shiva, head of the Research Foundation for Science, Technology and Ecology in New Delhi. "If this is what has happened already, we need to take a look at what we are doing."

She says that thousands of farmers have left the land because of debt, swelling India's crowded and impoverished cities. Others have sold a kidney or offered their children as domestic servants. The farm crisis has fuelled unrest in the rural Punjab region, which has led to much violence. "The farmers of the Punjab have fought off the Bengals, they've fought off the British. But with corporate debt, they are literally putting themselves up for sale," Shiva says.

Shiva dismisses the success of the Green Revolution in India as a "myth," saying that the measurements used to assess it did not take into account the biological diversity that was destroyed by its chemicals and monocultures. Traditional rice farmers, for instance, did not just harvest rice from their paddies. They also gathered snails from the bottom of the flooded fields, and greens from their edges – both of which they ate. The pesticides used in the Green Revolution, however, killed both these sources of food, leaving the farmers with just the less nutritious rice.

As well, Borlaug's dwarf wheats produced less straw than the taller strains. This, Shiva says, robbed farmers of feed and bedding for their cattle, and meant that other farm land had to be used to grow animal feed rather than food for people. Meanwhile debt pressures have forced millions of farmers from the land, encouraging neighbours to increase the size of their farms – increasing the debt loads further to buy the land, seed, and needed equipment. "When companies make a trillion dollars in royalties from seeds, that's a trillion dollars that has been stolen from poor farmers," Shiva says.

The changes that Borlaug made to cereal plants may be reaching their limits. Plants, after all, must put some energy into producing the stalks that hold them up and the leaves that capture both sunlight and rain. As well, the pesticides, artificial fertilizers, and irrigation on which the high-yield Green Revolution crops rely have so degraded the soil that farm productivity in many areas has actually dropped. In the Punjab, reduced organic matter in the soil and increased salinity due to heavy irrigation have caused gains in wheat and rice yields to slow, and in some cases even drop, according to a July 2002 report in the trade journal *Economic Development and Cultural Change* co-authored by a World Bank economist. "Although results achieved in Pakistan with Green Revolution technologies are impressive, the results of this study raise important questions about the sustainability of those gains," the report concludes. An August 2002 study in the journal *Nature* estimated that 17 per cent of the world's arable land was degraded after just a few decades of Green Revolution farming.

The big advances in yields on which farmers have come to depend as prices went down are no longer assured. Worldwide production of wheat dropped from 592 million tonnes in 1990 to 585 million in 1999. And while yields on individual farms jumped by 3 per cent a year in the early years of the Green Revolution, they increased only 3.8 per cent in the ten years of the 1990s, according to the United Nations Food and Agriculture Organization. That, coupled with rising output costs and dropping prices, has thrown agriculture into crisis.

The enigmatic Borlaug has come forward to defend his life's work in the last few years and to take a few shots at critics of the Green Revolution. "I have worked with many colleagues, political leaders, and farmers to transform food production systems," Borlaug said in an April 2001 speech at Tuskegee University in Alabama. "As a result of these efforts, food production has more than kept pace with global population growth. On average, world food supplies were 24 per cent higher per person in 1998 than they were in 1961 and real prices were 40 per cent lower." He stood proudly by the advances in food production that his crops – with the chemicals, irrigation, and machinery used to grow them – have produced and worried that critics would stop them from being adopted in other developing countries.

It angered Borlaug that his original sponsors at the Rockefeller Foundation had not supported his efforts to bring the Green Revolution to Africa. He blamed "elitist" environmentalists. "Some of the environmental lobbyists of the Western nations are the salt of the earth, but many of them are elitists," he told the *Atlantic Monthly* for a January 1997 profile. "They've never experienced the physical sensation of hunger. They do their lobbying from comfortable office suites in Washington or Brussels. If they lived just one month amid the misery of the developing world, as I have for 50 years, they'd be crying out for tractors and fertilizer and irrigation canals and be outraged that the fashionable elites back home were trying to deny them these things."

Borlaug and the Green Revolution faced criticism almost from the start. Even as he was taking his wondrous new crops to India and Pakistan, resistance was starting to build in the West. Starting with Rachel Carson's *Silent Spring* in 1962, Western society began to question the assumption that farm chemicals were harmless. By the mid-1970s, environmental groups were starting to be organized, and by the 1980s, governments were making the environment a central consideration in all of their operations. Despite industry protests to the contrary, scientists eventually proved that DDT, once a popular farm insecticide, was responsible for the thin-shelled eggs laid by bald eagles and other predatory bids. This made the eggs easier to crack and led to a decline in the population of many of the great birds of North America. Their populations rebounded soon after DDT was banned.

Until they started to study the effect of farm chemicals on the environment, scientists did not realize that chemicals could build up in the soil and in living organisms – a process scientists call persistent organic pollution. Before they knew about this form of pollution, scientists assumed that one or two sprayings of chemicals would not hurt larger living things such as birds or people. This assumption soon became an accepted fact and it took intense scientific scrutiny to debunk it. Once scientists realized that farm chemicals could accumulate in the body and in the soil over years and decades, the questions they asked changed. No longer could they just talk about the impact that one or two sprayings of chemicals might have. Now, they had to start asking what a lifetime – even generations – of exposure might mean.

A study in Mexico, where the Green Revolution was born, offered some disturbing answers.

Catching a ball. Jumping on one foot. Drawing pictures of your friends and family. These are the normal playtime activities of any child. For four- and five-year-olds, it is also how they learn. Ball catching hones hand-to-eye coordination. Jumping on one foot teaches children balance and a greater awareness of their bodies. Drawing pictures teaches them to translate the images in their heads into lines on a page – an essential tool for literacy. So when a team of researchers went to northern Mexico to study the effect of pesticide use on children in an agricultural region that uses a lot of pesticides, they asked them to perform these simple and playful tasks.

Five scientists took part: Elizabeth Guillette, an anthropologist from the University of Arizona; and María Mercedes Meza, María Guadalupe Aquilar, Alma Delia Soto, and Idalia Enedina García of the Instituto Tecnológico de Sonora in Mexico. Their work took them to one of Mexico's most intensive agricultural areas, the Yaqui Valley in northwestern Mexico, where the Green Revolution had arrived in the late 1940s. In 1990, pesticide residues were found in the cord blood of newborns and in mothers' breast milk. Guillette and her team wanted to find out what the effect of that, and of regular exposure to pesticides by the children as they grew up, might have on children's development.

The Yaqui Valley was a nearly perfect spot for the test. The children in the valley were exposed to pesticides on a daily basis. Farmers there harvested two crops a year, with each harvest being sprayed up to forty-five times. That's almost two sprayings a week of compounds such as organophosphates, which are derived from nerve gas and have been found to disrupt hormone functions; organochlorines, such as DDT; and pyrethroids. Between 1959 and 1990, thirty-three different compounds were used in the area, including DDT, dieldrin, endosulfan, heptachlor, aldrin, endrin, lindane, benzene hexachloride, and parathion-methyl. "Substances banned in the United States, such as lindane and endrin, are readily available to farmers," the scientists wrote. Canada has also banned endrin, but lindane is still used here to treat seeds. The Pesticide Action Network has included lindane and endrin among its "dirty dozen" of farm chemicals the group wants banned.

Exposure to these chemicals made the children of the valley ideal test subjects for the study. As well, people who lived in the foothills surrounding the valley shared a common heritage and genetic line with those in the valley. They also ate the same types of food, lived in similar houses, had similar-sized families, and also worked in agriculture. The only real difference between the two communities, the research team found, was that the foothills children were not exposed to pesticides, since the land was used for livestock grazing, not for growing grain.

The test results for the foothills children were dramatically different from those of the valley kids. "The longest a valley child jumped was 110 seconds, compared to 336 seconds for a foothill child," the researchers wrote. The foothill children were also markedly better at catching a ball, and 59 per cent of the foothill children were able to remember that they were promised a red balloon at the end of the testing, something only 27 per cent of the valley children could remember. But the most heartbreaking part of the study came with the drawing exercise. Both groups of children looked at their subjects while trying to draw a picture, but with wildly different results. The foothill pictures looked like typical kids' drawings of stick figures with happy faces and round eyes. The valley pictures were just scribbles. Even knowing what they were supposed to be, it was impossible to tell that these were pictures of people.

Drawing is used to test the cognitive abilities of children who cannot read, so the inability of the valley children to draw simple pictures may point to serious brain dysfunction in the children – as might the memory problems. "Environmental change has placed the children of the agricultural area of the Yaqui valley at a disadvantage for participating in normal childhood activities. Will they remain at risk for functioning as healthy adults?" the researchers wondered.

As in P.E.I., the incidence of spina bifida in Mexico was abnormally high – 17.6 cases per 10,000 births, one of the highest incidence rates in the world. In P.E.I., Labchuk heard about the Mexican study on CBC's *Nature of Things*. She contacted Guillette and received a booklet from the researcher so she could conduct a similar study on P.E.I. She was worried, however, about how long it might take her to secure the funding and the time to conduct the study. The school study, for instance, took more than two years and several missed deadlines to put together. It frustrated Labchuk, an uncompromising woman with little patience for those who doubted the health effects of pesticides, that P.E.I.-based studies were even needed before Islanders would take the threat seriously. "Do we have to wait until an entire generation has been damaged before we do anything?"

As we spoke, water from a storm a few days earlier that dumped up to seventy-one millimetres of rain on P.E.I. in just a few hours – flooding streets in Charlottetown – was draining from farm fields into the island's streams and rivers, including the nearby Wilmot River. It was early in July 2002, and most farmers had applied only one or two sprays of fungicide so far. There had been no fish kills the year before. A drought in 2001 meant that there were no big rainstorms to wash pesticides into the water, and the dry conditions meant farmers did not have to spray as often for blight. The summer of 2002 was already proving to be much wetter, creating ideal conditions for the spread of blight, and Labchuk doubted the farmers could count on another year without fish kills.

A few kilometres away, Barry Cudmore was watching the skies and monitoring the radio news. Like Labchuk, he feared the recent rains would bring word of another fish kill. He had applied fungicide to his potato fields just before the big rain and figured most of it had been washed off in the downpour. "That spray's pretty safe, but it's not good for fish," he told me. He had checked his fields after the storm, and was "pleasantly surprised" to find that his twenty-metre buffer – twice the mandated size – had kept the rainwater out of a stream running through his farm. "Had that storm happened two or three years ago, we would have had a lot of damage off the farm," he said.

That was on a Sunday night. By the following Wednesday, three hundred dead stickleback and brook trout were found on the banks of the Wilmot River just south of Cavendish. A week later, Labchuk led a march through Summerside demanding a halt to pesticide use. "The air's contaminated. The soil's contaminated. The water's contaminated," she told the Charlottetown *Guardian*. "The answer is not more regulation. There has to be a big-picture look and a big-picture solution – and that big-picture solution is organic agriculture." In a press release, she described 2002 as the "summer of pesticides."

For Labchuk, fish kills are only the most obvious, and unavoidable, evidence of a problem with pesticide use on the island. Buffer zones around waterways only mean that the pesticides are absorbed there instead of washing away in the water. In the buffer zones, the chemicals kill insects and birds instead of fish, she says. But dead birds and bugs scattered across wooded areas don't draw as much attention as thousands of fish washing up on shore in one afternoon. "People think that just because the fish aren't dying, that everything is okay. I don't think that's true."

Still, she was starting to get some support among the island's reluctant residents. "I can't believe I'm going to say this, but I'm starting to think Sharon Labchuk has the right idea," trout fisherman George Roach told a community paper after a 2000 fish kill. The Wilmot fish kill two years later, when the toll eventually hit 4,500, was reported by a sport fishing group, whose leader was upset that farm chemicals had wiped out years of work to bring trout to the river. "Our group has been working for over five years to get these sea-run trout to return only to have this happen," Robin Paynter, project coordinator for the Prince County Fly Fishers Association, told the Summerside *Journal-Pioneer*. He said it would take years to repair the damage and bring the trout back again.

Over the following month, there were five more fish kills, including another in the Wilmot – making 2002 one of the worst years yet despite three years of measures to keep pesticides out of rivers. Since 1994, twenty-six fish kills have been reported – nine in 2002 alone. Within two weeks of the first fish kill that year, 12,000 dead fish had washed up on the shores of P.E.I. streams and rivers. No charges were laid that summer, however, as Environment Canada inspectors could not determine the farm from which the chemicals had spilled.

In the summer of 2001 I stopped at a Green Revolution corn farm on Wellington County Road 7 in Ontario. It had rained the night before and the soil under the corn was as dry and hard as pavement, except for a few channels carved by the rushing rainwater. I tried to take a handful of soil, but couldn't. I used a rock to break away a chunk and it crumbled into sand. There were no worms, no rotting fibres releasing their nutrients into the soil to be taken up by the crops, and no moisture. There was no living material visible in the soil to hold it together, as there had been at an organic farm I had just visited down the road. Above me, the corn was maturing on full, plump cobs.

This is the wonder of the Green Revolution. There was nothing in that soil to produce that corn. Years of pesticides, artificial fertilizers, and monoculture farming had killed any organic matter that normally nurtures plants. This farm, and millions like it, now required the chemicals the farmer sprayed to grow anything at all. What was once a boost to nature has now replaced it. But unlike nature, which offers its nutrients for free, the chemicals had to be bought – making farmers dependent on large farm-supply companies to keep them in business. The soil and the farmers who tended it were addicted to chemicals. The cornfield I was standing in extended far beyond the rolling hills. Across the road, another cornfield dominated that horizon.

Such monocultures are the hallmark of the Green Revolution, and they destroy the rich biodiversity that once was one of agriculture's greatest strengths. Farmers seeking the efficiencies offered by growing huge fields of identical crops abandoned thousands of traditional varieties or plants. In North America, only 5 to 20 per cent of the crops grown a hundred years ago are still in commercial production. Ninety-one per cent of the tomatoes grown a century ago, and 90 per cent of the peas, are no longer available to farmers. According to the United Nations Food and Agriculture Organization, in China, 90 per cent of the wheat varieties grown sixty years ago have been lost, and in Mexico, where corn was first domesticated, only 20 per cent of the corn varieties harvested in the 1930s are still grown. The FAO reports that just 120 species of plants provide 90 per cent of the crops eaten by humans, and that 90 per cent of the agricultural diversity on farms a century ago no longer exists.

The same is true for animals. In 1986, the FAO identified six thousand breeds of farm animals. Since then, 300 have become extinct and another 1,800 are at risk. "Once you've lost a genetic resource, it's gone forever," says Ricardo Cardellino, the FAO's senior officer for animal genetic resources. The FAO's Hartwig de Haen blames industrial agriculture's demand for uniformity for the decline. "If you want tomatoes that can be taken to market and remain hard, are the same size, and don't mature rapidly, then you end up with just a few varieties."

Plant breeders rely on diversity, however, to provide them with the genetic resources they need to develop better crops, and at times even to save entire industries from devastation. In the mid-nineteenth century, for instance, foreign insects and fungi made their way to Europe, probably brought there on trading ships plying the Atlantic Ocean. The two combined to ruin the carefully cultivated vineyards of France, Italy, and Germany before three varieties of wild grapes from North America were found to resist the pests. Today, traditional varieties of grapes in Europe grow exclusively on the North American rootstocks to which they are grafted.

More than a hundred years later, in the 1970s, a virus began attacking rice paddies in Asia. Breeders had a tough time finding any rice that could resist the virus, finally discovering a small patch in Uttar Pradesh, India. The breeders crossbred the rice, *Oryza nivara*, with rice crops across Asia to make them resistant to the virus. It worked, saving millions from starvation. The breakthrough would not have been possible, however, were it not for the wonderful diversity that nature provides, but which industrial agriculture eradicates. Indeed, since that lucky find thirty years ago, breeders have not been able to find another patch of *Oryza nivara*.

In Mexico, studies have found the Green Revolution's industrial agriculture to be a threat to indigenous species of corn. A 1993 study by Garrison Wilkes of the University of Massachusetts found that teosinte – a sprawling annual grass in Mexico and Guatemala that is corn's closest wild relative – was in rapid decline, mostly because traditional farming methods had fallen by the wayside and livestock were being allowed to graze in fallow fields where teosinte tended to grow. The declining wild population threatens the resource that plant breeders used to improve the corn grown in fields around the world. "Genetic engineers cannot create genes," says John Tuxill, who wrote a study on biodiversity for the Worldwatch Institute. "They can only move them around."

We are witnessing, with the diminishing diversity of the plant life on which we depend, and the degrading of the soil in which it grows, the industrial model of agriculture pushed to the brink of collapse.

Until the mid-1990s, just before Cavendish expanded its island operation, Danny Hendricken's farm in eastern P.E.I. was a well-diversified operation. Working with his brothers and father, Hendricken grew seed and table potatoes, raised a few hundred hogs, grew feed for the hogs, and kept a strawberry patch that brought in a third source of income. Strawberries, which thrive in sandy soil and wet climates, were a popular cash crop on P.E.I. That popularity, however, drove up supply and pushed down prices. By the mid-1990s, Hendricken could no longer cover his costs in the strawberry patch and ploughed it under for potatoes.

A few years later, as industrial hog farms made their way onto the island, Hendricken had to decide whether to boost the size of his hog barn or get out of the business. At the time, he had about six hundred hogs. A new barn up the road had ten times that many, and Hendricken found himself unable to compete. "I really liked working with the hogs, but the money just wasn't there," he said in an interview. He sold off the hogs, converted the barns to other uses, and focused on potatoes and rotation crops. "It's unfortunate, but we're a monoculture now. Potatoes and grains."

Hendricken knows what he has lost, but the economics of modern agriculture left him no choice. He gave up the diversity that had given his farm an enviable level of stability in the past. If the price or yield of one commodity dropped, he could get by with good prices or good production in another. Now, he relied on one crop –

potatoes – and his fortunes were determined by its price and his luck in growing them.

In his work as the island's representative for the National Farmers Union, Hendricken has seen dozens of farmers forced by economics to make the same commitment to one crop. And as each one of those farmers decides to concentrate on one crop or one type of animal in hopes of stretching thinner margins over larger operations, he raises the stakes for all other farmers in that industry – especially those struggling to remain diversified. Each farmer's move to monoculture affects the economy of scale, making it more difficult for others and aggravating the very economic forces that made monoculture necessary in the first place.

Until the introduction of the mechanical potato harvester in 1965, farmers were limited to only about thirty acres of potatoes. That was about all a family, with help from some local schoolchildren and seasonal labour, could expect to harvest by hand each year. In New Brunswick, schools adjusted their fall schedules to accommodate the harvest, just as they once did in southwestern Ontario during the tobacco harvest. But such practices fell by the wayside with mechanical potato harvesting, which required at least eighty acres to operate efficiently. Anything smaller and the farmer could not grow enough potatoes to pay for the machinery. Over the years, both the machines and the farms have grown bigger. On P.E.I., the average farm was about 355 acres in 2001, an 18.5 per cent jump from 1996. At the same time the number of farms dropped 17 per cent to 1,845. Across Canada, the average farm has grown by 10 per cent since 1996.

The machinery needed to run such a farm doesn't come cheap. New tractors alone can cost $250,000, as can the implements they tow. Buying such machinery means borrowing from the bank – essentially gambling that future harvests will be big enough to cover the debt payments. It's a bet that P.E.I. farmers who borrowed heavily to expand their operations to supply the new french fry plants lost when the drought of 2001 drove down production by 30 per cent. "As we've moved to monoculture, farm debts have increased dramatically," says Hendricken, whose own equipment is worth about $1.5 million. Capital value on farms in P.E.I. averaged $869,985 in 2001, a 36.1 per cent jump since 1996. "All it takes is one bad year and you're in serious trouble," Hendricken said.

Getting into any form of agriculture is increasingly expensive, requiring an average investment of $800,000 in land, machinery, quota, buildings, and livestock, according to Statistics Canada. The most expensive operations are hog farming, which costs $1.4 million to get started, and dairy at $1.1 million. Making such an investment requires going into debt, making the farmer beholden to the big companies to which they sell their produce so they can keep a steady revenue stream to cover their debt payments.

Complicating things on P.E.I. was the position of the Irving corporation as a major supplier of chemicals, seed potatoes, and fuel for farmers, and, at the same time, being their biggest customer. Through its Cavendish Farms french fry plant, Irving claims 1 billion of the island's annual 2.8-billion-pound potato crop. McCain, the world's largest french fry maker, also has a plant on the island. During a tour of Irving's Cavendish plant in 2000, Mike Johnston, vice-president of operations at the plant, told me the company had developed several of its own varieties of potatoes for its contract farmers to grow. The farmers then sprayed those potatoes with chemicals bought at an Irving farm-supply outlet, using machinery run on fuel bought from Irving. "When you're in that kind of grip, how can you negotiate a fair price with that company? You can't," says Hendricken, who does not grow for Irving.

Scott Howatt, a young farmer working just south of the Cavendish plant, told me his father was disgusted when he went to work growing for the Irvings. "It gives you a set market," he said. "If you're able to produce, you know you'll be paid for it." His father had raised him to grow his own seed potatoes and sell them across North America. But that business dried up with the PVYn crisis of the early 1990s. "We were shipping to the U.S. and Quebec. All that left," Howatt said. The family also grew table potatoes and sold them in bags featuring the family's name – but that, too, has been scaled back as Howatt prefers to spend his evenings with his family instead of in the barn sorting potatoes. The spuds Howatt grew in 2000 were chopped, frozen, and sold in bags bearing the Cavendish name. He bought his chemicals from Irving, and his fuel. And at the end of the growing season, he would accept whatever price Irving was paying.

This is the essence of industrial agriculture. Just as a factory worker uses his company's tools and raw materials to produce the company's products, the industrial farmer uses a company's tools and raw materials to produce its products. Howatt, buying supplies from the same company he later sells to, is little more than an employee of the company. He produces what he is told, how he is told, and at what price.

The industrial model Tyson introduced to livestock farming was extended to the fields with Green Revolution economics and tools. Just as Tyson took control of the most profitable parts of the poultry industry, the Irvings extended their control of the potato industry on P.E.I. by investing in its most profitable parts – deciding what potatoes would be grown, supplying the chemicals used to grow them, and then selling the potatoes under their brand name.

Selling chemicals and fuel is a much more stable business than growing potatoes or any other crop. It also provides diversification for the company that the farmers – risking all on weather and growing conditions – no longer have. "The farmer assumes all the risk," Hendricken says, echoing the refrain of farmers across the country.

While the demands of large food companies such as Irving and Tyson drove farmers to abandon diversity in favour of the efficiencies offered by monocultures, the companies they serve are well diversified. Irving, for example, one of Canada's largest private companies and a powerhouse in the eastern provinces, has interests in lumber, shipping, oil and gas, newspapers, and food. McCain, besides producing one-third of the world's french fries, also sells frozen fruit juice, pizzas, desserts, vegetables, and waffles.

Farmers, however big they have become compared with previous generations, remain too small to bargain individually with food processors over the price of a pound of potatoes. "There's plenty of money in the system," Hendricken says. "Farmers have to stand together to get it."

Would You Eat Wormy Sweet Corn?
Regular Sweet Corn:
Insecticides: Carbofuran - Sprayed 3x
OR
Bt Foliar Spray - Sprayed 4x
Fungicide: Bravo - Sprayed Once
Herbicide & Fertilizer: 1 Application of each
* The weather this summer made it difficult to grow quality sweet corn. The rain and wetness reduced the effectiveness of the sprays.

Regular Sweet Corn

Signs on non-genetically modified
sweet corn, Hillsburgh, Ontario

---

*"We are assured that this is absolutely safe and that
no harm can come from us eating it. But if you
gave me the choice right now, I wouldn't eat it."*

Arpad Pusztai,
plant scientist

CHAPTER FOUR

WHAT'S GOOD FOR GM

M eeting Arpad Pusztai was a bit of an eye-opener. The scientist whose studies marked the beginning of the public debate over genetically modified, or GM, foods was visiting Canada after giving testimony before a New Zealand royal commission in February 2001. I had expected him to talk about why GM foods are bad and should be banned – or at least labelled. Greenpeace, the leading critic of GM food around the world, was, after all, shopping him around to the local media. The poster announcing his lecture sported the headline "Killer Potatoes," a reference to his research on GM potatoes in 1998.

But Pusztai turned out to be a reasonable man more interested in bridging the widening gap between critics and supporters of GM than scoring points against those who had left his career in tatters after he raised concerns about the safety of GM potatoes.

Pusztai worked at the Rowett Research Institute in Aberdeen, Scotland, for more than thirty years and published almost three hundred scientific papers. In the late 1980s, he began examining the snowdrop lectin – a protein found in snowdrop bulbs that would kill insects but was safe for animals to eat. The hope for many in the scientific community, Pusztai included, was that lectin could be somehow inserted into other plants to protect them from insects. At the time, there were no genetically modified foods on the market, and Pusztai hoped to be one of the pioneers in the emerging field. Other researchers, mostly in corporate labs in North America, were looking for ways to insert the *Bacillus thuringiensis*, or Bt, gene into crops to make them toxic to insects. Bt comes from a soil bacterium and is used as a spray by organic farmers when more benign methods of insect control prove ineffective. By the time Pusztai began his studies into potatoes that had been genetically modified to include the snowdrop lectin, Bt vegetables and cotton were already coming to market. Pusztai still held out hope for lectin, however, and began a series of studies into the safety of GM foods that would forever change the debate.

The tests he performed were simple. He fed four groups of six rats each four different potato mixtures for 110 days. One was fed regular potatoes. Two more groups were fed two varieties of potatoes that had been genetically modified to include snowdrop lectin, and a fourth group was fed regular potatoes with snowdrop lectin sprinkled on top. The first and last group responded as expected, showing few adverse effects from their diets. The other two groups, those eating GM potatoes, developed immune system problems, and their livers, hearts, and brains were not as big as they should have been. Since the rats fed lectin and potatoes were healthier, Pusztai thought that something about the genetic modification process, and not the lectin itself, had caused the rats' health problems. Still unwilling to give up on a technology he believed in, however, he wanted to do more studies and agreed to a television interview to help drum up the needed funding.

That's when the trouble began. With the Rowett Institute's blessing, he agreed to an interview with the British TV newsmagazine *World in Action*, which was working on a show about genetically modified foods. The technology had only begun to be used in Europe, and controversy about its adoption simmered just below the surface, involving a few activists and scientists, but attracting little attention from the general public. By the time the *World in Action* interview aired on August 10, 1998, Pusztai had largely put it out of his mind, having done the interview two months before. He still hoped, however, that it would help bring in some money to continue his research.

It didn't. Across Britain that night, viewers watched as Pusztai told them they were "human guinea pigs" in an experiment on their food. "We are assured that this is absolutely safe and that no harm can come from us eating it. But if you gave me the choice right now, I wouldn't eat it," he said.

The first reaction of the Rowett Institute was to back Pusztai's work, saying it was proud of his research. "For the first two days, I was the greatest thing since sliced bread," he told me. His boss, Philip James, even called him at home after the program to say he thought the interview had gone well. The next day, Pusztai's "guinea pig" comment was front-page news, with newspapers quoting scientists with ties to the biotech industry questioning his conclusions and, more seriously, the quality of his science. Pusztai was called into James's office that evening, where it was decided that the institute would put out a press release the following morning to clear up any questions about Pusztai's research. Pusztai went home assuming his boss still backed him and that staff would work late to prepare the release.

He was wrong. "I came in [the next morning] and I was suspended," Pusztai said, still hurt several years later by what he saw as a betrayal. The institute had decided that he had become a liability. "The easiest way was to gag me," Pusztai said, adding that he was too well known and respected in the scientific community to be discredited right away. He was forced into retirement and banned by the institute from speaking publicly about his work with GM potatoes. The institute confiscated his plants and data, refusing him access to his life's work. The British House of Commons eventually lifted the gag order, but not before industry scientists had called into question every aspect of what Pusztai freely admitted were very preliminary findings.

It was a one-sided fight. As Pusztai was banned from speaking, he and the quality of his science became the story instead of his findings. At one point, James even told reporters that Pusztai had not used genetically modified potatoes in his research and was just confused. He implied that Pusztai was old and senile, and no longer capable of the great science he had once conducted. By the time James's claims were disproved and it was acknowledged that Pusztai had in fact been experimenting with GM potatoes, the comments had undermined everything Pusztai had said.

Pusztai was eventually able to publish most of his results in the respected British scientific journal *The Lancet* more than a year later – despite threats to the editor of the journal from a senior member of Britain's Royal Society that he was risking his career by accepting the paper. The scientists who had criticized Pusztai for his TV interview had demanded from the beginning that any valid criticism of GM foods be published in a recognized scientific journal. Once that was done, however, they criticized *The Lancet*, accusing it of trying to boost circulation by publishing a notorious paper – and again deflecting attention away from the science to the source of that science. "It is clear from an editorial previously published by *The Lancet* that the editor or the magazine were strongly supportive of Pusztai before they had seen his science," Peter Collins, senior policy adviser at the British Royal Society, told the rival journal *Nature*. "I don't think *The Lancet* can present its decision to publish Pusztai's paper now as a routine scientific decision."

There certainly were legitimate questions about Pusztai's results. Rats can't survive on a diet of potatoes alone, and with such a small sample group it was possible only the bad diet led to his results. A larger sample group would have allowed him to account better for the bad diet in his results. As well, a similar study with tomatoes and using twice as many rats four years earlier in the Netherlands had the opposite results. The contradictory studies should have been the launching point for more study, but never were, Pusztai said.

The public dressing-down served as warning to other scientists to keep their mouths shut if they found anything askew with GM foods. "I was an independent government scientist. My independence only went as far as I said what they wanted me to," Pusztai's wife, Susan Bardocz said. She was a biochemist at the Rowett with

Pusztai and left when he did. They had both spent their careers laying the foundation for the biotech revolution and still believed in its potential, but they were concerned that reckless science would undermine all their efforts and those of their colleagues. They were worried that the biotech industry and governments were all focusing solely on the money to be made and dangerously ignoring any potential problems.

The industry showed little interest in repeating Pusztai's experiments, even if only to prove that its products were safe. As Alan McHughen, one of Canada's top genetic engineers and the holder of patents for GM flax, put it in his book, *Pandora's Picnic Basket*: "A repeat of Dr. Pusztai's experiments would tell us nothing we don't already know from the human experiment on American consumers." (McHughen's book was donated to libraries across Canada by the Council for Biotechnology Information.)

Across Europe, consumers have refused to take part in any such experiment, and several grocery chains won't stock genetically modified products. The first company to ban GM foods was Iceland Group, a frozen-food chain that hoped to gain some market share by taking advantage of consumer unease about GM foods. Iceland Group was followed by such industry stalwarts as Sainsbury and Marks and Spencer in the U.K. Across Europe, protesters have gone into test plots for GM foods, pulling the plants up by their roots or cutting them down with old-fashioned scythes.

Gregor Mendel, a nineteenth-century Austrian monk, grew peas in his garden and worked out the basics of the science we now call genetics: that traits could be purposely passed from one generation to another under the right circumstances. Think of it as forced evolution. Only the fittest survived, but man defined what was fit for survival. *New York Times* writer Michael Pollan called it the "botany of desire" in his book of that name. Plants offered us their latest innovations – a sweeter apple, a bigger potato, or a symmetrical tulip

– and we picked and bred only those we liked. We could speed up the evolution of plants, but only in ways that nature allowed us. We could encourage plants with characteristics we liked to breed with one another, but we couldn't control the outcome. And, as Pollan puts it, the plants held the "trump card" by controlling which plants they would breed with – only plants from their own species. "Since unrelated species in nature cannot be crossed, the breeder's art has always run up against a natural limit of what a potato is willing, or able, to do – that species' essential identity. Nature has always exercised a kind of veto over what culture can do with a potato," Pollan writes.

Genetic modification changed all that. As much as the biotech companies like to portray their new technology as nothing more than the latest stage of man's long history of plant breeding, it is not. We now have the power to tell plants what traits to offer us. We stole the trump card, forever changing the game.

Genetic modification allows the plant breeder to take genes from one species and insert them into another. This is most often done by first isolating – in a lab – a desirable gene, such as the Bt gene from a soil bacterium. The isolated gene is then used to coat slivers of gold or tungsten that are loaded into a gun and fired through the stem or leaf of another organism, such as corn. It has been described as a bully breaking into a line dance, or as throwing a vase through a store window and hoping it lands upright on a shelf. Since there is no way of knowing where the bully gene may break into the plant's dance, the gene gun is used several times on different plants. Cells from the target plants are then grown into new plants, and the breeders watch for ones in which the new gene seems to be active. This is where traditional breeding comes back into play, with the breeder allowing only those plants exhibiting the characteristic of the alien gene to survive. The plant is then propagated, seeds are gathered, and the experiment moves from the lab to the field.

Another method, used mostly with potatoes, involves Petri dishes instead of gene guns. In this method, an agrobacterium microbe is used to penetrate the cell wall, taking the new gene with it. It has been called the Trojan Horse method, since the agrobacterium, a pathogen that naturally penetrates gene walls, is used to transport something extra into the target plant's DNA. This method is more sophisticated than firing a gun at a plant, but no more precise, since the breeder still has no control over where the Trojan Horse drops its payload.

For reasons scientists still do not fully understand, the agrobacterium method does not work well with grains or grasses such as corn or wheat. Similarly, the gene gun doesn't work with potatoes. The lack of understanding, however, has not slowed efforts down.

This experimentation resulted in two classes of products: herbicide-resistant plants, such as soybean or canola, that can be sprayed with powerful weed killers and not die; and insect-resistant plants, such as corn or cotton, that contain the Bt gene, which means they can produce their own toxin.

John Queeny – a high school dropout and self-taught chemist – fulfilled a lifelong dream in 1901 when he founded Monsanto Chemical Works in St. Louis to make artificial sweetener. He fended off attempts by sugar companies and European sweetener makers to run him out of business and soon expanded his product line to include caffeine and sulphuric acid. By the Second World War, the company had expanded again to produce styrene monomer, a key chemical ingredient in synthetic rubber, and got rich feeding the war effort.

Thirty years later, Monsanto supplied another war – this time in Vietnam – with the defoliant Agent Orange. By then, Monsanto had invested its war profits to become a major producer of farm chemicals and the world's largest maker of polychlorinated biphenyls, or PCBs. Its association with such products tainted the image of a company that had until then remained largely anonymous by supplying ingredients to other manufacturers. Agent Orange was blamed for cancer, skin rashes, and birth defects, forcing Monsanto and other chemical companies to pay out $180 million (U.S.) to veterans of the Vietnam War. The defoliant's key ingredient, 2,4-D, is under review by Health Canada and may be banned because of health and environmental risks. PCBs were proven to be a carcinogen and were banned in the 1970s.

Further hurting Monsanto's image was the environmental damage caused by spills from its factories. In 2000, it began the cleanup of an area around its St. Louis plant known to locals as Dead Creek because of the chemical pollutants that had devastated the area. The company had for years denied responsibility for the mess. It also publicly denied that its PCB plant in Anniston, Alabama, had anything to do with the abnormally high cancer rates among the people living near the factory, despite company documents dating back to the 1950s showing it knew that PCBs were toxic. That evidence was kept from local residents, however, while Monsanto dumped up to 110 kilograms of PCB waste a day into landfill sites near one of the town's poorest neighbourhoods.

In 1966, the company dumped twenty-five healthy fish into the town's Snow Creek to see what would happen. Within ten seconds, none could swim, and all were shedding their scales. In four minutes, all were dead. A blacktail shiner the company pulled from the Choccolocco Creek, a popular fishing spot near the plant, had 7,500 times the legal limit for PCBs. In 1970, Monsanto bought up all the hogs from a woman living next to the plant but didn't tell her the pigs tested ninety thousand times the legal limit for PCBs. The plant stopped making PCBs two years later.

Throughout it all, Monsanto denied that its plant had caused any environmental problems. Finally, after years of court battles with its impoverished neighbours, Monsanto was found guilty in February 2002 of negligence. It paid out more than $40 million (U.S.) to local residents, with more claims pending, and spent tens of millions of dollars more in cleanup costs. The plant is still in operation, making pharmaceuticals.

Around the time it was getting out of PCB manufacturing in Alabama, Monsanto was developing a new product that would eventually transform the company – Roundup herbicide. The chemical spray was put on the market in the mid-1970s and proved popular with farmers, who could count on it to kill every plant it touched. Plants must produce amino acids to survive. Roundup binds itself to the enzyme that produces amino acids, effectively choking the plant.

In a process sometimes referred to as "burning off," farmers spray Roundup and similar herbicides on their fields before planting. An application leaves a field clear of all weeds or plants left over from the previous year, making it easier for the farmer to get a new crop in the ground. Traditionally, farmers prepare their fields for planting by tilling the ground to clear it of stubble. This loosens the soil, which encourages erosion of the topsoil. Roundup – together with crops modified to resist it – is promoted as a way to practise so-called no-till farming, in which farmers do not plough under each year's stubble. They just burn it off with chemicals and plant seeds into the dead stubble. The soil remains firm with such a method, and is not at as much risk of blowing away in a windstorm or running off in a heavy rain.

By the 1990s, Monsanto was worrying about the looming end to its patent on Roundup, one of its best-selling products. The solution came from what had until then been a small part of the company – biotechnology. Biologists working for Monsanto had been trying to figure out a way to make plants resistant to Roundup so farmers could spray the chemical *after* a crop had been planted. If the crop was resistant to Roundup, the weeds would die and the crop would thrive. Roundup was such a powerful weed killer, however, that Monsanto's scientists were not having much luck finding a plant that could withstand it.

In another part of the company, meanwhile, another group of scientists was collecting samples of bacteria that had managed to prosper in the sludge behind Monsanto's Roundup factory in Luling, Louisiana. They had hoped to use the bacteria as a tool in cleaning up spills of Roundup. But when the scientists in the biotech division heard about the bacteria, they knew they had found their answer.

The scientists isolated the gene that made the bacteria resistant to the sludge and inserted it into cotton, potatoes, canola, and soybeans. The seeds from those plants were put on the market in the mid-1990s, in a move that would transform both Monsanto and the seed industry.

Until then, seeds were sold mostly by small companies at relatively low prices, since the crops that came from those seeds would in turn produce their own seeds that farmers could use to grow another year's crop. The exception was Henry Wallace's hybrid corn. His corn seeds were the product of a carefully crafted breeding program that produced only one generation of high-yielding corn. This was known in the industry as "hybrid vigour." Seeds taken from hybrid corn are not high yielding, obliging farmers to buy more seed each year. Wallace's company, Pioneer, grew to be the largest seed company in the world and is now a division of DuPont, which hopes to use corn to grow a natural form of plastic.

Monsanto's Roundup-resistant seeds, however, were not hybrids and so were reproduced year after year in farmers' fields. To keep farmers coming back each year to buy seeds – a financial necessity for the company after it had poured millions of dollars into developing GM crops – Monsanto obliged them to sign contracts pledging that they would not save seeds from one crop for use the next year. This effectively ended a farming practice dating back thousands of years. Monsanto also required farmers to pay a technology fee that doubled the cost of seeds. Despite these conditions, GM crops proved popular with farmers, who are constantly on the lookout for new products that promise to increase yields and ease the workload on their ever-expanding farms.

Before long, the genetic revolution transformed Monsanto. It sold off the sweetener division that had been its foundation and transformed itself into a "life sciences" company focused on finding a way to use biotechnology to grow medicines in farmers' fields.

Within a few years, the dream wilted. In December 1999, the pharmaceutical giant Pharmacia & Upjohn bought Monsanto. Its drug division – whose flagship product, Celebrex, an anti-inflammatory, set sales records when it was introduced the previous January – was merged with Pharmacia's. Its agricultural division was hived off as a separate company, freeing the company's valuable drug division from the sagging farm division.

Analysts on Wall Street had been calling for the move for months. Deutsche Bank analyst Timothy Ramey had declared the previous summer that "GMOs are dead," saying consumer rejection in Europe had laid waste to the biotech industry's predictions of a glorious future. There, grocers and food processors, including Gerber, a division of European biotech giant Novartis, were racing to declare their products free of GM foods. The backlash had started to cross the ocean, Ramey warned, spelling an "earnings nightmare" for the companies. Share prices, buoyed by hopes of a biotech future, began to fall. Ramey said he still believed in the science and promise of genetic engineering, but stressed it would take consumers much longer than had been expected to come around. These sentiments were echoed later in the year by his colleague at Deutsche Bank, Frank Mitsch, who argued in a bulletin to investors that the North American public would have to engage in a thorough debate over biotechnology – as was happening in Europe – before there would be any gains in the industry.

A pillar of the GM revolution has been the biotech companies' assurance that the process is precise: one gene at a time is moved between plants, or even species, allowing the breeder to transfer only the desired traits to another plant. Traditional breeding requires several generations of plants and a decade or more of working in fields and greenhouses before breeders get the plants they want. Marquis wheat, developed in Ottawa in the early twentieth century and credited with opening the west, took more than twenty years to develop. The much-loved Yukon Gold potato – often described as looking and tasting like it has already been buttered – was the result of more than a decade of crossbreeding by Garnet Johnson at the University of Guelph. GM scientists, however, boasted that they could speed up the breeding process by moving genes around in the lab instead of the field. They could even move genes from one species to another, and because they could move one gene at a time, they could ensure the target plant inherited only the desired traits.

This should make anyone feel secure about eating GM food. But the theory is based on a faulty assumption that ten years of research into the human genome unwittingly called into question. When scientists embarked on the genome project, they set out to map more than 100,000 genes that would reveal what it is to be human. They expected to find one gene for every trait – one for eye colour, one for height, one for baldness, one for skin colour, and so on.

But when they announced their preliminary findings in February 2001, the big news was not that they had figured out a rough map of the human genome – the most anticipated announcement in the scientific community in decades – but that there were far fewer genes than they had expected. "Here is a real surprise: the human genome probably contains between 25,000 and 40,000 genes, only about twice the number needed to make a fruit fly, worm or plant," Gerald Rubin, a molecular biologist at the University of California, wrote in *Nature*. Scientists working on the genome project explained that it now appeared that genes worked together to determine hair or skin colour – and that the essential difference between people and other species was not which genes they had, but how those genes acted in combination.

The press marvelled at how little difference there was between humans and earthworms, and the scientists seemed happy to keep that the focus of their coverage. It was just as well, since the discovery undermined the foundation of the entire biotech industry, which was hoping the release of the genome, with its promises of curing Alzheimer's and Parkinson's diseases, would repair its tarnished image. *Nature*'s special edition on the genome was sponsored by the biotech firm Aventis, a leading producer of genetically modified food and was full of ads from other biotech companies hoping to get rich from the discoveries the genome would produce.

Within hours of the news conference, anti-biotech activists were sending e-mails around the world speculating what the existence of so few genes meant. If genes combined with other genes to express certain traits, they wondered, how could anybody guarantee that a gene artificially transferred from one species to another would act only in the way it was supposed to? Didn't this undermine the claims of the biotech industry that genetic modification is precise and predictable? What did this mean for the future of biotech?

It was a year before such questions reached the broader public. That happened with the February 2002 publication of an article by scientist Barry Commoner in *Harper's* magazine. Commoner, a biologist at New York's City University, said the genome project undercut the "central dogma" of genetic research: the "seductively simple" theory that each gene produces one protein with one specific function. The most important discovery of the genome project, he wrote, was not the gene map it produced, but the discovery that genes work together to produce the necessary proteins to distinguish a person from an earthworm. "The surprising results contradicted the scientific premise on which the genome project was undertaken and dethroned its guiding theory, the central dogma," he wrote.

Perhaps even more disturbingly, he wrote that other scientific tests had been calling the central dogma into question for more than twenty years but were ignored by the biotech industry, which had so much riding on the precision argument. Universities, which increasingly rely on private funding from biotech companies to keep their biology labs open in the face of reduced government funds, have also not been inclined to pursue anything that might undermine the central dogma on which much of their funding and prestige in the emerging biotech field are based. "The central dogma was simply too good not to be true," Commoner wrote.

Reaction was swift. As with Pusztai, the immediate response was to impugn both Commoner and his science. He was accused in the

St. Louis Post-Dispatch, the hometown paper of biotech giant Monsanto, of "twisting scientific fact" to further his own environmental agenda. "He's interpreting the world to vindicate his own belief," Bruce Chassy, dean of biotechnology at the University of Illinois, charged in an article made available worldwide by Channapatna S. Prakash, a plant breeder at Tuskegee University in Alabama.

Prakash runs a Web site called AgBioWorld.org, and a chat room where scientists in the industry can exchange ideas and keep up on the public relations battles over biotechnology. More than anything, though, Prakash's on-line efforts mark an attempt by biotech believers to fight back on the territory that had proved so effective for the activist community – the Internet. Prakash boasts that through his Web site, chat room, and listserv, he can find out right away if any newspaper in the country has published an article criticizing biotechnology and organize scientists to swamp the paper with letters to the editor. "I will call up my friends . . . and they will write letters to your newspaper," he warned Bill Lambrecht, the Washington correspondent for the *St. Louis Post-Dispatch*.

He has had plenty to organize letter-writing campaigns about. The January 16, 2002, dispatch from his listserv was dedicated almost entirely to the Commoner article, including a lead item by Prakash himself in which he called Commoner "irresponsible," criticized him for reviewing past research instead of conducting original research, and asserted that despite Commoner's warnings that the biotech industry had based its work on unsafe assumptions in order to pursue greater profits, "commercial and legal interests" ensured the products were safe. "Most of what he says can simply be dismissed as 'So What?'," Prakash wrote, describing Commoner's work as "bad science." In the eight pages that followed, the only uncritical article was a reprinting of the *Harper's* press release announcing the story. True to his warning to Lambrecht, the rest of the articles distributed by Prakash picked apart the Commoner article.

Probably the best-known debate about GM foods was sparked by a study from Cornell University showing that GM corn killed monarch butterflies, which newspapers called "the Bambi of the insect world." Cornell entomologist John Losey was trying to figure out if corn borers retreated to other plants to avoid Bt corn when he noticed milkweed growing in a number of cornfields. That got him wondering about monarch butterflies, whose larvae eat only milkweed. His experiment was much like Pusztai's. Monarch caterpillars were fed milkweed. Some caterpillars ate milkweed sprinkled with pollen from GM corn, others ate milkweed sprinkled with regular pollen. Like Pusztai, Losey made the reckless move of going public with his early findings, rather than waiting until he had more conclusive evidence.

Losey's findings were published in *Nature* in May 1999. He had also submitted the study to *Science*, which rejected it for publication. *Nature*, based in Britain, where the GM controversy had been stirring since Pusztai's television interview the previous August, agreed to publish an abbreviated form of Losey's paper in its correspondence section. Losey reported that 44 per cent of the caterpillars he fed milkweed sprinkled with Bt pollen died. None of the rest did. Losey went to pains after the article appeared to say that his paper was simply a public declaration that some interesting results had come from the early experiments in a lab and called for more research. Like Pusztai, he said he was not opposed to GM crops but just wanted to study their impact. "We can't forget that Bt corn and other transgenic crops have a huge potential for reducing pesticide use and increasing yields," he said at the time.

Even so, the study soon became a flashpoint for the debate over GM foods. Opponents held Losey's paper up as proof that GM food was unsafe, which the study was not. And proponents picked it apart as if it were a scientific paper open to intense scrutiny, which it also was not. "The industry said they would attack us as scientists, and they did," Linda Rayner, who supplied Losey with the monarchs, told Lambrecht.

Researchers from Novartis and Monsanto, the top two biotech companies, visited Losey at Cornell and warned him that he might be putting his career in danger by publishing his results and accused him of being more interested in publicity than science. In the coming months, rather than taking Losey as a jumping-off point to a wider series of studies into the environmental impact of GM foods, scientists with ties to the biotech industry set about picking apart Losey's lab methods. There were charges that he had not sprinkled the pollen evenly, that he put more Bt pollen on the milkweed than the caterpillars would ever encounter in the real world, that the sample size was too small, and that the entire experiment was questionable because pollen from cornfields rarely reaches milkweed.

Losey readily admitted that his conclusions were limited because the experiment had occurred in the lab, not the monarch caterpillar's natural environment. In the lab, the larvae had no choice but to eat the pollen-sprinkled leaves. In the wild, they might choose to eat other leaves. Losey stressed that no conclusions could be drawn from his preliminary work, but that more study was needed. "This study is just the first step, we need to do more research and then objectively weigh the risks versus the benefits of this new technology," he said. But by focusing on the methods used by Losey in his experiments, the biotech industry and its scientists diverted attention away from the broader and more important question of Bt's impact on the environment, particularly the question of how many insects it might kill besides the European corn borer. The debate, as a result, was soon limited to Bt corn's impact on monarchs, as if they were the only life-form that might be affected.

"Based on known migration behavior, even in those regions in which corn and monarchs co-habitate, only a small portion of the monarch population will be present when the corn is shedding pollen," the U.S.-based Biotechnology Industry Organization, or BIO, said in a press release the day Losey's letter appeared in *Nature*. The industry then paid for several experiments across North America over the next year that proved the conclusion it had reached within just a few hours of Losey's study being made public.

Mark Sears at the University of Guelph, one of Canada's oldest agricultural colleges, conducted one of those studies. Sears, a highly respected scientist, found that 90 per cent of the pollen from a field of corn goes no farther than five yards from the edge of the field, and almost all of it lands on something within ten yards. Arguing that milkweed tends to grow more than five or ten yards from the edge of a field, Sears said very little pollen would ever make it to a milkweed patch where monarch caterpillars would eat it. Farmers pride themselves on keeping their fields clean of all weeds, including milkweed, though they are not always completely successful.

Sears's studies received little public attention, feeding scientists' and industry's cynicism about the media, which was seen as too quick to jump on the Losey study while all but ignoring anything that disputed it. At the same time, the release of industry-funded studies that found Bt corn safe for butterflies gave critics a second chance to use the Losey study to their advantage – this time by arguing that the biotech giants were buying the science they wanted. Sears and other scientists continued their studies under the auspices of a committee put together by the United States Department of Agriculture that included representatives from industry and academia and Margaret Mellon of the Union for Concerned Scientists, an early and consistent critic of GM foods.

Those studies, like the earlier ones, found little threat to butterflies in the field, although, as a result, the most toxic form of Bt corn, Novartis Event 176, was taken off the market. Mellon said the work done by the committee was the sort of response that should have been made to Losey's study from the beginning. "This was a model way to go about getting information on whether or not a risk exists. It brought scientists, environmentalists, and government folks together with industry, found a pot of money, set a research agenda, got proposals, funded the research, and got it done," she told the Pew Initiative, an independent think-tank on biotech and other issues.

In a study to mark the third anniversary of the Losey study, the Pew Initiative found that while the controversy had dangerously politicized the biotech debate, it may have helped government and industry develop the sort of review process that would satisfy critics. Unfortunately, the model does not seem to be catching on. "This was a really important process that should be followed routinely by the government as it makes decisions about GM products – and it's not," Mellon says.

As good as the studies were at examining the threat to monarch butterflies, they were limited by their narrow focus on just one insect. By trying to figure out whether monarchs could ever get a chance to eat Bt pollen, the studies overlooked the question of what else might be eating it, whether they were dying, and whether it mattered. All insects are part of the food chain. How is this food chain affected when Bt corn wipes out all the caterpillars in a field? Is the bird population affected by losing a food source? How about the animals that eat birds? While the crops in a field of genetically modified canola or soybeans can survive a spraying of Roundup or other herbicides, wildflowers and other weeds cannot. When they are killed, the habitats for the insects that birds rely on for food are lost. We should be looking more at what effect that had on bird populations and other wildlife, and whether the impact was greater or less than chemical pesticides.

Industry-sponsored studies into GM's risks to monarchs have ignored such concerns, and they still have largely not been addressed. The results of a four-year study by the British government looking at the impact of GM crops on the food and habitat of skylarks are due in 2004. The skylark once thrived in Britain's farm fields but their numbers have diminished. In parts of the Punjab region of India, the earthworm, firefly, butterfly, peacock, and vulture populations have dropped to near extinction, as have some plants – including the neem tree – since the Green Revolution began.

In its report in 2002, the federal government's Canadian Bio-technology Advisory Committee called for more study of the long-term environmental effect of GM foods, both good and bad. "Currently, environmental impacts are primarily assessed using small-scale confined trials that may be too small in an area to detect impacts that would appear in larger areas or too short in duration to detect effects that would emerge in the longer term," says the committee's report *Improving the Regulation of Genetically Modified Foods and Other Novel Foods in Canada*. "These and other gaps need to be addressed."

Charles Benbrook, a U.S. agriculture consultant, said the real lesson from Losey was not what he found, but that he had bothered to ask what effect Bt corn had besides killing corn borers. "The government and industry were saying at the time, arrogantly, that this was the most tested technology ever, that all the tests had been done. Well, Losey blew that all away," he says. "And he did it by asking the most basic question that should have been asked a long time before." Losey's study showed that GM foods had not been as extensively tested as it seemed and raised the question of what other questions had not been asked, Benbrook says. And that, in turn, fed the idea that the products had been rushed to market.

The main criterion for approving genetically modified foods was a principle called "substantial equivalence." Because genetically modified foods were deemed to be substantially the same as foods already on the market (having only minor genetic differences), and because foods on the market were considered safe, genetically modified foods were also considered to be safe.

Years after Losey's study was published, the attacks reached truly silly proportions. Articles about a freak storm in February 2002 that wiped out millions of monarchs in their winter home in Mexico topped pro-biotech and agricultural listservs for weeks, as if to say that we shouldn't worry about Bt corn since the butterfly faces so many other threats from nature. In an interview with *Agricultural Research Magazine*, Mark Sears remarked that several butterflies splattered on his windshield as he drove out to the fields, and that his car probably posed a greater threat to the monarch than genetic modification.

Ann Clark, a pasture science professor at the University of Guelph, found herself the target of several attacks in the past decade as she emerged as one of Canada's foremost critics of GM foods. The most vicious came on January 18, 2000, when both a colleague at Guelph and her boss went on the offensive over a review she wrote of the scientific literature made available by the Canadian government on GM foods.

Clark's study was hardly controversial, finding simply that there was not enough information available on the Health Canada Web site to explain why Ottawa had approved forty-three GM products, and calling for more information to be released. The study was published on the Web site of the Council of Canadians, a vocal critic of GM foods. That association coloured my perceptions in the same way that the biotech industry's funding of the anti-Losey studies coloured perceptions of that work. I thought, however, that it would be worth trying to find out why there was not more information publicized about the approval of GM foods. The demand by biotech companies that their studies be kept from the public to protect corporate secrets was one of the main criticisms of the technology. Such secrecy denied people a chance to decide for themselves whether the food was safe and amounted to the companies saying "Trust us" to a society that increasingly trusted fewer people. The secrecy fed the public's suspicion that the companies had something to hide.

I managed to reach two people at the University of Guelph that afternoon: Doug Powell, who worked with Clark in the school's plant sciences department, and Rob McLaughlin, then dean of the agricultural college. They didn't hold anything back. Powell, a defender of GM foods and a favourite at biotech industry conferences for his studies showing that the public can be sold on the technology, called Clark's study "silly" and unworthy of a scientist. "It's just a superficial examination worthy of high school."

Almost from the beginning of the phone interview, McLaughlin was calling Clark "unethical" for having ventured into an area that was not her area of expertise. "The University of Guelph hires her and pays her to do research in pasture management and she's very good at it, but at the end of the day we do not hire her, and she is not considered by us, to be an expert in this area," he said. "I think her behaviour is unethical." I was taken aback. He had always been cordial in the past. This attack, however, was personal and aimed directly at Clark's credibility – the foundation of any scientist's career.

My next call was to James Turk, executive director of the Canadian Association of University Teachers. He said comments like McLaughlin's limited academic freedom, which he said was essential to universities being centres of debate and higher learning. "One of the ways in which there have been attempts to deny people freedom of expression and to cut back on academic freedom is to say, 'Well, academics should only be able to comment on the area in which they are experts'," said Turk. "If one took that seriously, it would muzzle most academics speaking about most subjects in this country if you define their areas of expertise narrowly enough." I had asked McLaughlin who at the university would be a better spokesperson on the safety of GM foods. He recommended Doug Powell, who taught risk communication at Guelph – not plant science.

As entertaining as such public spats can be, they tend to undermine the public's faith in science in general. This was something that the business world, it seemed, was slow to figure out in earlier attempts to manage the debate over such things as the dangers of cigarette smoke, global warming, and the use of pesticides. Worse, the public execution of scientific careers sent a chill through the biotech research community, making other scientists reluctant to pursue, much less publish, anything that might be critical of biotechnology.

Pusztai says he has been able to continue his work, albeit on a limited scale, thanks to the help offered to him by scientists who still have jobs. They want to remain anonymous, however, fearing they too could be ostracized if they are caught helping such a high-profile critic of GM foods. They offered him access to their databases, libraries, labs, and other research facilities, and he did the work they couldn't. "If you say you are going to do research into the potential dangers of genetically modified foods, you won't get any funding," he says. "As a scientist, I was always taught that we must be critical. We are asked to suspend this with GM foods."

In 1993, tobacco giant Philip Morris set up an agency called The Advancement for Sound Science Coalition through a public relations firm that would be paid $37,500 (U.S.) a month to attack what the company saw as "junk science." Junk science seemed to be anything concluding that second-hand smoke could cause cancer. The coalition commissioned studies from scientists showing no ill effect from second-hand smoke and paid experts in the field to write favourable newspaper columns that would be submitted to newspapers for use on their opinion pages. It was a classic third-party technique. A company, recognizing that its voice on an issue lacked credibility, arranged for a third party to do the talking.

With a name as innocuous as The Advancement of Sound Science Coalition, few would suspect that the group was a front for the tobacco industry. This cover was enhanced when the PR firm APCO Associates brought other industries to the coalition that were also interested in rebuking scientific discoveries that might hurt their bottom lines. By recruiting members of the farm, food additive, and biotech industries, Philip Morris was able to align itself with industries that the public might be more sympathetic toward, but which also had some interest in its definition of sound science. It could also hide the fact that it was funding the coalition almost entirely.

That the current arguments over sound science versus junk science – the missive now applied to anti-GM studies – have their roots in the tobacco battles was hardly surprising. Tobacco was, after all, an agricultural product – and one that relied heavily on the chemical fertilizers and pesticides made by the biotech giants. As well, Philip Morris owns Kraft, one of the world's largest food companies, and laid claim to 10 cents of every food dollar spent in the United States. Its interest in "sound science" extended far beyond the effects of second-hand smoke.

Current practitioners of the third-party technique on behalf of the biotech industry include the Council for Biotechnology Information, headed by former Monsanto Canada president Ray Mowling, the Food Biotechnology Communications Network,

Ontario Agri-Food Technologies, and Doug Powell's Food Safety Network at the University of Guelph, which is funded by the food industry, biotechnology companies, and the conservative Donner Foundation. Each organization portrays itself as an unbiased source of information on biotechnology and claims its pronouncements are based on sound science. Each can be counted on, however, to give unswerving support to GM foods and to dismiss any criticism of biotechnology as junk science, whether that criticism comes from as predictable a group as Greenpeace or as respected a body as the Royal Society of Canada.

In a surprise move in January 2001, the Royal Society issued a report harshly critical of GM crops and questioned the federal government's dual role as both regulator and proponent of GM foods. The report called it a "significant conflict of interest" for the Canadian Food Inspection Agency to be charged with protecting the public and the environment from risks posed by GM foods, while promoting the technology as safe. This conflict was aggravated by the agency's mandate to balance any risks posed by GM foods against the economic benefit they might offer Canada. "The claim that the assessment of biotechnology risks is 'science-based' is only as valid as the independence, objectivity and quality of the science employed," the report said. "The more regulatory agencies are, or are perceived to be, promoters of the technology, the more they undermine public trust in their ability to regulate the technology in the public interest."

Efforts by both government and industry to dismiss public concerns with "sound science" arguments have only fed public distrust when the source of that science was the industry itself or a government agency working as industry's "dedicated publicists," the Royal Society said. Sound science became corporate jargon for favourable science and lost any real meaning despite its linguistic appeal. More disturbingly, with industry backers arguing there is no scientific basis for labelling GM foods, science became a pretext to undermine the public's right to choose – the very foundation of a democratic society – even to make the "wrong" choice in the eyes of some.

From the point of view of the companies and their scientist defenders, including Powell, unease over GM food was irrational because there were no reported health problems among consumers even though 60 per cent of the food in grocery stores now contains GM ingredients. Other concerns, such as E. coli or food poisoning, deserved greater attention than GM foods, which dominated the food safety debate. "What frustrates me is all the time that is wasted," Powell told a meeting of the Biotechnology Industry Organization in June 2002. Of course, with no labels on the food telling us what is modified and what is not, consumers have no way of knowing what GM products they may be eating. If this was, as McHughen put it, a "human experiment," it was being poorly run.

Labelling has become a flashpoint in much of the debate over GM foods and has exposed some of the contradictions in the pro-biotech argument. Biotech companies argue that GM food does not need to be labelled because it is not substantially different from conventionally grown food. And yet the companies also argue that their products are unique enough to be patented and sued farmers such as Percy Schmeiser of Saskatchewan for patent infringement when they grew the products without permission.

It takes impressive intellectual gymnastics to simultaneously argue that a product is unique and thus requires a patent – and as such requires segregation, labelling, and expensive licences before it hits the farm gate in seed form – but also is so indistinct that once the seeds are grown into plants they require no such special treatment. But as impressive as such gymnastics are, they are not convincing. The process of genetic modification is not distinct from the products, as industry would have us believe. The process is the product. At least, that is how companies such as Monsanto sold their vision of the future to investors.

In a statement quietly tabled in the House of Commons in November 2002, Agriculture Canada expressed its fear that such investment could be jeopardized by the labelling of GM foods.

"The adoption of a mandatory labelling system by Canada could have a significant impact on its trade relationship with its largest trading partner, the United States," the statement said. "A disjointed approach with the U.S. on voluntary versus mandatory labelling could place both trade and investment at risk."

Both industry and government argue that a simple label on a product cannot tell consumers enough to be useful, since biotechnology is too complicated to be boiled down to a small tag on a package of food. Biotechnology certainly is complicated, but that hasn't stopped the industry from arguing for voluntary labels that would allow it to advertise any perceived benefits that might be engineered into the food. Joyce Groote, past president of the lobby group BIOTECanada, said the industry favoured voluntary labels because that would allow companies to call attention to any genetic modifications they thought might help sell products – such as enhanced nutritional qualities or flavour. Mandatory labelling, however, would force food companies to put labels on food from plants that produce their own insecticide or were modified to withstand strong doses of weed killer – qualities consumers might find less appealing. Such issues, Groote said, were too complex to be put on a simple label. "What meaningful information would you give consumers?"

At the BIO 2002 industry conference in Toronto in June 2002, the pro-biotech plant breeder and author Alan McHughen continued the industry argument against labelling. "Putting a label on it says that it's different. It's only different from a subjective standpoint," he said. Throughout the seminar, "Separating Fact from Fiction," chaired by Doug Powell, McHughen stressed that as a professor at a publicly funded university he worked for taxpayers. "Consumers will be more confused [by labels] and as a representative of taxpayers, I don't want them any more confused than they already are," said McHughen.

Speaking at the same seminar, Greg Pence of the University of Alabama said that once genetically modified products with traits that

consumers might want came to the market, the opposition to genetically modified foods would wither away. "I think once you have a
better-tasting tomato that sells for less, it will be over. Greenpeace
will say there are risks, but consumers will make their choice." When
asked how consumers would make that choice without labelling – or
would the tomatoes be labelled in the way Groote had outlined, he
said, "That's not labelling. That's marketing."

Jeff Wilson likes to refer to himself as Farmer Jeff. He grows
market vegetables just outside the village of Hillsburgh, northwest
of Toronto, and operates a small green grocery adjacent to his house.
At one time, the shop was little more than a vegetable stand at the
end of his driveway, like thousands of others dotting highways and
country roads across Canada. After a fire gutted his old shop, Wilson
rebuilt the store to rival the produce section of any city supermarket.
When fresh produce from his own fields is not available, he buys
fruits and vegetables from other farmers to keep his shelves and
coolers full. Wilson takes great pride in knowing most of his customers, talking to them about the growing conditions that brought
them their food, and providing the best-looking produce he can.
"This stuff is just gorgeous," Wilson said one afternoon as we toured
his cornfields. And, indeed, it was. As Wilson pulled back the husk
from a cob, he revealed plump, perfect kernels. There wasn't a
blemish or worm to be found. The Bt had done its job.
     Doug Powell used Wilson's farm and shop to test his theories on
consumer reactions to genetically modified foods. The two have
worked together for years. Wilson was an early head of AGCare, a
farm group set up in the 1980s to confront consumer fears about pesticides, but he has spent the last few years promoting GM foods.
Powell was active with the group as well, advising it on media and
consumer relations and speaking on behalf of the group to defend
genetic modification. In recent years, their experiments at Wilson's

farm have formed the basis of Powell's presentations at food and biotech industry conferences across North America, including two appearances at BIO 2002 in Toronto – at 15,000 delegates, the largest-ever gathering of the biotech industry.

Powell began his career at Guelph in 1996, when former Schneider's executive Ken Murray donated $100,000 to Guelph and the University of Waterloo to establish a two-year teaching and research project, called Science and Society, to be shared by the schools. As part of his work, Powell set up the Food Safety Network. He was later hired full-time as an assistant professor and was granted tenure. With more industry funding, including $320,000 from the Donner Foundation (which included $100,000 for *Globe and Mail* writer Stephen Strauss to become a Donner Fellow while he wrote a book) and another $250,000 from Murray, he expanded the Food Safety Network to include more listservs, more students, and more research projects. The network focused on farming and food issues, maintaining an archive of news items and studies about the food industry and generating its own studies and newspaper opinion pieces on agricultural issues, such as GM foods.

In 2000, Wilson turned over parts of his farm and produce store to Powell so he and his students could test their theories on communicating with consumers about GM food. The previous fall, the two men showed up at a Loblaws store in Toronto with AGCare to counter the arguments being put forward by Greenpeace and the Council of Canadians as they launched their anti-GM food campaign in Canada.

The Food Safety Network has consistently produced studies showing that consumers can be convinced to buy GM food, that organic foods are not as safe as conventional, and that GM crops are popular with farmers. In 2002, the network merged with a Saskatoon call centre set up in the late 1990s by Food Biotechnology Communications Network to field consumers' questions about GM food. Diane Wetherall of the FBCN told the 2002 annual meeting of

AGCare that the move made sense because calls to the centre were dropping off and Powell had all the information that her group wanted to hand out.

Powell's working theory was that if consumers were told more about GM food, they would buy it. "By actively engaging them through street theatre, through op-eds, we like to think we've had an impact," Powell told the BIO conference. "Canada is certainly not Europe." To explore his theory, he and Wilson grew both genetically modified and conventional sweet corn during the summer of 2000. After the harvest, the food was sold in Wilson's on-farm store in bins clearly marking which was modified and which was not. The modified corn outsold the conventional by a wide margin: 8,160 cobs to 5,430. A survey of 174 consumers found that 69 per cent said they would prefer GM corn over conventional, while 26 per cent would not.

I visited the model farm several times that summer, both with Powell or Wilson on hand and without them around. From what I saw, it was hardly surprising that the GM corn outsold the conventional. The sign over the conventional corn read, "Would you eat wormy sweet corn?" It is the only time I have seen a store label its own corn "wormy." The sign then went on to list the chemicals sprayed on the corn to kill bugs and weeds and the fertilizers used. Over the GM corn, the sign read, "Here's what went into producing quality sweet corn," and listed the fertilizers used to grow the corn. Another sign identified the corn as genetically modified. The descriptions of the corn as either "wormy" or "quality" were not mentioned in Powell's presentations to BIO 2002 or in his writings on the experiment. He did write, however, that "a few customers in the market were observed to fill their bags with regular corn and then pause to read the large signs above the bins, which explained the pest management regime for each type of corn. They then proceeded to empty their bags and refill them with Bt sweet corn."

In an interview, Powell said he saw no problem with the "wormy" sign. "It was a rhetorical question," he said. Rhetoric aside, when one bin was marked "wormy corn" and another "quality sweet corn," it was hardly surprising which sold more. Perhaps the choice by Wilson's customers to take home more than five thousand cobs of wormy corn rather than buy "quality" Bt corn showed some pretty deep misgivings about GM food.

An information table in the market contained press releases and pamphlets on Powell's experiment, as well as a number of pro-biotech fact sheets written by Powell and his students and industry lobby groups. There was no anti-biotech information on display.

On one visit, I asked a man why he was buying regular corn over GM. He said he didn't believe that GM was good for the environment and was worried about its health effects. As he walked to his truck, Powell talked to him about Bt corn – describing how it did not need insecticides because it produced its own and that it had been approved as safe by the federal government. Powell then told me I should talk to the man again. I did, and he said he would buy GM corn the next time he was at the store. Powell stood nearby with his arms crossed and a smile on his face.

The incident convinced me that the only conclusion that can be drawn from Powell's experiment was that, fed a lot of pro-biotech sales pitches, shoppers could be convinced to buy GM products. Any marketing man could have told him that. Certainly, the industry has already figured that out, judging from Groote's concept of pro-biotech labelling once food companies have engineered their products in consumer-friendly ways.

Percy Schmeiser speaking at a
Mississauga school, April 2002

---

*"There is no food in their world. There are
no farmers in their world. There are no
consumers in their world. There's just products
and market share."*

Vandana Shiva,
Indian activist

CHAPTER FIVE

MIXED VEGETABLES

One of nature's miracles is its ability to reproduce itself. A bit of pollen caught on the wind or a seed eaten by a bird or a squirrel later finds itself far away from its place of origin, mixing with related plants and its new environment to build new life. This force, which is the essence of life on earth, does not stop just because a biotech company has taken out a patent demanding that its genes flourish only in the fields of farmers who have paid for that right. Modified canola, popular with farmers because it has been engineered to resist weed killer, is now one of the most intrusive weeds on the prairies. Farmers who have never bought GM canola find it in their fields and cannot get rid of it because it is genetically modified to survive herbicides.

In northern Alberta, researchers found weed canola that was resistant to three different kinds of herbicides made by three different companies – Monsanto's Roundup, Aventis's Liberty, and Cyanamid's Pursuit – just a few years after GM canola was put on the market, and two years after the farmer facing the new weeds had planted it. "We knew this was going to happen," Alberta Agriculture canola specialist Phil Thomas told *The Western Producer*. "It was only a matter of when." An Agriculture Canada study of eleven fields in 1999 found that all of them contained canola that could resist more than one brand of herbicide. Those eleven fields, and the "triple-resistant" canola, as it is called, show both how quickly plants can mix and match genes, and how easy it is for GM food to contaminate the environment around it. An Australian study published in *Science* in July 2002 found that pollen from GM canola could travel up to three kilometres.

A more controversial study was published in *Nature* in late 2001. It found that wild corn in the southern Mexican state of Oaxaca, where corn was first domesticated more than four thousand years ago, was contaminated with genetically engineered DNA. Mexico banned GM corn in 1998 in hopes of protecting its ancient wild varieties from just such contamination. The study's authors, David Quist and Ignacio Chapela of the University of California at Berkeley, wrote that they had found evidence of the cauliflower mosaic virus in four out of six samples of wild corn taken from the mountainous Sierra Norte region of Oaxaca. The virus was used in GM corn as a "promoter" to switch on the transplanted genes. Two of the six samples contained the nopaline synthase terminator sequence, which shuts off the transplanted gene and is another leftover from the genetic modification process. One even contained the Cry 1A gene that was spliced into Bt corn to kill worms. "I repeated the tests at least three times to make sure I wasn't getting false positives," Quist said at the time. "It was initially hard to believe that corn in such a remote region would have tested positive."

Like earlier critics of GM foods, Quist and Chapela were soon attacked. For weeks, the Prakash listserv was dominated by criticisms of the study and its authors. Their methods used to test for the foreign genes were questioned, and the motives of the authors impugned. In 1998, Chapela led an unsuccessful fight at Berkeley against biotech giant Novartis's offer to donate $25 million (U.S.) to the university in exchange for having the first option on much of the school's genetic research discoveries. The method used by Quist and Chapela to screen for foreign DNA, a very sensitive genetic test called the inverse polymerase chain reaction, has been known to result in false positives because the samples being tested can become contaminated with the material for which they are being tested.

Critics said the pair should have used other methods to confirm their results.

By April 2002, the pressure of such criticisms had become too great and *Nature* took the unusual step of publishing an editorial saying that the Quist and Chapela study should not have appeared in the journal, saying, "The evidence available is not sufficient to justify the publication of the original paper." It published three criticisms of the study, and a rebuttal by Quist and Chapela. The critics especially took issue with the original study's conclusion that foreign genes were "jumping around the genome" of Mexican corn. One of the scientists writing in the April 4 issue of *Nature*, Nick Kaplinsky of Berkeley, said charges of jumping genes stretched the credibility of the study, since it "would have changed some of the basic assumptions of biotechnology, if correct."

Despite his criticisms, Kaplinsky admitted that Mexico's repository of heritage corn varieties may one day be contaminated with foreign genes, and perhaps is already. "I think at some point soon, someone will come up with good scientific evidence that [GM corn] is growing all over the country." Three other scientists reviewing the original paper questioned the methodology, but only one called for a retraction. The other two agreed with Kaplinsky that corn in Mexico was probably contaminated, but that scientific proof was still lacking. Even Denis Avery, a senior fellow with the conservative Hudson Institute who called the *Nature* study a hoax, wrote in a column for Knight Ridder news service that, "while Quist and Chapela's contention seems highly doubtful, it's likely that transgenic corn will turn up in Mexico eventually." He saw nothing wrong with that, however.

Quist and Chapela stood by their original conclusions. "To read *Nature* you would think our entire research had gone south. That is not the case. Our main statement, that there is GM contamination, is not contested by the critics," Chapela told the Glasgow *Herald*. The two lamented that they and their methods, not the ramifications of genetic contamination, became the focus of the discussion. Chapela admitted that his study was limited but said the best response would have been to do more research. "We would call for other researchers to produce more data and not simply harp on the limited amount of data that we had," he said to reporters. Quist told Reuters news service, "Politics have entered too far, made too many inroads into the scientific process."

Two of the strongest and earliest critics on the Prakash listserv were Mary Murphy and Andura Smetacek, who described themselves as ordinary citizens. "Chapela, while a scientists [sic] of one sort, is clearly first and foremost an activist," Smetacek wrote in the top item in the November 29, 2001, edition of the listserv – the same day the Quist and Chapela study appeared in *Nature*. Another dispatch from the listserv that day was topped by an e-mail from Murphy pointing out Chapela's connections to the Pesticide Action Network, an environmental group. "Not exactly what you would call an unbiased writer," she concluded. The two made more than sixty submissions to the AgBioView listserv. I could find none that identified who they were or who they worked for.

Shortly after the 133-year-old journal's semi-retraction, however, *Guardian* columnist George Monbiot (drawing heavily on an earlier article in *The Ecologist* magazine) revealed several connections between both Murphy and Smetacek and a public relations company hired by Monsanto. The Bivings Group specializes in using the Internet and listservs to a client's advantage. A paper on its Web site called it "Viral Marketing: How to Infect the World" and said the tactic worked best when nobody realized it was happening. "Once you are plugged into this world, it is possible to make postings to these outlets that present your position as an uninvolved third party," the report said. "Sometimes only the client knows the precise role we played."

Monbiot also pointed out several connections between Bivings and AgBioView. For instance, anti-GM activist Jonathan Matthews stumbled across a connection between the two while searching the AgBioView Web site, when a message popped up saying, "Can't connect to MySQL server on apollo.bivings.com." Monbiot wrote,

"Apollo.bivings.com is the main server of the Bivings Group." Prakash denied any ties to Bivings, which in turn denied any connection to Murphy and Smetacek. In an interview, Prakash said he makes no effort to verify the identity or qualifications of those who submit comments to his listserv and does not restrict the use of pseudonyms. "You need to take this with a pinch of salt," he said of his listserv. "This is not a refereed journal."

Amid the controversy, the Mexican government continued with its own investigations. It had initially rejected the Quist and Chapela study, which challenged the country's ability to protect its valuable wild corn varieties. In a study released about two weeks after the *Nature* retraction, however, the Mexican environment ministry said that it had found the cauliflower mosaic virus throughout Oaxaca and Puebla states. Contamination was found in 95 per cent of the sites where 1,875 seedling samples were taken. In all, 8 per cent of the seedlings were contaminated. The worst contamination was near main roads where corn was sold to villagers, Jorge Soberón, executive director of the ministry's national commission on biodiversity, told a United Nations meeting on biological diversity at The Hague.

In some fields, up to 35 per cent of the samples analyzed by the environment ministry and Mexico's National Autonomous University were contaminated. "This is the world's worst case of contamination by genetically modified material because it happened in the place of origin of a major crop," Soberon said. "There is no doubt about it." The mosaic virus was used in GM corn by Monsanto, Sygenta, and Aventis, but Soberon said he could not determine which company's version of the virus had made it into the corn since they all refused to release the information needed, claiming such information was proprietary. "I find that extremely difficult to accept," he told the *Guardian*. "How can you monitor what is going on if they do not allow you the information to do it?"

The Mexican environment ministry said the foreign genes probably came into the country with imports of American corn, which have increased dramatically under free trade. American corn, thanks to generous subsidies, can be sold in Mexico for less than domestic corn, making it popular with consumers.

The scientific advances of the Green Revolution that had enabled Mexico to feed itself had been overcome by economic forces. In 1982, President Miguel de la Madrid was forced by a debt crisis to abandon Mexico's efforts to help small farmers boost production of corn, wheat, rice, sorghum, and soybeans. The plan had been implemented two years earlier in hopes of enhancing the country's food security by ensuring it grew all the food it needed. Under directives from the World Bank and the International Monetary Fund, Madrid cut subsidies to small farmers and allowed interest rates to rise – further hurting farmers. Under the prescribed structural adjustment program, farm subsidies dropped by 80 per cent in the 1980s, and nutritional assistance to the poor was abandoned. Food policy, the World Bank and the IMF said, would be decided by market forces. That led to large imports of cheaper, subsidized American corn.

Mexican farmers, however, tended to not make the same distinction as North Americans between corn kernels intended to be used as seeds and those intended to be food, and may have planted imported corn in their fields. The Mexican government planned to submit its study into GM contamination to a scientific journal for publication, but only after a thorough review by independent scientists. Exequiel Excurra, president of the environment ministry's National Ecology Institute, told the Mexican newspaper *La Reforma* that the government wanted to avoid a repetition of the dispute that plagued Quist and Chapela's study. In November 2002, however, *Nature* said that it would not publish the Mexican study.

In Canada, the threat of genetic contamination has been of particular concern to organic farmers, who worry that GM crops will breed with their non-GM crops. Organic farmers work under strict certification requirements that do not allow them to use any synthetic fertilizers or pesticides. They also cannot use GM seeds, and GM contamination from a neighbouring field could cost an organic farm its certification and so the higher prices paid for organic crops. That's why a group of Saskatchewan organic farmers filed a lawsuit in January 2002 against Monsanto and Aventis, charging that genetic drift from fields growing GM crops threatened their organic crops. That would cost them customers, the farmers argued. "Any kind of science, whatever it is, if it's infringing on our rights, they don't have a right to do it," Arnold Taylor, one of the farmers and president of the Saskatchewan Organic Directorate, told Reuters. With GM canola so prevalent on the Canadian prairies, it was impossible to grow non-GM canola and prevent it from being contaminated, he said. Monsanto's spokesperson Trish Jordan said the organic farmers should be prepared to tolerate some level of GM contamination in their crops.

Two days before Christmas 2002, Monsanto applied for approval of its latest product, genetically modified wheat. Like the canola at the centre of the Saskatchewan suit, the wheat is modified to withstand Roundup. And like the canola, it will be impossible to keep it from contaminating the non-GM crops across the prairies. That's why the Canadian Wheat Board wants Ottawa to reject the application. Gord Flaten, director of market development for the wheat board, told Dow Jones that more than 80 per cent of the board's customers have said they would not buy from Canada if GM wheat is allowed in our fields. "We need to be sure that if customers don't want this product, and the handling and segregation system cannot satisfy customers requirements, then it should not be introduced at all." Monsanto's new grain could be in Canadian fields by 2005, making Canada the first country in the world to allow GM wheat. Monsanto's Jordan said, however, that the company had not yet decided whether to release it commercially. "While regulatory approval will certainly provide an important level of confidence across the wheat industry, it doesn't mean we're going to be ready to introduce the product." Greenpeace and the Council of Canadians joined the Wheat Board in urging Ottawa to reject Monsanto's bid and keep Canada free of GM wheat as a market advantage. Farmers, meanwhile, worried that with little standing in its way, the new wheat would be approved, costing them customers. And organic farmers worried they would lose yet another crop altogether if GM wheat were to follow canola's destructive path.

The threat to organic farming goes beyond gene contamination and the loss of a potential crop. Organic farmers use Bt, which the biotech companies have inserted into the DNA of corn, as a spray to kill insects. They don't use it very often, preferring such methods as crop rotation to keep insects in check, but need it whenever infestations get out of control. As such, it is one of the most important tools organic farmers have. The sparing use of Bt by organic farmers for more than thirty years prevented insects from building up a resistance to the pesticide.

With half of Ontario's corn estimated to be genetically modified, Bt-resistant corn borers are assumed to be developing already, despite encouragement by farm groups, agriculture ministries, and biotech companies for farmers to leave parts of their fields Bt-free to slow such a development. Numerous laboratory tests have shown that Bt resistance can develop within just a few generations. Monsanto itself figures that Bt resistance will render Bt corn useless within thirty years. All this, of course, represents a tempting marketing opportunity for biotechnology companies, now developing new types of Bt corn that can kill the Bt-resistant worms created by the first wave of GM crops. Monsanto, for instance, is researching ways to insert two types of the Bt gene into one variety of seed, betting that few insects will be able to develop a resistance to both types. Such measures cannot prevent resistance from developing, however, they can only delay it. Monsanto has said it does not see any particular problem with this, since it can just find another gene to splice into the corn to produce a new pesticide. Organic farmers, meanwhile, would be robbed of a safe and effective insecticide.

Rene Van Acker, a plant scientist whose interests in agriculture extend far beyond his lab at the University of Manitoba, fears that biotechnology and industrialization are robbing farmers of something

vital. For centuries, agricultural skills were passed from one generation of farmers to the next. Farmers were taught as children what
combination of plants would keep insects and weeds at bay, and how
crop rotations would thwart the development of large insect populations while replenishing the soil with needed nutrients. Industrial
agriculture, and its reliance on chemical pest and weed killers and
fertilizers, makes such skills obsolete. Farmers need only follow the
protocols set out by the chemical companies and their field representatives to keep their farms producing well. Biotechnology,
which further simplifies operations, makes traditional skills even
more useless. Van Acker and some of his students set up "learning
circles" in rural Manitoba through which young farmers could
learn the skills used by older farmers before the Green Revolution
swept them aside. "Once these old guys are gone, so are their skills,"
lamented Van Acker.

Another Winnipegger, founder of the Rural Advancement
Foundation International, Pat Mooney, worries that farmers are losing
not only the skills that once made them so vital to the food industry,
but their traditional rights, as well. Mooney set up RAFI in the 1970s
after a stint at the United Nations Food and Agriculture Organization,
where he became aware of the plight of small farmers and their rights.
Traditionally, farmers saved a portion of each year's crop to use as seed
for the coming year. By choosing seeds from their best-performing
plants, over time, they improved the quality of their crops as they
propagated only those that did well on their farms. It was also a cheap
way for farmers to keep their farms operating – an especially important safety net when times were tough. There has long been a thriving seed industry, of course, which farmers used to find entirely new
varieties of crops and hybrids that could boost production. Farmers
bought seed when the cost could be justified by added production.
Hybrids, for instance, typically return about $3 to the farmer for
every dollar invested in seed. That is a solid investment.

With genetically engineered seeds, farmers not only have to buy
the seed itself, but must also pay a "technology fee" that effectively

doubles the cost. For the fee, the farmers buy the right to use the crop for one year. After that, the farmer must buy more seeds and pay the fee again. This is how the biotechnology companies hope to recoup the money they spent developing the seeds. "Without patents to provide some period of market exclusivity, the hard, cold fact is that researchers and investors would never dream to recoup their investment in R&D," Carl Feldbaum, the head of the Biotechnology Industry Organization, said in his keynote address to the group's annual meeting in June 2002. Through the World Trade Organization's Trade-Related Aspects of Intellectual Property Rights agreement, or TRIPS, patents granted in one country can be extended to another, a system Feldbaum said was also necessary. "Without stable national and international systems of intellectual property protection, biotech enterprises and the benefits they bring are simply not possible."

But to critics of GM crops, the patents and technology fees are a threat to farmers' independence that will drive small-scale farmers from the land. Because of the higher cost, only those farming on a large scale could take full advantage of the technology and gain an advantage over smaller farmers. Critics of GM do not concede that GM seeds boost production – and there are several studies questioning this notion put forward by the industry – but the simplicity of using GM crops is never questioned.

Roundup Ready soybeans, which have been genetically modified to withstand spraying of Monsanto's powerful Roundup weed killer, allow farmers to kill all the weeds in their fields with just one chemical. Conventional soybean fields require three or more different chemicals to get all the weeds.

"Weed management was becoming a real problem in the soybean industry, and then along comes a product that massively simplifies the system. No wonder it caught on so quickly," Charles Benbrook, an agricultural consultant in the United States, says. "Roundup Ready soybeans have made it possible for farmers to divert a lot of their managerial skills away from weed management to other areas," such as land acquisition and expanding their farms.

Crops that produce their own insecticide save the farmer the time needed to spray for insects. "On my farm I explore any production practice . . . that can make my farm more efficient," Ontario farmer Jeff Wilson wrote in a guest column for the *Globe and Mail* entitled "Why I Grow Genetically Engineered Crops." Without genetic engineering, farmers must use a variety of sprays to control weeds, adding to their work. A 2002 study by the George Morris Centre in Guelph found that farmers growing genetically engineered soybeans made 1.7 fewer passes over their fields than they did three years earlier.

With their work in the field simplified, farmers could take on more acres to achieve economies of scale that otherwise would not be possible. Past technological advances that increased the productivity of farmers' work in the field – tractors, combines, and chemical fertilizers and pesticides – led to similar jumps in both farm size and productivity.

But for many farmers, saving seeds is much more than a cheap way to replant a field year after year. It represents the passing of the farm's genetic and cultural heritage from one year to the next – just as farming skills were passed from one generation to the next. In India, activist Vandana Shiva says, saved seeds represent a living bond to previous generations. "The poor of the Third World have been custodians of this resource," she says. For a biotechnology company to add just one gene and claim a patent on the seed is nothing less than robbery of that heritage, she says. "You rob them and make them buy it back," Shiva says. "I have called it stealing the loaf while sharing the crumbs."

Basmati rice is one such case. Through generations of cross-breeding, Indian farmers developed twenty-seven distinct varieties of the aromatic grain, each suited to different growing conditions and tastes, and none protected by patent. In 1997, Texas food company

RiceTec Inc. was granted U.S. Patent No. 5,663,484 after crossing a strain of basmati with another and claiming that it had developed a "novel" rice to be sold under brand names such as Texmati and Jasmati. Shiva says the original patent – which granted RiceTec intellectual property rights over "basmati rice lines and grains," not just the new varieties it had developed – threatened the livelihood of 250,000 Indian farmers growing basmati. Because the patent extended to all basmati, any farmers growing any variety could have been forced to pay a patenting fee on a variety of rice they had helped develop. "It was piracy," Shiva says, still angry about it years later.

Shiva's organization launched a court challenge, saying the patent was applied too far and infringed on the rights of Indian farmers. In August 2001, the group won a partial victory when RiceTec lost all but three of its twenty basmati patent claims, keeping patents only on the specific varieties it had bred. As well, its original patent was amended to remove the reference to "basmati rice lines and grains," leaving Indian farmers free to keep growing and selling their varieties without having to pay a patent fee. While the victory meant that RiceTec could no longer claim ownership of all basmati varieties, the granting of three patents allowed the company to profit from centuries of work by Indian farmers. "They did not develop this. It belongs to the Indian people," Shiva says. "Patents should never be granted to living organisms."

In central Saskatchewan, Percy Schmeiser has fought Monsanto using a similar argument. After fifty years of careful crossbreeding and selection, Schmeiser developed a breed of canola that prospered in the soil and climate conditions of his thousand-acre farm. He never took out a patent on the seeds he developed but considered them his, nonetheless. But since the summer of 1998, he has been in a legal battle with Monsanto, which claims he infringed on the company's Patent No. 1,313,830 by growing canola that is modified to resist Roundup.

Schmeiser's troubles began the previous summer, after he sprayed Roundup around telephone poles on his property, a common practice among farmers, and noticed the canola was not dying. A few days later, he sprayed a three-acre patch of canola to see just how far this resistance spread. After a few more days, a definite pattern emerged: plants near the road survived, but those farther away died. Schmeiser then went about the business of farming and in the fall harvested his fields.

The following spring, as he had done for decades, Schmeiser took an eight-thousand-pound batch of seeds from his field, had them treated in nearby Humboldt so they could be used as seeds, and planted them in his fields. In the meantime, Monsanto had heard rumours about Schmeiser's three-acre experiment and sent investigators to check them out.

Speaking to a group of high school students in Mississauga four years later, Schmeiser described what it is like when a farmer gets a visit from a Monsanto investigator: "The first thing they say is 'We're ex-RCMP.' They try right from the beginning to intimidate people. Most farmers don't hear the 'ex' part." Monsanto ends up on a farmer's doorstep usually after being tipped off by another farmer calling the company. "Someone phones and says, 'I think my neighbour is growing Roundup Ready canola,'" Monsanto's Trish Jordan said in an interview. Schmeiser paints a much darker picture, saying Monsanto has turned farmer against farmer with its patent investigations. "They are destroying the fabric of rural Canada. A farmer gets one of those visits and he starts to wonder who reported him. Was it this neighbour or that neighbour?"

Monsanto sent investigators to Schmeiser's farm to take a few plants for testing. Then came visits from the former RCMP officer from Robinson's Investigations of Saskatoon and a letter from Monsanto's lawyers demanding compensation for infringing on the company's patent. When Monsanto first filed its suit against Schmeiser in 1998, it accused him of stealing its patent, but offered to drop its court case if he paid the company $300,000 (U.S.) – twenty times the $15 (Cdn.) an acre Monsanto charges as a technology fee for its canola. The company had dropped the theft charge by the time of the trial but still wanted the money. The company still believed Schmeiser came about the Roundup Ready seeds illegally. It was not, however, pursuing a case against the man it believed sold Schmeiser the Roundup Ready seeds.

Schmeiser's case was heard for three weeks in June 2000 in a Saskatoon federal court. Schmeiser claimed that the patented genes came to his farm accidentally, either via pollen blowing in the wind, or via seeds falling off a truck or moved about by birds or other wild animals. "A deer can rub up against a plant and pick up something, then go to another field and rub up against another plant," spreading the genes of one field to another, Schmeiser told the Mississauga students. Monsanto admitted that some cross-pollination was possible, but not on the scale that its tests showed occurred on Schmeiser's farm, where it claimed that 90 per cent of his nine hundred acres of canola was Roundup Ready. "It was commercial grade," Jordan said.

Monsanto insisted to the court that it had no intention of "tricking" farmers into paying fees on crops that contained the patented gene because of accidental pollen spread. Schmeiser said there was no way to make a claim of 90 per cent contamination by just testing plants from the edge of his field plus twenty-seven random samples from a thousand acres of canola, as Monsanto admitted it had done.

But whatever the level of contamination in the field was, in the end it didn't make any difference to Judge Andrew MacKay. He ruled that it did not matter how the patented genes got into the field, all that mattered was that they were there and that the crop was "known or ought to have been known by Mr. Schmeiser to be tolerant to Roundup." After weeks of deliberation, Schmeiser and Monsanto settled on a damage claim of $19,832 – still more than the $15,000 technology fee for a thousand-acre field. A year later, the same judge ordered that Schmeiser pay Monsanto $153,000 in court costs. In its initial claim for costs, Monsanto wanted Schmeiser to cover the $35,000 paid to two Agriculture Canada scientists to testify against him. With his own court costs topping $200,000, Schmeiser emptied his retirement fund to fight the case and turned to fundraising to keep going. The case returned to court in May 2002 for Schmeiser's appeal, which he lost. He vowed, however, to take his case to the Supreme Court. "If you can patent a plant, what about birds, bees, and animals – and ultimately humans? Where does it stop?"

Jordan said Schmeiser should have called Monsanto as soon as he discovered the genetically modified canola around the utility poles, rather than saving the seeds and replanting them. The company would have come out to remove the plants and compensated him for the lost crop. "If he didn't want it, why did he plant it?"

Schmeiser told the Mississauga students he is often asked if he opposes GM crops altogether. He said he does not but is against the patenting of lifeforms and against technology agreements that require farmers to give up their traditional right to save seeds. The technology agreements also require farmers to allow Monsanto's investigators to come onto their property for three years to test for patented genes. "It's one of the most repulsive contracts on the face of the earth," Schmeiser said. "It's a reign of terror. Not in some banana republic, but right here in Canada."

Anti-GM activist Pat Mooney saw worse things on the horizon. Mooney dubbed one of Monsanto's most notorious patents the "Terminator." U.S. Patent No. 5,723,765 is a gene-based patent licensing agreement. Under the technology agreements signed when they buy GM seeds, farmers promise to not save seeds from the crops to plant again without first paying the required fee.

The Terminator would make such agreements unnecessary by preventing the patented plants from propagating. The Terminator gene produces a toxin to kill the embryo inside the seed, obliging farmers to return to the company every year to buy seeds. They would no longer be able to save and develop their own seeds, as Schmeiser and farmers around the world have done for centuries. During the uproar that followed Mooney's Internet dispatches about the patent, Monsanto announced in 1999 that it would not pursue the Terminator technology.

Mooney took little delight in Monsanto's decision. The fine print on the announcement said the company would not pursue the Terminator "at this time." That has left the door open to their pursuing it later, once the controversy had passed. But Mooney sees something even worse on the horizon, which he has dubbed "traitor" genes. This new generation of genetically modified plants would need to be sprayed with a company's proprietary chemicals before they can sprout or flower or develop any other desirable traits. With Roundup Ready seeds, farmers had the option of not using Roundup on their fields (though most used it after having paid the technology fee for the seeds). With the traitor seeds, farmers must buy and spray the chemicals if they want a crop at all, making them dependent on the companies for their livelihood. "We're going back to a feudal system," Schmeiser told the Mississauga students.

That kind of talk frustrates Per Pinstrup-Andersen, head of the World Bank–funded International Food Policy Research Institute. Pinstrup-Andersen, like many defenders of GM foods, likes to turn analogies to colonization and serfdom back on opponents of genetic modification, saying those of us in rich countries can afford the time to debate the merits of the technology, but millions of starving people need access to GM crops as soon as possible. "I don't presume to speak for the farmers in the developing world, but I want to at least give them the choice," he says. "I don't subscribe to the romantic notion that subsistence farming is a great thing. Those who say that should visit one of these places. Their lives are miserable. They can't feed their children. They want out." Countries are better off growing food for the export market, which gives them the money needed to buy a wider variety of food for their people, he says. "I'm not going to [tell] the woman who just lost her crop to drought that we haven't developed a drought-tolerant crop because we just didn't want to," he said.

Brian Halweil has heard such economic arguments before; he just doesn't believe them. Halweil is a researcher for the Worldwatch Institute, an agricultural think-tank set up by Lester Brown, an official with the USDA under John Kennedy. The growing and aching poverty in countries that have turned their economies over to the export market under the instructions of the World Bank and the International Monetary Fund is ample proof that such theories don't work, he says. "Just look at Mexico." In a quest for foreign money, the country's agriculture was turned over to cash crops such as tomatoes and cucumbers to sell into the rich North American market. "It worked for a while," Halweil says. "Then the peso crisis hit."

In December 1994, the Mexican government said it could no longer afford to prop up the peso and allowed the value of the currency to drop by almost half. The rapid devaluation doubled the price of imports – including corn – and cut in half the value of exports, including cash crops. "Those farmers who had committed to those crops were hurt very badly," Halweil said. "They are very vulnerable to swings in the market."

Charles Benbrook has made his living questioning the assumptions of the biotechnology industry after leaving Washington to set up shop in Sandpoint, Idaho, where he works as a consultant. He spent eighteen years in Washington, working for the Carter administration, for Congress, and for the National Academy of Science. His studies have looked into the environmental impact of GM foods, the quality of the plants grown, and the effect they had on the farms that grew them. While the biotechnology industry promotes GM crops as an environmentally friendly way for farmers to cut pesticide use and boost their returns, Benbrook's studies have found otherwise. Like Arpad Pusztai, Benbrook is not completely opposed to GM foods. He is just not convinced that they are properly tested, or that they live up to their hype.

I met Benbrook at an integrated pest management conference in Toronto in March 2002. IPM is a way of farming that involves using a mix of methods to control pests and weeds – much as P.E.I. was pushing farmers to do through its Foodtrust program. GM crops,

Benbrook says, are one such pest control method, a very useful one. A study by the Canola Council of Canada, for instance, found that between 1997, when GM canola was first introduced, and 2000, farmers were making about $10.63 more an acre than they would have growing regular canola. Such studies, and most commodity groups have them, have encouraged more farmers to switch to GM crops. Today, between 90 and 95 per cent of Ontario canola fields are genetically modified, and half the corn. But with that rapid spread has come diminishing returns.

GM crops, like any new technology, gave great advantages to those who jumped on the bandwagon first. They got a boost in yields while prices were still high, greatly simplified their operations – allowing them to plant larger fields with little extra effort – and had fewer weeds or insects to spoil a good harvest. But as more farmers have adopted the new technology, the advantage has declined. Farmers attracted to the crop by the high prices and simplicity swamped the market, driving prices down. After less than a decade, GM crops dominated the markets, with the majority of corn, canola, and soybean farmers paying Monsanto and other biotech companies $15 or so an acre, but with none any longer having an advantage over the others.

The same thing happened a generation before with chemical fertilizers. Those who adopted the innovations early had a great advantage over others for a few years, but in the long run margins for everyone soon became unsustainably thin, and the advances that once made farming simpler became a way to make farms bigger as farmers left the industry. "Once the [innovation] works itself through the system, you're more or less back where you started, waiting for the next innovation," Richard Gray, a farm economist at the University of Saskatchewan, told *The Western Producer*. A 2002 USDA study found that those farmers who adopted GM crops first extracted the only economic advantages, and that the major benefit seemed to be the ability to run larger farms than would otherwise be possible, and to provide some "insurance" against weed or insect infestations. A study by the European Union painted an even bleaker picture. It found that over the long term, GM crops would boost costs for farmers by between 10 and 41 per cent, since contamination would force them to stop saving their own seeds.

The qualities that give GM its big advantage over conventional varieties may already have begun to wear off, Benbrook found. He uncovered some disturbing problems with the crops. They seemed to have an increased susceptibility to fusarium, a fungus that has been the scourge of farmers across Canada the last few years, and sudden death syndrome. "Sudden death" is a bit of a misnomer. The death actually takes a long time, but the disease develops below ground at the root level. By the time the farmer notices anything, the disease has progressed quite far and the plant dies soon after – giving sudden death syndrome its name.

Benbrook found that modifying soybeans to withstand Roundup suppressed parts of the plant's natural immune system, leaving the plant open to stresses such as disease and fungus. The effect seemed to be especially acute in the days following a spray of Roundup. Until recently, even Monsanto did not fully understand exactly how Roundup worked to kill plants. Because of that, Benbrook wrote, the impact the chemical had on modified crops was also not fully understood, so such adverse effects could not be anticipated.

Soybeans, for instance, have a symbiotic relationship with a bacterium called *Bradyrhizobium japonicum*, or *B. japonicum*, to feed nitrogen from the atmosphere to the soybean. Soybeans and *B. japonicum* work so well together, in fact, that many farmers use soybeans in their crop rotations to replenish the nitrogen in their soil. While GM soybeans can tolerate the Roundup sprays, the *B. japonicum* cannot. When a farmer sprays Roundup, he kills one of the key micro-organisms that helps his beans grow. Most farmers spray Roundup soon after the soybeans poke above the soil in hopes of getting rid of the weeds that might compete for nutrients with the young plants. Citing a 2001 study at the University of Alabama, Benbrook said such early applications hurt the plants when they are

at their most vulnerable, potentially damaging both their root development and their ability to get the needed nitrogen. Seedlings on
farms with good soil and good weather conditions were able to
bounce back, he found, but as much as a quarter of beans growing in
poor soil or exposed to bad weather were lost. He says it was remark-
able that no studies of this problem were conducted earlier, since
nitrogen and root development are the two main concerns for
farmers growing soybeans.

With Roundup killing the *B. japonicum* needed to put nitrogen
into the field, farmers were forced to buy nitrogen fertilizer and
apply it to the fields themselves. What was once a natural process
before GM crops has become another task for farmers to perform and
another input they had to buy. "It's like a tax on farmers," Benbrook
says. Applying nitrogen involves running the tractor over the fields
again, burning fossil fuels, and calling into question the environmental benefits the biotech companies claim for their products.

The unexpected stresses caused a drop in yields for many farmers
growing Roundup Ready soybeans, Benbrook found. He calls it
"yield drag." As disease, fungus, poor root development, and a lack of
nitrogen spread through the fields, the initial spikes in production
credited to genetically modified crops dropped off. In parts of Indiana
during the 2000 growing season, for instance, fields of Roundup
Ready soybeans produced 15.5 per cent fewer beans than those
planted with conventional seed, according to independent studies
cited in *Farm Journal* magazine. In Iowa, the difference was 19 per
cent, Benbrook says. In fields in other parts of the United States,
yields were relatively close across both GM and conventional crops. A
2002 study by the George Morris Centre found that Ontario yields
were virtually identical between conventional and Roundup Ready
soybeans, even though many of the conventional farmers surveyed
were growing typically lower-yielding crops under contract.

Since only those farmers with ideal growing conditions could
count on GM fields having comparable or slightly better yields for
their extra investment, Benbrook said planting Roundup Ready

beans really only makes business sense when weeds are a serious problem. Farmers, he says, should assess the impact of weeds on their yield in the past years and compare the lost revenue to the added cost of buying GM seeds and paying the technology fee before deciding to switch. That's how integrated pest management works. He suggests that farmers try everything they can to get rid of weeds before resorting to GM seeds, which can cost twice as much as conventional seeds.

Instead, GM seeds have been used even when weeds have not been a problem – just as antibiotics are routinely fed to chickens to prevent disease, rather than used only on ailing fowl. The rapid drop in price for Roundup since Monsanto's patent on the chemical expired has encouraged more farmers to spray it, Benbrook says. Several studies have found that the use of agricultural herbicide sprays has increased dramatically since the introduction of herbicide-resistant crops. For instance, a survey by the Canola Council of Canada, released in March 2001, showed that western Canadian farmers between 1997 and 2000 made an average of 2.13 herbicide sprayings on GM canola, compared with 1.78 applications on non-GM.

A study by John Losey, whose studies of monarch butterflies set off a firestorm in 1999, and a colleague at Cornell, John Obrycki, found that widespread plantings of Bt corn had not cut the use of insecticides in farmers' fields. "Bt plantings are not used as a replacement for insecticides, but in addition to them," the two said in their study, published in the May 2001 edition of the journal *BioScience*.

The problem is that farmers use Bt corn as a preventive measure, just as those growing Roundup Ready crops. Few farms, however, need to use Bt all the time. Losey and Obrycki found that planting Bt corn makes financial sense only if the infestation is bad enough to justify the higher cost of the Bt seed. Ann Clark at the University of Guelph has made similar calculations in her studies. Even when Bt corn boosts a farmer's production, it might not be a good financial move. Benbrook found that American farmers spent $659 million (U.S.) in patent licensing fees for Bt corn between 1996 and 2001 and managed to boost their production by 276 million bushels, worth $567 million. "The bottom line for farmers is a net loss of $92 million," Benbrook wrote. "The economic value of using Bt corn depends largely on whether infestation levels of European corn borer impact yields." That's how organic farmers use Bt spray.

As the biotechnology industry was meeting in Toronto in June 2002, some of its harshest critics were holding a much smaller meeting at the Greenpeace offices just a few blocks away. Fresh from a weekend counter-conference challenging the assumptions of the biotech industry, the leaders of the anti-GM movement discussed whether to keep the focus on the growing power of the food and farm-supply companies or to focus on keeping genetically modified wheat out of farmers' fields. A campaign against GM wheat had brought the activists into alliance with farm groups that had previously viewed them as the enemy, such as the Canadian Wheat Board. "Agricultural groups that hate our guts are sitting down with us at the table," Nadege Adam of the Council of Canadians said later. They all agreed to work closely with groups in the United States to mobilize consumers and to coordinate continent-wide campaigns.

The movement had slowed after Monsanto was taken over by Pharmacia. For a while, it seemed the industry itself was on the ropes. Poll after poll told the industry that both North American and European consumers did not want to eat GM food and wanted it labelled. Major food makers also said they didn't want it. Monsanto was forced to pull its New Leaf potato – which used a Bt gene to kill the Colorado potato beetle – from the market.

Then, in the fall of 2000, an alliance of environmental and consumer advocacy groups in Washington acted on a hunch. They wanted a way to expose shortcomings in the food system and knew that a brand of GM corn called Starlink was supposed to be used as animal feed only. The Environmental Protection Agency, fearing that it might be allergenic to humans, had approved it only as animal feed and had placed strict rules on its handling to keep it out of the human food chain. Knowing this and suspicious that the rules were not being followed, the activists took a chance. Larry Bohlen of Friends of the Earth visited a Safeway grocery store in Silver Spring, Maryland, a Washington suburb, and filled his cart with all the corn-based products he could find – from taco shells to tortillas to corn chips. The products were sent to a lab in Iowa for testing and retesting. The results were always the same: taco shells made by Kraft contained the Cry9C Bt gene used in Starlink corn to kill the corn borer. Later more products were discovered containing the gene. After the scandal broke, more than three hundred products had to be removed from U.S. grocery store shelves, at an estimated cost of more than $1 billion.

Many activists hoped the scandal signalled the beginning of the end for the GM food industry. It was not to be. With no conclusive proof of adverse health effects associated with the Starlink corn, the industry was able to dodge the bullet. Aventis, the maker of Starlink, paid $30 million in compensation to farmers and eventually withdrew Starlink from the market rather than suffer more public relations problems.

The industry recovered somewhat after announcing apparently beneficial plants such as golden rice – engineered to contain beta carotene to help reduce blindness in the developing world – and releasing the rice genome to help researchers working with the developing world's most important crop.

By the time of the BIO 2002 conference, boastfulness and optimism had returned to the industry. Two years earlier, an agricultural biotechnology conference held in the basement of a downtown Toronto hotel attracted only five hundred delegates and got little media attention. BIO 2002 was held in Toronto's largest convention centre and attracted 15,000 delegates and 2,000 reporters from around the world. *The Times of India* sent a reporter from Bangalore and a marketing representative to sell ads for the paper. "We're in a zone now where we're getting over the initial hump," Carl Feldbaum, president of BIO, said. He argued that it was time to explore new frontiers, such as going to the developing world with products like golden rice and treatments for diseases such as Ebola and dengue fever, and using the World Trade Organization to challenge Europe's refusal to allow GM crops. "The industry is mature enough now to have a foreign policy," he said.

But talk of a foreign policy did little to soothe the industry's critics. "Industry is not yet a government, but they can speak the language and usurp that role," Vandana Shiva said in a speech to launch the activist conference running the weekend before BIO 2002. Holding up a pamphlet from the industry conference, she read aloud from its boasts of new products that would give companies increased market share, then commented: "There is no food in their world. There are no farmers in their world. There are no consumers in their world. There's just products and market share."

Barry Hamilton outside the closed
Rose Valley grain elevator, July 1999

---

*"There is no free market. There is only
government policy."*

Brian Doidge,
farm economist

CHAPTER SIX

A SLICE OF BREAD

On July 26, 1999, I met Barry Hamilton in the back room of Lea's Corner Crafts in Rose Valley, a farming community clinging to life in central Saskatchewan. He had just come in from the fields. Mud caked on his fading jeans and worn workboots. Sweat stained both his threadbare T-shirt and the ball cap that shielded his eyes from the harsh July sun. The fields he was working that day, however, were not his own. They were his neighbour's. To make ends meet, Hamilton hired himself out to other farmers – helping them seed, spread pesticides and fertilizers, and bring in the crop. He did all this while tending to his own five hundred acres of grains and oilseeds, land originally homesteaded by his grandparents. In past years, Hamilton had hired himself out to the oil fields of Alberta to bring in cash. Oil companies like to hire farmers when they can. They work hard, shun unions, and aren't interested in long-term careers. They just want a quick source of cash to supplement their real jobs – farming.

The summer I met Barry Hamilton, tough times had meant that he could not find work in the oil fields. In the past, his wife Lorna's job at the Rose Valley hospital had helped tide them over during such times, but government cuts had closed the hospital. The local grain elevator had closed that summer as well. The closest elevator was now forty kilometres away, adding to both the cost and time Hamilton and his neighbours invested in farming. Hamilton was concerned that he might lose the farm. The Hamiltons had farmed for generations, before they came to Canada one hundred years ago. But Barry Hamilton was facing the prospect of ending for his family and all future Hamiltons that long and rich heritage. That hot afternoon, tears welled in Hamilton's eyes.

The Canadian Wheat Board, founded in 1935 after some of the toughest years ever to face grain farmers, has its roots in the pool movement of decades earlier. Farming far from their markets, early prairie farmers found themselves captive to the grain traders, rail companies, and elevator operators who stood between them and their customers. They began to resent the power wielded by the entrepreneurs who, like them, had flocked west to prosper from the growing wheat trade. The Winnipeg Grain Exchange, where traders speculated on the price of wheat, oats, rye, and barley, became both the financial centre of the private interests taking grain to market and the target of farmers' scorn. Farmers soon looked for ways to bypass these entrepreneurs to get their grain to market on their own.

An early advocate of such efforts, farmer and teacher Edward Alexander Partridge in 1905 wrote in an open letter to prairie farmers that "a thousand farmers controlling 10 million bushels of wheat and selling through a single accredited agent would be in a position of a single person owning 10 million bushels." Efforts by men like Partridge led to a wave of cooperatives being established across the Prairies. The first was founded in 1902, with the Territorial Grain Growers Association, followed by the Grain Growers Grain Co. in 1906. The Saskatchewan Cooperative Elevator Company was founded in 1911, and in 1917, the United Grain Growers pool system was set up with the merger of the Grain Growers' Grain Company and the United Farmers of Alberta. The Saskatchewan Wheat Pool, the largest elevator company on the Canadian prairies, was formed in 1924, the same year the Manitoba Wheat Pool was born.

By 1930, the pools had more than six hundred elevators across the three Prairie provinces and controlled about half the grain trade, largely achieving their goal of bypassing the private speculators at the Winnipeg Grain Exchange. They even had their own Central Selling Agency, a precursor of the current wheat board, marketing Canadian wheat through offices around the world. The head of that agency, John McFarland, who had built a fortune trading wheat before joining the pools at no salary, became the founding president of the wheat board after becoming disillusioned with the ability of the private sector to meet the needs of Canadian farmers – and convincing his friend Prime Minister William Bennett of the same.

McFarland was a late convert to the idea of a wheat board. In 1933, he lobbied in Canada and abroad for a cut in wheat production to raise prices. The argument is similar to that put forward by Ottawa today, that we must use world trade negotiations to cut subsidies abroad while keeping farm aid at a minimum at home. McFarland wrote to Bennett with his plan: "Our governments and farming organizations should take every step to urge acreage reductions upon other countries, while insisting on similar measures at home. While this may be considered impossible, it must be done." Bennett agreed, and a deal was signed between Canada, the United States, Argentina, and Australia to cut wheat exports in hope of boosting prices by limiting supply. The Winnipeg Grain Exchange, however, rejected the idea, saying the market alone should decide such things.

This was the turning point for McFarland, who wrote to Bennett that the exchange's rejection made him "all the more determined to have a government wheat board." He also chastised the Winnipeg exchange for refusing to recognize the role the federal government had played in keeping the market stable by buying up excess wheat during the three previous years. Farmers – hit by the now-familiar double whammy of low prices and bad weather – yearned for a way to bypass the exchange altogether. They blamed the traders for keeping prices low and fondly remembered the 1919 Canadian Wheat Board, set up for one year to keep trade stable after the war. With an election looming, Bennett set up the new Canadian Wheat Board that would market all Canadian wheat sold abroad, despite the objection of the exchange and its members.

Today, the board remains as the only marketer of Prairie wheat abroad or sold at home for human consumption and enlists as agents in its work the grain elevator companies, the grain exchange, and the train companies it was meant to bypass. The basic job of the wheat board is to sell Canadian wheat and barley, pool the returns, and divide it among farmers according to how much grain they brought to the board. It does that through sales agents around the globe, including full-time offices in Tokyo and Beijing.

Once a contract to sell Canadian wheat is signed, the board buys the wheat from farmers through the privately held grain elevators that dot the prairie landscape. The elevator companies test the grain to see how much it is worth and store it until a train can come to pick it up. It is then transported by rail to the grain terminals in Vancouver, Prince Rupert, Churchill, Thunder Bay, or Montreal. From the terminals, which are owned by the elevator companies, it is shipped overseas.

Each of these services exacts a fee paid by the farmer or the board. The board's expenses, as with revenue from sales, are pooled and used in calculating the price that is eventually paid to the farmer. When he delivers his wheat, the farmer is given an "initial payment." It is only a partial payment for the grain, based on the board's best guess of what the grain will be worth at the end of the year. It tends to be a conservative estimate, with the difference made up over the course of the following year. Farmers in the United States, by contrast, get all their money up front when they deliver their wheat, but are paid only what the price of grain happens to be on delivery day. If the price goes up the next day, week, or month, the farmer cannot benefit – unlike Canadian farmers.

The initial payment is so conservative that, at times, it is less than the price farmers in the United States are paid up front. This has led to some grumbling in farm circles that the wheat board is not getting farmers the best price it could. "I should be able to sell my wheat wherever I want," says George Godenir, a southern Saskatchewan wheat farmer. A bumper sticker on his pickup reads, "CWB: Confiscating Wheat and Barley."

The payment system helps smooth out wheat delivery to the elevators. Because all farmers get the same price for their wheat, depending on the quality, there is no incentive for them to rush to the elevator if the price of wheat suddenly spikes or to hold back deliveries if it drops. This means that farmers tend to deliver wheat to the elevators when it is most convenient to them, or when they run out of storage space on their farms.

This makes for a much more efficient operation, since grain is delivered when it best suits the entire farm. It also ensures that the wheat board has a steady supply of wheat available to it, since farmers do not hoard wheat in hopes of getting a better price. This, in turn, has enabled the board to guarantee delivery of wheat to its customers – a strong bargaining chip in sales negotiations.

Even the board's harshest critics and closest competitors in the North Dakota wheat industry concede that American pasta companies preferred to buy Canadian durum wheat because they knew they could count on regular deliveries of consistent high quality. A study commissioned by the wheat board in 2000 found that Canadian farmers made a total of $160 million more through the board than they would have made under the same growing conditions without the board.

Food processors, like any manufacturer, rely on consistency to keep their plants operating efficiently – consistency in delivery times and consistency in quality – and are willing to pay a small premium for supplies if they can maintain the efficiency of their operations. Any deviations add costs to their operations and hurt profits. By being able to guarantee consistency, then, the wheat board improves the efficiency of all the companies it sells to around the world.

*

Marcel Bouchard, who farms 4,500 acres near the optimistically named town of Fertile, Saskatchewan, has told his children to find something else to do with their lives besides farming. Across the Prairies and across the country, farmers have told their children the same thing. More than a quarter of all farmers left the industry between 1998 and 2001, according to Statistics Canada. Saskatchewan alone has lost more than two-thirds of its farmers since industrial agriculture began to make its way onto the prairies after the Second World War, a clearance unprecedented since the crofters of Scotland were driven from the land to make room for sheep. "In Redvers, they had a graduation for twenty-five kids and every one of them said they were going to Alberta," said Godenir, a neighbour of Bouchard's.

The summer I visited Hamilton in Rose Valley, Bouchard was able to seed barely half his land because of widespread flooding that took 1 million acres out of production. The next year, a bumper crop was ruined by a late summer rain that lasted a week and caused the kernels of grain to sprout just as they were being harvested. Since then, drought has stunted his crops. He tried diversifying, growing sunflowers and peas to lessen the impact of low grain prices, only to find prices down for those crops as well. He had a small beef operation, which he tripled to two thousand head of cattle to help out the beleaguered farm. But with drought ruining crops across the province in the summers of 2001 and 2002, the price of feed skyrocketed. Across the Prairies, farmers were forced to sell off their cattle rather than pay the huge prices for feed, driving down the price of beef and further eroding the ability of a cattle operation to make up for grain's shortcomings on farms like Bouchard's. Eastern farmers sent hay west, and politicians jumped on the campaign for the photo opportunities, but only those few farmers winning the lotteries for the free hay ever benefited.

Bouchard did have a bit of luck growing birdseed, which one year spiked to $17 a bushel due to sudden shortages elsewhere. He had only a few acres growing the bird feed, however, so the one-year doubling in price wasn't the windfall he needed. But it did get him wondering about society's priorities. "People are willing to pay $17 to feed their birds, so why not pay a decent price for wheat?"

In 1999, average farm incomes in Saskatchewan fell into the red for the first time since the 1930s. Government help for farmers to weather the crisis proved woefully inadequate. Bouchard paid an accountant $700 after the floods in 1999 to fill out the forms for emergency relief and got back a letter saying that because of his live-stock operation he didn't need any money – despite losing $150,000 that year. "I guess they figure that the cattle offset the grain," he said, shaking his head. "I'm still trying to figure it out." The basic problem was that farmers were compensated only if their income fell below 70 per cent of the average income over the previous three years. Farm groups blamed that provision for help being denied to those farmers hurting the most. "After three bad years in a row, there wasn't room left for my income to fall far enough to qualify," Bouchard said, won-dering how an aid program could exclude farmers who have been hurting the longest.

As well, the so-called whole farm income approach to aid pro-grams – in which farmers like Bouchard are denied help if one part of their operation does better than others – discourages farmers from diversifying. If Bouchard had bet his entire farm on rye or barley, two crops wiped out on his farm, he would have qualified for substantial government aid. Federal agriculture minister Lyle Vanclief, whose tough-love approach to farm aid earned him few friends in the country's farm fields, told me the federal government wanted to ensure the money went to the best-run farms. It did that by exclud-ing farmers who had been losing money for a number of years and perhaps should be thinking of another line of work.

The flooding and bad prices of 1999 briefly rekindled the farm protest movement on the Prairies. Farmers took to the highways in their combines to protest the inadequate aid they were being offered while farmers in the United States and Europe enjoyed increasing subsidies. Canadian farmers held rallies in Regina and Ottawa, and one farmer drove his combine all the way to Parliament Hill in a plea for more help. The protest didn't last, and Ottawa rode out the storm by bumping up subsidies by $500 million, less than half what the farmers said they needed. Since then, the combines have been kept in the fields, and the farmers have given up on holding rallies. "It didn't do a damn bit of good. We spent our own money and didn't get anything for it," said Godenir, who organized many of the protests. He said the protests backfired when city people saw farmers holding up traffic with expensive machinery as they cried for more money.

Then a group of large grain farmers held their annual meeting at a Mexican resort. Godenir said he could feel support for grain farmers seeping away after that, with no amount of talk about cheap airfares and off-season rates able to overcome the image of farmers demanding bailouts from a Mexican beach. "That was probably the low point," Godenir said, his voice dropping. Internal bickering among farmers organizing the high-profile protests and a feeling that the issue was slipping away left Godenir and others too disheartened to keep up the fight.

But the central issue – heavy subsidies elsewhere – had not gone away. Farmers had no problem competing on the open market, Godenir said, echoing farmers across the country; they just want a level playing field. That meant that if Canada could not convince the United States and Europe to cut their subsidies, it must match them. The cause was taken up across the country. Most farmers had supported Ottawa's focus on negotiating a drop in subsidies at the World Trade Organization – until the Seattle trade talks failed in December 1999.

A few days later, Bob Friesen rose at a meeting of the Canadian Federation of Agriculture. As president of the CFA, he had carefully stitched together a common front among Canada's often disparate farm groups to work with the federal government in its fight against subsidies abroad. But after Seattle, Friesen announced a change of course. "It's time to stop chintzing us on aid," the CFA president said to the applause of farmers. His demand set off a firestorm of similar demands across Canada from virtually every farm group and shattered a hard-won alliance with the government on the issue of subsidies.

The demands did not end when trade talks resumed two years later at the WTO meeting in Doha, Qatar, where 144 countries agreed to negotiate a cut in farm subsidies. The Seattle talks, had they continued, would have taken three years. By the time the Doha talks began, then, negotiations were already two years behind schedule and farmers could wait no longer. While Ottawa clung to the hope of using the WTO to help them, farmers demanded that Ottawa match foreign subsidies until it had negotiated the promised cuts. Saskatchewan premier Lorne Calvert outlined the demands in a column for *The Western Producer* newspaper: "While achieving partial success at the WTO – an extremely difficult task – will help our farmers, it will not be sufficient. To really level the international playing field, Canada must commit itself to redesigning its national farm programs to ensure that our farmers receive a level of income support equivalent to that of our main competitors." Ottawa preferred the much cheaper option of keeping a lid on subsidies, while hoping to convince other countries to do the same.

Clearly, the battle over trade subsidies would not end with the launch of WTO talks. The U.S. aid package announced in May 2002 topped $190 billion (U.S.) over ten years for 2 million farmers, 70 per cent more than its former aid package. Canada provided a little over $1 billion (Cdn.) in aid a year for 270,000 farms. Vanclief flatly rejected matching the U.S. package, pro-rated for Canadian farmers, saying it would cost $10 billion or more to do so. With so many other demands for federal money, he said, there just wasn't enough money. "People want money for health care, for education. We've got municipal politicians in the audience tonight who want money for infrastructure," he said at a meeting with farmers in Belleville, Ontario, in the summer of 2000.

At the time, farmers in Ontario were dealing with the same sort of flooding that prairie farmers had faced the year before and had organized a series of town-hall meetings to discuss compensation.

Farmers told heartbreaking stories of planting their crops twice because rain had washed away the first seeding, and then watching helplessly as mould and disease ruined the second planting. "This is shaping up to be one of the worst years for the Ontario crop farmer," Bruce Webster, then local director of the Ontario Wheat Board and one of Vanclief's constituents, told him. It was the same message Vanclief had heard from western wheat farmers a year earlier, and he was no more moved to action this time.

Once again, Vanclief rode out the storm without making significant increases in aid. He stuck to his argument that the best way to deal with subsidies was to use the WTO to ban all subsidies. But progress on that front was slow. Trade negotiators have met for more than two decades trying to cut subsidies, saying they encourage farmers to overproduce and drive down prices for all farmers. Brian Doidge, a farm economist with the University of Guelph and the Ontario Corn Producers Association, says the low prices are more the result of government policies creating an artificial trading environment than of market economics. "There is no free market," he told a gathering of Ontario corn farmers in September 2000. "There is only government policy."

On his way to the 2002 Salt Lake City Winter Olympics, U.S. president George W. Bush stopped in on the national convention of the National Cattlemen's Association in Denver, Colorado, and used the terrorist attacks of September 11 as an excuse to change his mind on cutting farm subsidies. "It's in our national security interests that we be able to feed ourselves," Bush said. "Thank goodness we don't have to rely on somebody else's meat to make sure our people are healthy and well-fed." It isn't the first time national security has been used as a reason to help farmers. The U.S. school lunch program was set up after the Second World War by the Department of Agriculture in response to government concerns during the war that its army recruits were malnourished. The school lunch program now costs $5.6 billion a year – money used to buy American produce, guaranteeing stable markets for the country's farmers.

Three months after his May 13 speech in Denver, Bush signed the Farm Bill, detailing the subsidy packages available to American farmers. He came under almost immediate attack. The *Washington Post* called the bill "a low point in his presidency," while the *Wall Street Journal* called it "a bucket of slop that has left even Washington agog." Canada, Australia, the European Union, Brazil, and Mexico all threatened to drag the United States before a WTO disputes panel – like the one Canada has faced over the Auto Pact – over the subsidies. "Frankly, I find it gross," said Canada's trade minister, Pierre Pettigrew, outside a meeting of trade ministers in Paris, where U.S. delegates were greeted with chants of "hypocrites" as they entered. Pettigrew said the bill threatened to derail the Doha round of talks.

In fact, if all the threatened challenges took place and the United States followed through with its plans to keep challenging the existence of Canada's wheat and dairy boards, the real action at the WTO would shift from the negotiating table to the disputes panel, which involves only a handful of countries. This would make the development of the world rules for trading an even more secretive process than it has been in the past.

The disputes panel takes place in camera. No part of its proceedings – not the submissions made to the panel, not its deliberations, and not even the names of the trade experts sitting on the panel – are public. Yet these unelected panels have the power to overturn laws passed by democratically elected, national governments. With such slowly shifting emphasis from the negotiating table to these secret panels, the members of the WTO – Canada included – are eroding what few democratic controls remain on the development of international trade rules. This holds serious implications as the WTO and its panels turn their attention to both health care and education – two sectors in which the United States, Canada, and Europe have all said they would like to see freer trade.

For farmers like Vickie Dutton, the biggest problem is the U.S. Farm Bill. Dutton is a grain farmer and trader in Saskatchewan who finds more than just the size of the Farm Bill offensive. For years, without the benefit of subsidies given to U.S. and European farmers, Canadian farmers diversified their operations. A favourite for prairie farmers has been pulse crops – field peas, dry beans, lentils, and chickpeas. Prairie production of field peas and lentils doubled from 1996 to 2001, while dry beans jumped fivefold. Chickpeas, unheard of on the prairies in 1996, claimed 1.2 million acres by 2001. The prices were never great, said Dutton, but at least they weren't being driven down by other countries' subsidies. The 2002 U.S. Farm Bill changed that. "Now they're subsidizing pulse crops, too. We find a crop that can help us out, and now it's gone," Dutton told me. She is worried that nobody east of Manitoba cares, and is frightened she might lose her farm. "For the first time, the other day, my husband said that maybe we should sell the farm," she said, forcing back tears.

In Europe, the Farm Bill slowed efforts to limit subsidies as Eastern European countries were brought into the Economic Union. Ten countries – Poland, the Czech Republic, Hungary, Slovenia, Estonia, Slovakia, Lithuania, Latvia, Cyprus, and Malta – expected to join the EU by 2004 and wanted to cash in on the union's generous farm subsidies. That encouraged Brussels to talk about cutting its subsidies, but not about eliminating them. The U.S. Farm Bill, however, dampened even that enthusiasm. Franz Fischler, the EU's agriculture commissioner, called the bill "a blow to the credibility of U.S. policy in the WTO." Like Pettigrew, he said it could only hurt the trade talks. "We cannot negotiate on the basis of 'do as I say, not as I do.'"

Bob Friesen of the Canadian Federation of Agriculture said the Farm Bill was so big that he had to wonder if it was meant to scuttle the WTO talks entirely so the United States could keep giving its farmers an advantage. "It's a complete farce."

The U.S. Farm Bill played into the hands of the Europeans, who have dragged their feet for decades on any meaningful cuts to subsidies. Having been through two wars in the twentieth century in which millions went hungry, Europe long ago made the same connection between national security and food sovereignty that Bush drew for the cattlemen in Denver. Once Canada's largest customer for wheat, Europe is now among the world's top exporters, thanks to subsidies that guarantee a profit for grain farmers. Besides, farm subsidies are a substantial part of the European Union. Forty-eight per cent of the union's 92-billion-Euro budget goes to the Common Agricultural Policy, or CAP, reflecting the continent's commitment to its farmers.

Nowhere was that better illustrated than in Doha, where the Europeans threatened to kill the launch of a new round of talks by refusing to negotiate an end to farm subsidies. France's trade minister, François Huwart, was the EU's point man, saying he would never agree to anything that committed Europe to gutting the CAP. At one point, he threatened to walk out of the talks, which would have ended any hopes of reaching a deal and would have been a devastating blow to the entire WTO two years after its failure in Seattle.

The sticking point became the wording of the deal's clause on farm subsidies. Canada and the United States wanted the clause to read, "Building on the work carried out to date we commit ourselves to comprehensive negotiations aimed at: substantial improvements in market access; reductions of, with a view to phasing out, all forms of export subsidies; and substantial reductions in trade-distorting domestic support." France objected to the use of the phrase "phasing out" and even refused to replace it with a commitment to "substantial" cuts in subsidies, saying this would weaken its position in the coming talks. Doha was about setting an agenda for the talks, Europe argued, and any commitment to phasing out subsidies should be saved for the real negotiations to take place over the following few years.

In the end, a deal was signed that gave Europe an escape clause by inserting the phrase "without prejudging the outcome of the negotiations" into the clause, effectively gutting the commitment of the negotiators to eliminate subsidies. The negotiations of that week were also a warning of what was to come. As the *Washington Post* observed in an editorial, "The summit only laid out an agenda for trade talks, and the fact that even this was difficult suggests the scale of the challenge ahead."

What lay ahead were more subsidies. Long before the launch of the talks in Doha, University of Guelph economist Brian Doidge warned Ontario corn farmers that both the United States and Europe ramped up their subsidies packages to farmers during the last round of world trade talks and could be expected to do so again. He was right, and that's kept Canadian farmers caught in the same squeeze they have been in for two decades of trade talks over subsidies – unable to collect subsidy cheques themselves, but forced to live with the low prices caused by subsidies to others. The big difference this time, however, was that Canadian farmers were also contending with year after year of bad crops. Not only were prices low, but Canadian farmers had less to sell. And what they had was often of poor quality. Low prices, low yields, and low quality added up to a crisis on Canada's Prairies with no end in sight. As Marcel Bouchard lamented, "Sometimes, it seems we just can't win."

While the United States was handing out subsidies to its farmers, it was launching a fresh attack on the Canadian Wheat Board, saying it gives Canadian farmers an unfair advantage on the world market. In a reversal of the rhetoric most Canadians are used to hearing – that the much-larger Americans can outgun us in any market – North Dakota congressman Earl Pomeroy has argued for years that the wheat board gives Canada too much clout on the world market. "The wheat board takes better care of farmers than can be done in the U.S.," he told me. "It is an enormously big player." Pomeroy, whose home state draws 40 per cent of its income from agriculture, mostly grain farming, is the congressional face of the attack on the wheat board. He insists he has nothing against Canadian farmers themselves. Growing up in Grand Rapids, North Dakota, Pomeroy was a regular visitor to Winnipeg – the nearest big city and home of the wheat board – as a boy. "I played rugby against a lot of big Canadian farm boys," he said.

But however fondly he remembers the farm boys of his youth, it is the North Dakota farmers in his home constituency whom he represents in Congress, and they are in direct competition with Canadian farmers like Bouchard and Godenir, whose farms are only forty kilometres from the border with North Dakota.

The soil and weather conditions are the same in Saskatchewan and North Dakota. The seed varieties, the pesticides, and the fertilizers are the same. The only difference is the wheat board, and Pomeroy blames it for the tough times the farmers in his home state are facing.

The problem with the wheat board, from the U.S. perspective, is that it is good at its job and is not privately run. The wheat board's sales account for about 20 per cent of the world's grain exports, according to the best estimates, less than half the market claimed by the wheat trading division of the large U.S. grain company Cargill and slightly less than Archer Daniels Midland's (ADM) grain division. That clout allows the board to lure buyers away from American grain, including buyers in the United States, Pomeroy said. A 2001 complaint filed in Washington by the North Dakota Wheat Commission, which represents 28,000 farmers, claims Canada uses its market power to secure contracts with American pasta companies that would otherwise buy North Dakota wheat. "We've just been absolutely buried in a flood of Canadian wheat," Pomeroy said.

The argument is that the wheat board, because of its strong presence in the international market, drives down the price of grain and hurts U.S. farmers. In the jargon of trade politics, this is known as a "Section 301 case," so-named because Section 301 of the U.S. Trade Act of 1974 authorizes the U.S. trade representative to retaliate against any trade practice deemed unfair by the International Trade Commission, a quasi-judicial agency in Washington that advises the White House, the trade representative (the American equivalent of

Canada's trade minister), and Congress on trade matters. Its job is to assess the effect imports have on American industries, to determine whether other countries are trading unfairly, and to recommend what action to take. In the case of the wheat board, it determined that, if anything, the wheat board drove up the price of durum wheat by negotiating better deals for Canadian farmers. American farmers were also able to take advantage of the higher prices, the ITC found. For other types of wheat, the price negotiated by the wheat board was sometimes lower than the U.S. price, but was most often higher.

Despite its own findings, the ITC ruled that the wheat board gave Canadian farmers an unfair trade advantage, since it gave farmers clout in the market and operated with government backing. The wheat board's loans were guaranteed by the government, ensuring it got a good interest rate, and there is a minister responsible for the wheat board sitting at the federal cabinet table. As a government-sponsored agency, the Americans argued, the board's dealings should be open to public scrutiny. No such requirement was suggested for its private competitors, however.

As the United States was putting its massive Farm Bill into place, it was preparing to launch a WTO challenge to the wheat board that could spell the end of one of the best programs Canadian wheat farmers have. "The administration is committed to ensuring fair treatment for U.S. farmers, and this investigation addresses important issues concerning Canadian Wheat Board sales practices," U.S. trade representative Robert Zoellick said in a statement a few weeks before the launch of trade talks in Doha.

A week earlier, Zoellick testified before the House Ways and Means Committee in Washington that he believed the wheat board was engaging in "unfair pricing" and that the United States should push for an elimination of these practices, or at the very least force an end to the board's control of grain exports. He told the committee, which was deliberating on whether to give Bush a free hand to negotiate a WTO trade deal, that he was a "strong supporter" of the North Dakota case. At that point, the ITC was still three months away from ruling on the case, but Zoellick was ready to declare that the wheat board gave Canadian farmers an unfair advantage.

It was beginning to look like the Bush administration had already decided that it did not like anything that cut into the business of big American companies and was dressing up its objections in a veneer of commission rulings it knew it could count on to decide in its favour. Testifying before the same committee five months earlier, before the ITC had even begun holding hearings, Neal Fisher of the North Dakota Wheat Commission said his group's complaint would "serve as a model for solutions to the unfair trading practices of export trading enterprises in the WTO." In November 2002, the ITC gave the U.S. government the ammunition it needed to launch a WTO challenge to the wheat board when it contradicted its ruling of eleven months earlier by declaring that the wheat board sold grain in the U.S.A. at "less than fair value."

A year before the North Dakota farmers started making noises around Washington about the wheat board, the United States Department of Agriculture, in one of its regular publications, took a look at U.S.–Canada trade in wheat and decided that American imports of Canadian wheat had nothing to do with wheat board practices. "Geography and market economics, not governments, are the most fundamental determinants of current U.S.–Canada wheat trade." According to the USDA document, Canada's elimination of the Crow Rate, which for almost a hundred years subsidized the cost of getting Canadian grain to overseas markets, had forced the wheat board to look for markets closer to home. That meant more exports to the United States.

The USDA assessment found that any advantages the board had in its marketing were "small or negligible in the highly competitive commercial world wheat markets" since the board had no control over production besides offering farmers money to grow wheat instead of other crops. In short, the USDA in the summer of 1999 reported that the wheat board was not stealing American markets, was not undercutting American prices (and might even be raising the price of wheat), and was selling more wheat to the United States because it was right next door and because American companies wanted to buy it. The fact that officials in Washington one year later came up with a contrary assessment shows just how politically driven the current objections to the wheat board really are.

That's certainly the opinion around the board's headquarters near Portage and Main in downtown Winnipeg. Staff there have grown weary of the constant attacks from midwestern U.S. politicians hoping to score a few points and a few votes by attacking the wheat board. "A political dance between influential American senators and U.S. president George W. Bush could have serious consequences for western Canadian wheat farmers caught in the middle," the wheat board wrote in its bimonthly publication *Grain Matters* as it waited for the trade commission to make its decision on the North Dakota complaint.

Brian White, the board's vice-president of commodity analysis, says big American companies like Cargill and ADM wield far more influence on the world stage than does the wheat board. Cargill alone has twice the world export grain trade, and ADM about the same as the board; they also both deal in other crops, livestock, shipping, and feed manufacturing with dozens of countries. The wheat board, by contrast, deals only in Canada with Canadian farmers and only sells wheat and barley for export or domestic human use. Its power pales by comparison to Cargill and ADM, which do not attract the same attention from our trading partners. "What we really should be concentrating on is the influence of trading enterprises, whether state trading enterprises or not," White says.

The board has been through nine trade challenges with the United States and survived them all. But however politically driven American attacks on the wheat board might be, the fact remains that the board has become a bargaining chip at the world trade talks. That much was made clear a year before the current round of trade talks began in Doha. The Cairns Group – a loose group of eighteen countries that tend to support each other at trade talks, including

Canada, Australia, New Zealand, and Brazil – had just concluded a meeting in Banff which included a visit from Franz Fischler, Europe's trade commissioner. He made jokes all week about "walking into the lion's den" by attending the meeting where his defence of farm subsidies was the main topic of conversation and much derision. After the meeting, Fischler said Europe was being demonized in trade talks because it paid its subsidies directly to the farmer, while other countries used more roundabout methods.

Europe, he said, would cut its subsidies if Canada would do the same by gutting the Canadian Wheat Board and the marketing boards for milk, eggs, and poultry. "We don't accept, really don't accept, that only the European form of subsidization is trade distorting, and the others are not," he said. "It seems to me sometimes there are camps arguing that trade liberalization is a good thing for others, but not for themselves."

Three years after we first met, I spoke with Barry Hamilton on the phone. In many ways, little had changed. He was still behind in his SaskPower bills and dodging phone calls from the local John Deere dealership wanting the $5,700 payment that was now six weeks past due. He was still cutting hay for neighbours and having trouble collecting the money he was owed for the work. "One guy offered to pay me in hay, but I said I don't think John Deere wants hay." Rose Valley was still suffering as well, having lost its Imperial Oil dealership, while the Petro-Canada service station had converted from a full-service operation with a convenience store to a card-lock system that required no staff. Hamilton's son still lived off the farm, working at cutting meat in a Regina supermarket and hoping to return to farming.

But despite all that, Hamilton's voice was filled with an optimism absent three years earlier. "I've gone organic," he said, as surprised as anyone raised on the teachings of the Green Revolution. His last chemical spray was in June 2001, and he was nearing the end of his farm's conversion to organics. He suffered through tough years of low yields and low prices as his fields adjusted to producing crops without artificial boosts and pesticides. Those were some of the toughest years he had ever faced in thirty years of farming. But the promise of higher prices for his next crop gave bounce to his voice. He had found a way to make his small farm viable and spoke hopefully of his son being able to return to the farm, after all.

After a life on the land marked by a continual loss of control over his destiny, as trade disputes and subsidies in far-off countries made it harder to make a living, he was taking action. And just as prairie farmers of previous generations bypassed the big companies they saw as standing between them and the prosperity they had gone west to find, Hamilton had found a way to do the same.

At first, some of his neighbours had laughed when he went organic. They had grown up together and embraced the Green Revolution together. But when they heard about the $20,000 a year he saved on chemicals and the expected higher prices for his crop, they became interested. His brother-in-law decided to follow his lead, and a few of his old friends have asked what life is like without chemicals. "I just tell them that it's nice to sit back at night and not have to worry that Monsanto will come knocking at the door looking for money."

Calves at Mason Dixon Farm,
Gettysburg, Pennsylvania, March 2000

*"The WTO allows multinationals to grow and
grow and grow in the name of free trade. But
when farmers get together, it is called collusion
and anti-free trade."*

Leo Bertoia,
Dairy Farmers of Canada

CHAPTER SEVEN

A COLD GLASS OF MILK

L unch at the Old Country Buffet in York, Pennsylvania, was huge. I had fried chicken, french fries, a thick slice of bread, mixed vegetables, and a glass of milk. I shared my table with a group of Ontario dairy farmers, part of two busloads of farmers touring Pennsylvania and New York in late March 2000 to witness a future they did not want, one of big farms with thousands of cows and unstable milk prices. One in which they managed staff instead of working with the cows themselves and had to compete with milk imported from the United States. It was the third day of our trip, and we had already been to seven farms, with four more scheduled over the next day and a half.

The smallest had three hundred cows, about six times the size of the average Canadian farm. The largest had 2,300 – forty-six times the average in Canada. The Ontario farmers were impressed by the efficiencies on these massive milk factories, and it made them all the more nervous about the future. Back home, in their own well-run barns, they could occasionally convince themselves they could compete with the biggest and the best in the world. Here, confronted with efficiencies of scale they could not apply on their own farms, the truth was sinking in. Over lunch and on the buses, they spoke with sad amazement at the scale of the farms they feared they might one day have to compete against.

As we washed our hands after lunch and prepared to get back on the buses, Reg Gilmer, one of the farmers, approached me. Throughout the trip, I had been talking to as many farmers as I could, asking them about the future of dairy farming in Canada, and the way farmers are paid for the milk they produce. Gilmer wanted to know why I was on the trip and what I hoped to get out of it. Why had I asked him on the first night of the trip for his thoughts on the future of Canada's milk marketing boards? My question had clearly been bothering him ever since, and his questions explained the cautious glances he had been throwing me during the farm tours and the hesitant answers to my questions – so different from the frankness he had displayed that first night.

Finally, Gilmer asked what I thought about marketing boards – and waited nervously while I considered my answer. Such questions are tough for reporters. We're not supposed to display bias. But I've never been a good liar, thankfully, and decided to tell him the truth. I support marketing boards, I said. I told him that I believe in ensuring that farmers get a fair share of my grocery money and that marketing boards did that. I told him that as far as I could tell, Canadian milk didn't cost any more than American milk, even though American farmers get less than half what Canadian farmers are paid. I told him that our marketing boards should be models for the world, not a target at trade talks.

Gilmer visibly relaxed. It had been bad enough seeing the sort of stiff competition he would be confronting if – and, he feared, when – marketing boards could no longer protect him from the big American farms. But having me on the tour, a reporter from the city, had added the worry about what I might say to my readers.

Marketing boards had been taking a beating at the World Trade Organization, both through the trade talks and complaints by the United States and New Zealand, but fighting those complaints was only half the battle. In the two generations since Canada introduced marketing boards, consumers have forgotten why they were set up in the first place. And so had consumers in other countries such as

Great Britain and Australia, where elimination of the boards in the 1990s wiped out half the industry. Fearing a similar future for himself – a fear that had pushed him to go on that tour – Gilmer, and the other farmers taking a little longer to wash their hands as they listened to our conversation, needed to know who was a friend and who was a foe. They had enough enemies on the international scene. They didn't need any at home, too.

In the 1960s, with expensive milking machines making their way onto Canadian farms, dairy farmers were looking for a way to bring some stability to the industry so they could afford to make the needed investments to keep the industry up to date. As well, dairy companies struggling to keep up with booming demand wanted to ensure a steady flow of milk to their plants. Farmers could not hold on to milk, a perishable product, for weeks or even months hoping the price went up. On-farm milk storage was expensive and limited. And because cows must be milked two times a day, the milk had to be shipped out on a regular basis – forcing farmers to take whatever price they could get. That left dairy farmers of the mid-1960s in a dilemma: specialization had made it possible for them to invest in better barns and milking machines, but had robbed them of the stability that came with diversity. "Milk is a perishable product, and we don't have the option of packing up and moving to another product," Leo Bertoia, head of the Dairy Farmers of Canada, said at the 2002 meeting of the Ontario Milk Marketing Board.

The answer Canada came up with after years of federal and provincial studies was marketing boards that would regulate the supply of milk and, in so doing, the price. The first board was set up in Ontario in 1965, with other provinces soon following suit. The boards would determine, in negotiations with dairies and cheese companies, how much milk would be needed in the coming year, and farmers would produce only that much. Each would have a quota to fill and could buy and sell quotas on exchanges run by the marketing boards. Farmers would be paid a set price for the milk, as long as they kept to strict quality measures. The boards would collect the milk from the farmers and deliver it to the dairies and cheese companies according to their needs. Just as U.S. and European farm policies – mostly in the form of direct subsidies – were set up to serve domestic needs, so too was the milk marketing system. Limits on imported dairy products helped maintain the stable supply of milk and, conse-quently, the price for Canadian farmers.

The milk marketing boards brought a stability to the dairy industry that has been shaken only by recent challenges at the World Trade Organization – challenges that had farmers like Reg Gilmer worried. He and other dairy farmers grew up with supply manage-ment. They know the good it has done, and they don't want to lose it. And they don't want to own farms like the ones they saw on their trip to the United States, but they feared they would be forced to if they lost supply management. "These farms are ten years away in Ontario without supply management. Maybe fifteen," Gilmer said.

What caught the attention of the United States and New Zealand, the two countries complaining to the WTO about Canada's milk boards, was the low price Canada's farmers got for their minus-cule milk exports. The price farmers receive for their milk applies only to milk sold in Canada under the quota. Anything the farmer produces over the quota is exported at the going world price – which for the past few years has been about a half to a third the price of raw milk in Canada. The United States and New Zealand complained to the WTO that the high domestic price was subsidizing the farmers, allowing them to dump milk on the world market at low prices.

Their problem wasn't just that the farmers had a two-price scheme for selling their milk, but that they were doing it through a body appointed by the government. This, they argued, meant that the Canadian government had interfered in the market to give Canadian farmers an advantage. If there is one underlying principle behind all the WTO's rules, it is that governments must not interfere in the market to the advantage of their own people. It is a principle that ignores the fact that fifty-one of the largest hundred economies in the world are not countries, but corporations.

Despite vigorous denials to the WTO by both Canada and the dairy boards, a trade disputes panel at the WTO's Geneva headquarters ruled in the fall of 1999 that the milk boards were – in effect – agencies of the government. That was because the governments mandate the boards to carry out a specific role – ensuring a safe and stable supply of milk. The government does not tell the boards what to do, but delegates responsibility for the industry to the boards. That was enough for the WTO to consider the boards an arm of the government, even though a farmer-elected team of managers runs the provincial boards. And as arms of government, anything the milk boards do to help farmers in Canada is considered a government subsidy and a violation of WTO rules. The boards and the farmers were left struggling to figure out how they were agents of a government they were constantly at odds with over agricultural policy, but they had little choice but to find a way to comply with the WTO ruling without gutting the system that had made the Canadian dairy industry among the most stable in the world – or face $70 million in trade sanctions.

Before the 1999 ruling, Canadian milk was sold abroad through the milk boards. The board would keep a tally of the milk each farmer produced and pay the domestic price for anything up to the farmer's quota. Anything over the quota would be sold on the world market at whatever price the board could get. The farmer never knew how much milk he or she was exporting until the cheque came at the end of the month, and never knew where the milk was going.

It was a simple, efficient system that could not survive the WTO ruling. Farmers did not produce much over-quota milk, since the price was generally too low to justify the effort. But most produced some. "I'd rather produce too much milk than not use up all the quota I've paid for," Neil McCannell, a dairy farmer near Orangeville,

Ontario, said after the 1999 ruling. Only about 4 per cent of Canada's milk production is exported. For most farmers, exports are an after-thought in a system built around serving the local market.

At the first meeting of the Dairy Farmers of Ontario after the WTO ruling, nervous farmers gathered in Toronto to hear what the marketing board was going to do. There had been brave words in the farm press from dairy leaders saying they were confident the milk marketing boards would survive the WTO challenge. Now, Canada had to file a response to the WTO outlining how it would address the ruling. Ottawa had been meeting with the marketing boards for months to figure out a way to do that without taking away the stable prices farmers in Canada regarded as their best asset.

John Core, the long-time president of the Dairy Farmers of Ontario (he has now retired), rose at the meeting with a sly grin on his face. He had a plan, one that skirted the whole issue of subsidies and dealt only with the issue of how the board handled exports. From now on, farmers would have to arrange their own contracts, he said. The boards would collect contracts from foreign – mostly American – dairies and cheese companies interested in buying Canadian milk at world prices, just as they always had. The boards would let Canadian farmers know about these offers and leave it to them to negotiate con-tracts. The boards would then deliver the milk according to the contract. Under this arrangement, the milk boards would just be an information exchange for those interested in entering into export contracts and a delivery service for those who negotiated such deals. Core said the new plan would shield Canadian farmers from the WTO, since the boards would no longer be involved in the price negotiations. "That gets us right out of the way," he said.

But getting out of the way was not enough. The following summer, I was in Washington to meet with Tim Galvin, then the U.S.'s top negotiator at the WTO. I told him about the new arrange-ment Canadian farmers had come up with to counter the WTO chal-lenge. He took a deep breath and let me know this fight was only just beginning. He was too much of a diplomat to be too forthright in his criticism of the marketing boards, but he made it clear that anything that gave Canadian farmers a higher price for milk sold domestically would be a problem for the Americans. And if that meant gutting the marketing boards, which had brought stability to Canadian farming without factory farms, so be it.

The worry, he said, was that high domestic prices gave Canadian farmers the flexibility to undercut American farmers when bidding for American contracts, thereby driving down the price U.S. farmers could get. "If you have a domestic support program that helps keep the farmer in business, then there's always the concern that it will allow them to be more aggressive on the export side," he said, after carefully considering his words. He said the United States, like New Zealand, didn't care what Canada did to meet its domestic milk needs, but wouldn't stand for anything that gave Canadians an export advantage.

But there was, it seemed, more to it than just Canada's milk exports, which were much too small to have any effect on world prices. The weekend before the Seattle meeting of the WTO, the Dairy Farmers of Canada held an international meeting of dairy farm groups in Vancouver to discuss trade issues. There were farmers from Africa, Europe, South America, Asia, and, of course, the United States and New Zealand. Each delegation was asked to explain how dairy farming worked in their country, and what they hoped to get from the world trade talks scheduled to begin a few days later. It was a little over a month since the WTO had ruled against the Canadian dairy boards, so I was most interested in what the Americans and the New Zealanders had to say. The Americans were split on the issue. Some said they supported the efforts of their government to bring "fairness" to world dairy trade, and others said they might like to have marketing boards themselves.

It was the New Zealanders, however, who gave the meeting the clearest sense of what Canadian farmers were up against. "Your quotas are bad for everyone," said Earl Rattray, a member of the New Zealand Dairy Board. Canadian farmers, he said, are held back by the price of quota – the $20,000 a farmer must pay for the right to milk a cow for domestic consumption – from becoming truly world-class farmers, and New Zealand would help free them. He showed little of the restraint Galvin had displayed as he outlined his country's free trade philosophy and its belief that using the WTO to force an end to the marketing boards would be good for Canadian farmers. "You have much to gain."

The Canadians hosting the meeting were taken aback by the zeal of their guests. "It's like a religion for them," Richard Doyle, executive director of the Dairy Farmers of Canada, commented later. This wasn't just about trade. The New Zealanders made that much clear. It was about spreading the gospel of free trade. Doyle said farmers around the world envied the Canadian system because it provided farmers with a good income. The United States and New Zealand were pushing their case at the WTO to make sure other countries didn't adopt our system, he said.

Two years later, even Canadian farmers were shocked when the WTO tossed out its earlier ruling against Canada. An appeals body at the WTO ruled that the United States and New Zealand had failed to prove that the new system used by dairy boards to handle exports violated any trade rules. The ruling overturned all previous judgements. "We won, it's as simple as that," Doyle said. Agriculture Minister Lyle Vanclief told the House of Commons that the dairy industry would continue with business as usual.

The ruling, however, was not the clean victory Canada wanted. It did not say that Canada's milk marketing boards complied with WTO rules, just that the United States and New Zealand had not *proven* that the boards violated any rules and that they had not properly calculated the amount of any subsidy to Canadian farmers. It was, in effect, an invitation for the two countries to keep up their fight, and within weeks a fresh challenge was launched at the WTO. "This is not a victory for Canada, far from it," said New Zealand trade minister Jim Sutton. There is no double jeopardy in trade complaints, and countries can keep launching trade challenges until they get what they want.

The euphoria of the WTO victory had worn off by the time of the annual meeting of the Dairy Farmers of Ontario a month later. The new milk board chair, Gordon Coukell, warned the six hundred farmers at the meeting to prepare themselves for months, even years, of trade challenges and uncertainty about the future, bemoaning a system that allowed an "endless amount of litigation." The only thing that could stop the constant challenges, he said, was explicit WTO rules allowing supply management. "The fact that the appeals keep on coming is a definite indication that better defined rules need to be negotiated," he said.

Supply-managed farms in dairy, poultry, and eggs are the most stable and profitable in Canada, Coukell said, and needed no government subsidies. The government should be looking for ways to spread supply management around the world, not just defend it at home. "Government negotiators and officials need to be very careful not to get caught up in the global marketplace concept and free trade rhetoric of the U.S.," he said. "The WTO is about rules of trade, not free trade. . . . We must remain vigilant that our very effective system for dairy and poultry production is not negotiated away one piece at a time." Leo Bertoia, head of the Dairy Farmers of Canada, commented, "The WTO allows multinationals to grow and grow and grow in the name of free trade. But when farmers get together it is called collusion and anti-free trade."

There is little reason to believe that milk and cheese prices would drop if the dairy boards were eliminated. What is more likely are continuing increases in both the price of food and the size and environmental risks of the farms used to produce that food. That has been the experience with other industries and countries where farmers lost similar protections.

At one time, hog farmers in Manitoba had a clearing house that sold all the pigs produced in the province to whatever slaughter-houses wanted them. It was called single-desk selling and it got farmers the best prices it could. Farmers were not always happy with the prices, of course, but once the system was gone they realized how good they had had it. As Maple Leaf Foods made plans to build its hog slaughtering operation in Brandon, the province's Conservative government eliminated single-desk selling in 1996.

At the time, farmers were getting $70 to $90 per hundred pounds. By November 1998, the price had dropped to a range of just $25 to $30. Prices have since recovered somewhat, thanks to heavy demand from Japan in the wake of that country's mad cow scare, but the dramatic drop and instability wiped out up to half the hog farmers in the province. For the most part, only massive factory farms survived.

And yet the prices paid by consumers for pork did not drop. In fact, over the past twenty-five years, once inflation is taken into account, the price paid to farmers has steadily declined – falling most dramatically after single-desk selling was eliminated – while the prices at the grocery store steadily increased. Consumers failed to benefit from the low prices that caused such hardship on the farm and led to the development of factory farms.

The big food companies who buy low and sell high on the pork market were the only ones to reap the benefit. Maple Leaf acknowl-edged this in its first-quarter financial results in 1999, saying, "Maple Leaf Pork benefited from favourable commodity markets." The money that was once paid to farmers was transferred to the company's bottom line and used to finance a restructuring of the industry. Without single-desk selling, the remaining farmers were left on their own to negotiate with the slaughterhouses. With perhaps millions of dollars invested in new, big barns, the farmers were not in a strong bargaining position, so they took what price they could. It kept the price of pork down and drove farmers to find more and more ways to achieve economies of scale.

There can be little doubt that this future awaits the milk industry in Canada if dairy farmers, like pork farmers, lose their form of single-desk selling. In 1994, as its farmers were struggling to come to grips with the devastation of the mad cow crisis, Britain got rid of its milk marketing boards in a bid to improve the efficiency of the industry. The move drove thousands of farmers out of business. Losing the marketing boards cost British dairy farmers their clout in the marketplace, and prices dropped. Within a few years, prices were the lowest in the European Union, and by 1999 they were at the lowest level in ten years. Once inflation was taken into account, the prices paid to farmers in the post-marketing board era were the lowest in generations.

The savings enjoyed by the dairy companies were used to finance a massive restructuring of the industry. Mergers and acquisitions in both the processing and retailing industries strengthened the bargaining power of the companies, which ignored a cooperative that some farmers set up to replace the marketing boards. "This reduced the influence that producers had on the market," commented the International Federation of Agricultural Producers. "Processors have consolidated, giving themselves greater market power and thus reducing the competition for supplies. Retailers also consolidated and have taken a firm stance in negotiations [on the price of milk.]"

A British Competition Commission study looking into the grocery trade heard heartbreaking testimony about the turmoil caused by the low price of milk. Farmers, who must pay grocery store prices like the rest of us, seemed particularly upset that their low wholesale prices were not being reflected at the retail level. One farmer from Devon told the inquiry that she did not know how much longer her family could hold on with such low prices. The two main dairy cooperatives in the United Kingdom – Milk Marque Limited and United Dairy Farmers Limited – both testified that grocery chains cut the number of milk suppliers they would deal with after the industry was deregulated, giving farmers fewer places to sell their milk and less negotiating power. The result, according to Marque, was a drop in the prices paid to farmers of 5.6 pence per litre from 1996–97 to 1998–99.

Meanwhile, the price of milk delivered to the door (milk is still delivered door-to-door in about 35 per cent of the British market) increased marginally, and the price of store-bought milk decreased only 2.6 pence. The result was that the farmer's share of the retail price of milk dropped by 10 per cent for delivered milk and 17 per cent for store-bought milk. As the commission noted, "There seemed an inequity between that which the farmer received and that which the farmer paid."

Marque also pointed out that dairy farmers, producing an easily perishable product, must stick to strict quality and food safety standards on their farm that are harder to maintain with dropping incomes.

The United States does not have supply management and has been losing dairy farms at a rate of 5.6 per cent a year as the industry shifts from the traditional dairy states of Wisconsin, Minnesota, Michigan, New York, and Pennsylvania to California, Arizona, New Mexico, Idaho, and Washington. The average dairy farm in the United States milks 108 cows, about twice the average in Canada. That number is expected to grow as factory farms come to dominate the industry.

Despite some very large farms, the industry in the east is still dominated by farms roughly the same size as the average Canadian operation of around fifty cows. Out west, however, the industry is controlled by large operations of several thousand cows each, and California recently surpassed Wisconsin – dubbed the Dairy State on its licence plates – as the U.S.'s top milk producer. The post-war industrialization of the American poultry business is being repeated in dairy.

This is what the Canadian farmers saw for themselves during their one-week tour of New York and Pennsylvania dairy farms in March 2000. The largest farm we visited was Mason Dixon Farms

Inc., where 2,300 cows a day are milked. In addition to milking cows, every dairy farm has a number of calves, heifers, and full-grown cows that normally give milk but are not doing so at the moment. For comparison purposes, dairy farmers count only the cows milked each day, but the total herd could be twice that number when all the non-milking cows are counted. There were about five thousand cows of various ages and production stages on Mason Dixon Farm the day we visited. We had already been to several farms, but none quite like this. Each Ontario farmer, as he got off the bus, stopped to take an amazed look at the massive barns and work sheds that make up the farm.

I had driven to the farm with the owner, Richard Waybright, a little earlier than the rest so we could talk about an operation that he boasted was the future of farming. As we drove down the country road to the farm, Waybright waved at the children waiting at the end of each laneway for the school bus to arrive. I commented on how he seemed to know every child in the area. "I should," he said. "They're my grandchildren."

He and his family have bought every farm along the road – which was now, it seemed, a driveway for his farm. Almost all the Waybrights work for the family farm, as veterinarians, accountants, engineers, and marketing experts. Only one of Richard Waybright's five children does not work on the farm, and Waybright expected that most of his grandchildren would stay in the family business. At seventy years old, after a lifetime of building his father's small operation of twelve cows to a business of five thousand, Waybright was most proud that he had lifted his family out of traditional farming and away from anything that got their hands dirty. "When I was a kid going to school, you were ashamed to be a farmer. It was dirty and you were poor. Now, my grandchildren go to school with other farm kids and they know they're not just farmers any more. Their fathers make as much as doctors and lawyers."

Hired hands, mostly from Mexico, work in the barns and in the fields. Waybright also likes to hire staff locally, boasting that some of his workers have been with him for more than a generation. He has full-time mechanics on the forty-five-person payroll to keep the equipment running. We were touring the mechanic's garage when it occurred to me that the farm was like a town inhabited by cows. It wasn't just the number of cows, but the infrastructure involved in housing and milking them. This town of cows was serviced by a public works system that would be the envy of any human settlement. The skyline was dominated by a 176,000-litre water tower, which feeds into underground pipes that deliver fresh water to all the barns. The barns, in turn, are kept clean by a sewer system, which transports manure to a composting facility that generates 1.5 kilowatts of power from the methane gas coming off the manure. That is enough power to meet all the farms' needs, with excess sold to the state utility. Despite the composting, however, a massive sewage lagoon is still needed for liquid waste. The mechanic's garage was impressive, as well, with every tool needed by mechanics.

The farm also has its own fleet of four milk trucks, with nine drivers who keep them on the road constantly. Waybright decided that rather than invest in storage facilities on the farm, he would buy trucks. The milk goes straight from the cows into one of the trucks. It is then driven a thousand kilometres south to Florida, where one of Waybright's sons had negotiated a better price for the milk than they can get in Pennsylvania. Waybright said that while one truck was always at the farm ready to receive milk, a second was in Florida delivering milk, a third was on the way to Florida, and a fourth was on the way home to pick up more milk.

Economist Mark Stephenson of Cornell University told the Ontario farmers during their trip that milk in the United States flows south as the ability of cows to produce milk decreases with higher temperatures. This means that a farmer in Pennsylvania, who also has more access to pasture land and feed than a southern farmer, can produce milk more cheaply than a Florida farmer.

The most extreme example of the southern flow of milk we saw was at Frey Dairy Farms Inc. in Conestoga, Pennsylvania. The thousand-cow farm is run by Tom Frey, whose cousin Quintin runs the Turkey Hill Dairy next door. Tom and Quintin are the grandsons of Armor Frey, a dairy farmer who began selling his excess milk door to door in the 1940s. His business grew into one of the most successful independent dairies in the state and was eventually broken off from the farm as a separate business. It has since expanded into producing ice cream and yogurt and owning a chain of convenience stores across Pennsylvania. Once the tie to the dairy farm next door was broken, the Freys running Turkey Hill saw no need to keep buying milk from their cousins, and the Freys running the farm saw no need to keep selling milk to Turkey Hill if they could get a better price elsewhere. The result is that every day a truck pulls into Tom Frey's barn, loads up with milk, and drives past the Turkey Hill entrance to deliver milk hundreds of kilometres south to a dairy in Virginia. Meanwhile, trucks from New York State idle in the parking lot of the Turkey Hill Dairy, waiting to deliver milk.

Clearly, neither business would do this if it didn't make economic sense. But for the farmers on the tour, the idea of long-haul trucks delivering milk hundreds of kilometres was crazy. That's because Canadian farmers tend to supply their local markets. With the marketing boards providing stable prices in each province, there is no economic incentive to ship milk to faraway markets. Most milk is consumed close to where it is produced. Ontario and Quebec have Canada's largest dairy industries, then, because they also have the largest populations and are home to some of the country's largest cheese factories.

The emphasis on local consumption is one of the reasons marketing boards were first set up, since at the time there was little ability for farmers to ship their milk to faraway markets, making them captive to local buyers. But while advances in transportation and refrigeration technologies have made long-distance shipping possible, as Waybright and the Freys proved, they have not made it desirable. Fossil fuels must be burned to run a tanker of milk several hundred kilometres to another market, contributing to air pollution and global warming. While it might make economic sense for an individual company to ship its milk far away, it makes little environmental sense. The profit the milk producers gain from selling their milk to the highest bidder in a far-off market is a cost to consumers and other companies who pick up the tab for pollution controls. Other farmers also pay, since the cost of sending milk south drives down the prices.

The problem with the American system of dairy production is that it is based on individual needs, on the assumption that a number of individuals acting in their own interest will result in a better system as a whole. The Canadian system, by contrast, takes into account the needs of the dairy industry as a whole and figures out the best way to balance individual needs so the system operates to the benefit of all.

The difference is reflected in a number of ways. All Canadian farmers belong to a provincial marketing board, which collects their milk and delivers it to the milk and cheese companies. Marketing board trucks drive up and down Canada's country roads every day picking up milk from each dairy farm along the route. In the United States, farmers either contract directly with a dairy or with a co-operative to sell their milk. The farmers along any country road could easily be members of different co-ops or be selling to different companies – each with its own milk collection system. The result is that two or three trucks ply the same roads every day to collect milk for two or three different processors. It is hard to see where the overall efficiency is in having three trucks do the work that one truck does in Canada.

There are those, of course, who argue that Canadian consumers would pay less for their food if only we got rid of supply management. The Fraser Institute, a right-wing think-tank, is among the most vocal critics of supply management. In November 2001, the institute published a study arguing that milk prices were too high in Canada because farmers got too much money for their raw milk. Author Owen Lippert, who later joined the office of Canadian

Alliance leader Stephen Harper as a trade and immigration policy adviser, said that if supply management were done away with, farmers would be paid less for their milk. If those savings were then passed on to consumers – which is certainly not guaranteed – $1 billion could be shaved from the nation's milk prices. That works out to a little over $30 a year for each person in Canada, or about 57 cents a week – enough for a family of four to buy one large coffee, if they pool their savings. Lippert estimated that Canadian milk prices were about 6.5 per cent higher in Canada, or about 9 cents a litre, than in the United States, which he blamed on supply management paying farmers 41 per cent more for their milk.

Lippert admitted that abolishing supply management would lead to a "period of adjustment" for Canadian farmers. He pointed to New Zealand and Australia as examples of countries that went through this adjustment and assumed that Canadian farmers would have the same experience. If we did, we would be in for some turbulent times. Deregulation of those markets forced thousands of farmers off their land as low milk prices made it impossible for them to stay in business. Lippert estimated that 25 per cent of Australia's dairy farmers left the industry soon after the market was deregulated in 1990, with the remaining farms becoming larger to make up for the lost production. New Zealand saw a similar adjustment. Through the 1990s, both countries converted what had been domestic-oriented markets into export-oriented industries, shipping half their production abroad.

Lippert assumed Canadians would be able to duplicate this feat even though we were next door to the world's largest dairy producer. By contrast, both New Zealand and Australia are next door to the fastest-growing economies in the world – the so-called Asian Tigers. Without such markets on our doorstep, but instead a voracious competitor, it is easy to see why Canadian farmers like Gilmer fear the dismantling of a system that has served them so well in the past. As well, Lippert failed to mention that the period of adjustment in Australia cost taxpayers there $1.5 billion (Cdn.) to bail out farmers after deregulation chopped their incomes in half. Ten years after they were deregulated and told they could enjoy a better future as a result, the Australian government was still paying out $78 million a year to struggling dairy farmers.

Not surprisingly, the milk marketing boards have their own studies showing that Canadian shoppers are well-served by supply management, with prices in Canada 17 per cent lower than in the United States, according to an ACNielsen Canada survey. A June 1999 survey looked at nine Canadian cities, comparing their milk prices with those in cities it deemed similar in the United States. Toronto was compared to New York, for example, Montreal to Boston, Ottawa to Washington, Calgary to Dallas, and Vancouver to San Francisco. In each market, Americans were found to be paying more for a basket of dairy products that included whole and skim milk, cheese, yogurt, butter, and ice cream. The biggest price difference was between Toronto and New York, with New Yorkers paying 38.65 per cent more for their dairy products. The smallest difference was between Winnipeg and Tulsa, with the Oklahoma shoppers paying just 4.06 per cent more. An investigation by *Canadian Grocer*, an industry journal, in October 2002, found that, while Canadian milk was 3.7 per cent more expensive than American (in Canadian dollars), butter was almost twice the price and ice cream was 10 per cent more expensive in the U.S.A.

Rick Phillips, a policy director at Dairy Farmers of Canada, an umbrella group for the provincial milk marketing boards, says that the lower prices reflect efficiencies built into the Canadian system, such as having just one fleet of trucks running up and down country roads collecting milk from farmers, rather than the overlap of two or three trucks plying the same roads in the United States. "It's a cheaper way to run a system," he says. As well, supply management keeps the price of raw milk relatively stable, so milk companies don't need to factor "risk premiums" in their retail prices to cover any sudden spikes in the price paid to farmers.

A former Turkey Hill convenience store manager in Pennsylvania explained to me how risk premiums work. Consumers consider milk a staple and buy it on a regular basis. They keep a close eye on the price and notice any sudden swings. As a result, stores hoping to keep a steady stream of customers do whatever they can to keep the price stable. "There's no way I'm going to change that price if I can avoid it," the manager explained. At the same time, his margins are so thin that he cannot afford to sell milk at a loss should the wholesale price suddenly spike. So to keep his prices stable, he sets one price, based on the upper range of what he expects to pay for wholesale milk and keeps the retail price at that level as long as he can. The result is a price for milk comparable to that in Canadian stores. "I've been up to Canada. I didn't notice much difference in the price," he said.

During the tour of U.S. factory farms and other trips to the United States, I visited a few supermarkets and convenience stores to check out the price of milk and dairy products. What I found was somewhere between what the Fraser Institute concluded and what ACNielsen told the Dairy Farmers of Ontario. Sometimes, American prices are higher. Sometimes they are lower. But they were never so low that I felt I was getting a raw deal in Canada, and never so low that I would be willing to inflict on our farmers the turmoil that would result from doing away with supply management so that I might save a few pennies on a litre of milk.

Polls have consistently shown that most Canadians support supply management and tough restrictions on imports and do not feel they are paying too much for their milk. Waybright made it clear during our visit that big American farms would start shipping north if they got the chance, and that they would soon start pushing smaller Canadian farms out of business. "You're in Gettysburg, where brother turned against brother, and in an hour and a half, 35,000 people were killed," he said. "We're not afraid of a fight."

In December 2002, the WTO ruled on the latest U.S.–New Zealand challenge to Canada's marketing boards, declaring that they provide an unfair advantage to Canadian farmers. Canada was out of appeals and left with no option other than to cut all milk exports, said Richard Doyle of the Dairy Farmers of Canada. Only 4 per cent of Canada's milk is exported. "We won't sacrifice 96 per cent of the industry to save 4 per cent," he said.

Protest against industrial farming,
Horse Thief Canyon, Alberta, July 2001

"This is a natural selection process at work."
David Nelson,
Credit Suisse First Boston

"The free market is disappearing."
Jerry Waters,
Washington agricultural consultant

CHAPTER EIGHT

THE INDUSTRIAL CHEF

As you walk through the aisles of a supermarket, with its dizzying array of products and brands, you can marvel at the wonder of choice available in a market-driven consumer economy. Or you can look deeper and see beneath the apparent choice, the few companies providing us with food. Two American companies, IBP and Cargill, control 74 per cent of the Canadian beef-packing industry with slaughterhouses in Alberta. Three companies, Borden, RJR Nabisco, and Italpasta, produce 89 per cent of the pasta eaten by Canadians. Four companies, Archer Daniels Midland, Robin Hood, Dover Industries, and Parrish and Heimbecker, mill 80 per cent of our flour. One company, Archer Daniels Midland, an American-based giant that has former prime minister Brian Mulroney on its board of directors and that likes to refer to itself as the "supermarket to the world," alone accounts for 46.3 per cent of our flour. Five supermarket chains control grocery sales: Loblaw, Safeway, Metro-Richelieu, Sobeys, and Pattison. One company, Cargill, controls almost half the world's international sales of wheat. Another U.S. company, Archer Daniels Midland, controls about one-quarter.

These are the realities of the modern food industry, dominated as never before by only a handful of companies that control almost all the brand names we see on the shelves and give us an illusion of choice.

The force behind this consolidation of power is as old as the market itself: the bigger, more efficient operations bought out the smaller, less efficient ones. "The agri-business companies have merged themselves to greatness over the last fifteen years," says Darrin Qualman, executive secretary of the National Farmers Union. Farmers lost clout in the marketplace as the companies they dealt with grew into some of the largest companies in the world.

David Nelson, a senior analyst with Credit Suisse First Boston in New York, says consolidation of the food industry was both "normal and necessary" as narrow profit margins forced companies to merge, find new efficiencies, and keep share prices up. In March 2000, he took Wall Street's analysis of the industry to a Senate committee in Washington looking into corporate concentration in agriculture. "This is a natural selection process at work," he told the congressmen. He presented 114 exhibits, but none of the charts, pie graphs, and financial projections gave as stark an assessment of the food industry as Exhibit 33, an 1874 portrait of Charles Darwin. The caption underneath read "Adapt or die," in three words summing up the prevailing philosophy of the food industry.

At a Toronto food industry conference called Moving the Markets, Maple Leaf head Michael McCain spoke about the importance of consolidation and vertical integration in building shareholder value, and how that increased share price could in turn be used to pay for more consolidation. "The engine is shareholder value," he told the two hundred industry executives gathered. By vertically integrating the chicken industry, he said, Maple Leaf can boost its stock price, enabling the company to dip into the stock market to raise more money for more consolidation. As he spoke, a slide flashed on the screen behind him reading, "1 + 1 = 3." In Maple Leaf's 2001 annual report, he pledged, "We enthusiastically commit to create shareholder value."

Another speaker at the conference, John Risley of Clearwater Foods, said food companies must brand their businesses if they want to attract investors to pay for consolidation. "There is only one determination of value, and that's shareholder value," he said. The trick is to develop a plan for the company that can be sold to investors, and in today's market that means coming up with a plan to vertically integrate the industry, just as Tyson and Maple Leaf have done. "The market loves a good story," Risley said. A well-sold story could even carry a company through otherwise bad times with investors. "You can screw up a few times and people will stay with you."

In his presentation to Congress, Nelson said that food companies need to consolidate because of thin profit margins. "Essentially, we have too many companies fighting for too few profits." With tight margins, the growth demanded by the stock market is best achieved by merging with other companies, Nelson argued. This, in turn, satisfies the investment analysts demanding that companies keep growing if they are to earn the analysts' seal of approval.

Nelson outlined a joint venture by Wal-Mart, the world's largest retailer, and U.S. meat packing giant IBP to sell packaged, or case-ready, beef in 180 Wal-Mart stores, with more stores to be added later. This was a massive undertaking, with IBP investing $400 million (U.S.), doubling its capital expenditures in just one year, to meet the contract. Other companies, such as Smithfield, owner of Kitchener-based Schneider, were expected to make similar investments to supply Wal-Mart with pork and chicken. Nelson believed these contracts and the resulting capital investments by the suppliers would lead to a revolution in the meat packing industry that could wipe out the in-house butchers at neighbourhood supermarkets within two to three years, as the stores switched to packaged meat. "This announcement, inspired by concerns over unionization, will provide the critical mass necessary for case-ready meat to finally become the industry standard," he said.

The message was not lost on workers at those stores. In the United States, the United Food and Commercial Workers union fought Wal-Mart's plans to bring case-ready meat into stores. The company denied union charges that it introduced packaged meat first to stores where workers had tried to unionize, as a way to get rid of union organizers. "Case-ready meat is simply becoming the best way to deliver quality at an everyday low price for our customers," Wal-Mart chief executive Lee Scott said.

Store workers aren't the only ones affected by the move to case-ready meat. The pressure the retail sector brought to bear on food manufacturers was soon passed on to the farmers who supplied them. If a food company is going to supply a grocery store chain with a consistent product for all its stores, it has to demand a steady and uniform flow of produce from the farmers with whom it deals. Like the supermarket chain that found it easier to deal with a small number of large food companies, the food companies found it simpler to deal with a few large contract farmers than with a number of smaller ones. "There are logical cost savings in dealing with one big supplier," says Brian Halweil of the Worldwatch Institute.

Just as the Industrial Revolution shifted manufacturing from craft shops to factories, the industrialization of agriculture concentrates power in the hands of a few industrial giants, taking it from farmers and skilled tradespeople. When Tyson industrialized the poultry industry, it took control of processes that had traditionally been managed by the farmer, such as breeding and feeding. The Tyson model is now being repeated in Canada by Maple Leaf, and extended to pork. "Many of the current changes in the pork industry resemble past changes in the broiler industry. In both industries, new methods of vertical coordination are associated with new technology, geographical shifts in production, growth in farm size, and improved production efficiency," says Jerry Waters, a Washington food industry consultant who has studied the poultry industry in the United States. In a February 2002 conference call with stock market analysts, McCain said he expected branding, and the vertical integration that goes with it, to transform the pork industry, just as it had the chicken industry. Waters estimated that hog production was about two-thirds of the way down the road to being fully industrialized. The beef industry is only starting to adopt the Tyson model.

In the January 2000 issue of *Fedgazette*, a publication of the U.S. central bank, district news editor Ronald Wirtz predicted that the trend would keep moving throughout the livestock industries and into field crops. "To guarantee a steady supply of high-quality inputs, processing firms have turned to forward contracts – buy/sell agreements for future crops or livestock – to keep processing plants operating at high capacity and efficiency." He estimated that 70 per cent of the U.S. pork industry was under farmer contracts, up from 10 per cent in 1990. In the Canadian beef industry, he wrote, contract farming – unheard of in 1990 – had captured about one-third of the market. Between 15 and 25 per cent of the grain market is conducted under contracts, which he called the "cousin of consolidation." Larger farms, he said, filled such contracts, with smaller farms tending to be "gamblers," hoping to get a better price on the open market.

As the Tyson model moves throughout the food industry, farmers, whether they produce chickens, turkeys, pigs, cattle, cucumbers, tomatoes, or grain, will have to submit to similar contracts. It is a future of fewer and larger farms. As farms become bigger, however, they become more difficult and time-consuming to tend. Farmers have had to employ labour-saving devices, such as herbicides to get rid of weeds, and have turned to outside advice on what crops to plant and what animals to raise. Chemical, seed, and animal breeding companies provide much of that advice as cost-cutting governments close the farm support offices that once helped farmers.

Monsanto, for instance, was keen to fill the void left by closing government offices. In a pullout supplement to farm newspapers, the company told farmers, "You are not alone," and featured a photo of a field of soybeans under a stormy sky with a ray of sunlight shining on the farmhouse. It told farmers that the company had field representatives across the country ready to answers farmers' questions about weeds and seed choices – just the sort of advice they could once count on from provincial outreach offices. "Your field rep comes equipped with a deep technical and research database, and analytic tools that will help assess and solve most weed challenges on your farms," the ad read. "We have more reps in the field than anyone else."

The farmer's job now involves sorting through sales pitches that push the industrial farm model. Bob Stirling, a sociologist at the University of Regina, calls this a "hollow" skill that displaces farmers' traditional knowledge. "Increasingly this knowledge base is embedded in the non-farm inputs and marketing relationships," he writes in *Writing Off the Rural West*, a collection of essays on the effects of globalization on prairie farmers, published by the University of Alberta's Parkland Institute. "Farm management skill today requires one to determine whether or not the company supplying the input will make good on its advertising promises, and whether the market broker is reliable. Skill at the work of actually growing something becomes secondary in this new set of practices."

At a trade show in Toronto for pork and poultry farmers, a Quebec company displayed a "boar cart" in which male pigs can be moved with minimal handling. The remote-control cart – which sells for $8,500 – is used to move the boar around the barn so he can detect which sows are in heat and ready for artificial insemination. The cart eliminates the need for anyone skilled in either pig handling or detecting when a sow is ready for breeding. As a flyer handed out at the trade show says, "The Contact-O-Max boar cart allows for efficient working technique even when using unskilled farm workers."

Today's farmers need not even know the idiosyncrasies of their own land. Tractors fitted with a satellite-based global positioning system can sweep the fields as computers assess the quality of the soil metre by metre. A second sweep with a fertilizing machine, also hooked up to the GPS, uses the computer analysis to put precisely the right amount of fertilizer on every square metre of the field. Where once only a farmer with an intimate knowledge of his fields could tell where fertilizer was needed, now anyone who can drive a tractor can do the job – and with more precision. This eliminates the need for skills traditionally held by the farmer and goes hand-in-hand with a loss of power in the marketplace and a dwindling share of the consumer's food dollar.

In 1973, for instance, 13 per cent of the cost of a loaf of bread eventually made its way into a farmer's pocket. By the end of the century, however, that had dwindled to just 4 per cent. "The balance of power has shifted toward processor and retailers, and away from farmers," the Prime Minister's Task Force on the Future of Farming reported in April 2002. "Primary producers have fewer market options and must accept the highest of the low prices offered by these buyers." Farmers are squeezed from the other end too, with the cost of supplies rising faster than increases in the money they receive for their produce. In the last quarter of the twentieth century, gross incomes on Canadian farms tripled as farms grew in size, but net incomes fell as expenses increased by four and a half times over the same period. Fertilizer costs – a major expense as the Green Revolution ate away at the quality of the soil – increased by 75 per cent.

Under free trade, the Heinz corporation has been able to gain an upper hand in the Canadian tomato industry, centred in Leamington, Ontario. I travelled through the Leamington area shortly after Canada's free trade deal with the United States was signed and met tomato farmer Walt Brown, who was heading the farmers' negotiations with Heinz. Before free trade, he said, there were several plants in the Leamington area that bought local tomatoes. That gave farmers some power in the market since they could switch companies if they felt they could get a better deal. A 15 per cent tariff kept American tomatoes out of Leamington's processing plants.

But four of the area's twenty plants closed soon after the free trade deal was signed. Farmers were left with only Heinz, whose plant dominates Leamington's main street, and a few smaller operators as customers – and very little bargaining power. "The processors came to us and said if we can't do something, we're gone," Brown said at the time. "And we listened." The result was a Tyson-styled vertical integration of the tomato industry, with Heinz deciding what strains of tomatoes farmers would grow, and how. Heinz stepped up its tomato breeding interests and by the turn of the century controlled 30 per cent of the worldwide processing-tomato seed market.

Ten years after meeting Brown, I returned to the area to meet John Lugtigheid, then chairman of the Ontario Processing Vegetable Growers Marketing Board, at his farm north of Blenheim. "Some of the processors wrote us off with the free trade deal," he said. "They all ran off to California." Before free trade, contract talks were often adversarial, with farmers bargaining long and hard to get the best price they could. After free trade, with plants shutting down, the mood changed.

Faced with losing their biggest customers, farmers were more open to change, and so change came quickly. "It was that understanding of economics that has made all the difference," Heinz Canada president James Krushelniski told me. Krushelniski began his career in Leamington as a plant breeder for Heinz and spent nine years at the company's head office in Pittsburgh fine-tuning its vertical integration strategy before taking over at Heinz Canada. "I am extremely proud of what has been accomplished," he said. Half of Canada's processing tomatoes, 300,000 tons, now pass through the Heinz plant in Leamington each year.

Almost immediately after free trade began, Lugtigheid said, prices dropped about 12 per cent, driving many farmers from the industry. "A shock wave went through the community," he said. Small farmers were forced out of business. "There are virtually no hand-pick guys left." Those still farming are now part of a very different industry. Today, contracts to grow tomatoes specify exactly what variety of tomato a farmer would plant (one for juice, a meatier one for salsa), when the seedlings are put into the ground, when they are harvested, and how they are protected from disease, insects, and weeds. "We have a very strict pesticide policy," Krushelniski said. Farmers made few, if any, of the management decisions for their own farms. For proprietary reasons, they would not even know what kind of tomatoes they were growing, or what sort of product they would be used to make.

By deciding when to pick up the tomatoes, Heinz is able to ensure a steady flow of tomatoes to its plant – much as an auto assembly plant takes delivery of parts just as they are needed to make cars. Krushelniski said the vertical integration he helped implement kept Heinz in Leamington. "There is a real understanding that we need to work together to be successful," he said. "Together, we have got to ensure that we are competitive with imported tomatoes. If not, there's always the option of imported paste."

The transition of Leamington's tomato industry made economic sense, of course, but marked another step away from the farmer's control of his own operations. More and more, he became an employee of the tomato factory, more a foreman of its field operations than a farmer. Like the livestock farmers who lost control of their operations, the tomato farmers are contract employees who enjoy no benefits, no assurances of steady pay, and yet assume all the risks of growing tomatoes.

There is no doubt that the changes make for a much more efficient tomato industry. That is, after all, why Heinz stayed in Canada while others left. That, and the fact that Leamington is within a day's drive of many large cities in Canada and the United States. Both Brown and Lugtigheid are proud that they were able to keep the Heinz plant operating, and justifiably so. Had they been unwilling to adapt to free trade, they would have seen their industry wiped out as mass farms in California undercut their prices. Instead, the big farms came here. Where more than three hundred farmers supplied the Heinz plant twenty years ago, by 2002, the company had contracts with just fifty-five, despite expanding production at the plant.

"Those who were less efficient are no longer growing for us," Krushelniski said.

In March 2002, Heinz announced that it would move production from a newly acquired Borden tomato sauce plant in Montreal to Leamington. Krushelniski credited the vertical integration of the Ontario tomato industry for the move, calling it a "partnership" among farmers, the company, and government. "A partnership of employees, management, Ontario tomato growers, and the provincial government has played an important role in Leamington's growth and strong standing for the future," Krushelniski said as he announced the move. "It is their collective contributions that have allowed Heinz Canada to expand our business prospects in the U.S." The move boosted production in Leamington by 5.4 per cent to 23 million cases of ketchup, chili sauce, tomato juice, baby foods, canned beans, and pasta sauce.

Growing only the varieties of tomatoes Heinz dictated, the fields around Leamington went from producing eighteen tons of tomatoes per acre in 1988, to 37.8 tons in 1997. At the same time, prices dropped, leaving farmers no further ahead despite more than doubling production. Heinz, however, ended up with more tomatoes for its money. The George Morris Centre, the Guelph think-tank, estimates that the company's farm-level costs dropped 30 per cent in the 1990s.

In March 2002, Brown told a farmers' meeting in Leamington that they would get slight increases of between 2 and 5 per cent in the prices paid by Heinz. The increases came after two years of cuts and raised prices to between $97 and $109 a ton, a little less than they were when I first met Brown eleven years earlier. Free trade and cheap California tomatoes were blamed for keeping prices down, as well as the prospect of even cheaper Chinese tomatoes coming onto the market once China was admitted to the World Trade Organization.

Heinz's adaptation of Tyson's vertical integration model to Canada's tomato industry has worked so well, it has attracted attention from industry players in the United States and Europe. "I had a guy from France sitting at this very table," Lugtigheid said as we finished our lunch.

In another part of Leamington, another branch of the vegetable industry was pursuing yet another form of industrialization with North America's largest concentration of greenhouses. Leamington has almost a thousand acres under glass, producing tomatoes, green peppers, and cucumbers. With the area's greenhouses valued at a total of $180 million, the town accounts for 80 per cent of all hothouse production in Canada. Under the perfect growing conditions that are created indoors, the produce is plump and unblemished, perfect for attracting consumers in grocery store produce sections. "Consumers like the quality," says Darrin Didychuk, chief operating officer of Mastron Enterprises, the largest greenhouse company with fifty-five acres of greenhouses and sales of $68 million.

Greenhouses cost between $700,000 and $1 million an acre to build, but the returns are greater than on outdoor farms. The average farm income in Leamington is about three times the provincial standard, and double that in surrounding Essex County, thanks to the $150,000 in revenue from each acre of greenhouse. The farms generate so much revenue that some farmers don't need to borrow to come up with the money to expand their operations. The greenhouse sector grew by about 20 per cent a year in the 1990s and tripled in size from 1988 to 1999. In 2000, building permits for greenhouses worth $29.3 million were issued for the area. Growth slowed in 2001 as operators awaited the outcome of a trade dispute with the United States, but were expected to jump again after the disputes panel had dismissed the complaint. Three-quarters of Leamington's greenhouse produce is exported, and Didychuk says that the town's greenhouses supply 60 per cent of the United States' $600-million market for hydroponic tomatoes.

In 1999, the Leamington town council, worried about the heavy water use by hydroponic greenhouses (about 100,000 gallons a day per acre), commissioned a report with nearby Kingsville to study their economic impact. The researchers found that greenhouses generate about $325 an acre in municipal taxes, compared with $7.25 for vacant farmland. The towns then looked for ways to help the industry expand, including an $8-million expansion of the local water system. The federal government did its bit, too, and spent $2 million expanding its greenhouse in nearby Harrow to house a research station. Here, scientists develop plants for greenhouses, as well as computer programs that regulate pesticide and fertilizer use and control temperatures inside the greenhouses.

But despite their size and economic impact, because they are classified as farms, none of the health and safety laws, none of the overtime rules, in fact, none of the labour laws protecting other workers, apply to greenhouses. That makes it tough for the green-houses – like most agricultural enterprises – to attract enough local workers, especially during the harvest. So they have turned to migrant workers, mostly from Mexico, who come here through a program run by the Canadian and Mexican governments.

As many as three thousand migrants work in Leamington's greenhouses. They come for up to eight months at a time to work for minimum wages producing fresh vegetables for their Canadian hosts. "It's difficult work," Didychuk says. "It's very hot and humid, but the Mexicans are used to it. You go into the greenhouses, and the Mexicans are in long sleeves and pants." They work long hours, six days a week. On the seventh day, they venture downtown for a special Spanish mass at St. Michael's Roman Catholic Church. Most Sundays in the summer of 2002, a group of activists and students waited for them outside the church, calling them aside to discuss their rights in Canada. They heeded the call cautiously.

Juan was one of the first to come forward the day I was there. The summer of 2002 was his last in Canada, so he was less afraid of reprisals from his boss, but not so confident as to give his full name. After nine years, he'd had enough of not seeing his two sons and daughter grow up. He'd had enough of seeing his wife only between

November and February when the greenhouses were closed. "I come here to make a bit of money," Juan said through a translator. "I leave behind the love, the affection, the respect of my family."

In his nine years in Canada, Juan had grown tomatoes, peppers, and cucumbers. Before that, he was a farm worker in Mexico, earning $15 a day on the Green Revolution grain farms of central Mexico. The life was hard, and money tight. His family moved several times in search of work. It caused great disruptions, but nothing compared with his absence for eight months of the year. After almost a decade in Canada, Juan looked back fondly on those days. "Here, we have no rights," he said. "There, we work. They treat us like humans." Leaving his family every February, he said, was the toughest part of the job.

He worked ten hours a day, six days a week for $7.25 an hour. The farmer provided him with a place to sleep, but the cost of food was deducted from his paycheque, as was his flight from Mexico, under rules negotiated with the Mexican government. He also had the standard deductions for taxes, pensions, and employment insurance – even though he wasn't eligible to collect E.I. if he lost his job. One activist he spoke to, Consuela Rubio, told astonished workers they could collect Canadian pensions when they retired in thirty or forty years and have the cheques sent to them in Mexico. "You paid into this plan, so make sure you collect the money," said Rubio, a legal worker with the Centre for Spanish-Speaking Peoples in Toronto. "And be sure to remember to ask for your first paycheques before you leave." Greenhouse owners routinely withhold the workers' first cheques to ensure they stay for their contracted times.

Four years earlier, Juan said, he fell off a truck while unloading boxes and hurt his leg. His boss wanted him to keep working, but Juan said he couldn't. He went to a doctor, who told him to stay off the leg for a few days. His boss still wanted him to work, so he complained to the Mexican consulate. "The only thing they did was come to an agreement between consulate and the employer that I should go home. It's very unjust," Juan said through an interpreter. The farmer put him on the next flight to Mexico. He had learned his lesson and has since tried to avoid being sent home early for complaining.

In 2001, though, he got a rash on his leg and asked his boss for help. He refused. The rash spread, and within a week, Juan needed help getting out of bed and into the greenhouse. His leg became infected, and finally Juan's boss sent him to the hospital in an ambulance. "Before he sent me he insulted me. He humiliated me, like it was my fault I got sick," Juan said. "He said that I am an imbecile, that I did not want to work." At the hospital, the doctor said the rash had become seriously infected because it had not been seen to early enough and ordered Juan to stop working for a week. Juan got the week off, but without pay. He never found out what caused the rash, but like many of his co-workers, he suspected pesticides were to blame. The most popular pamphlet handed out by the activists visiting Leamington was one in Spanish outlining the chemicals used to grow vegetables and their side effects.

Under the migrant labour program, the Mexican workers, no matter how long they have been working in Canada, are not eligible to apply for citizenship. A man like Juan, who spent more time in the last decade working and paying taxes in Canada than in Mexico, is not welcome to stay and find work that pays better or would allow him to put down roots and build a better life for his family. Like the Chinese migrants who paid a head tax to come to Canada but were not allowed to bring their families, the Mexican labourers remain second-class residents of Canada. "We're like slaves," said Juan. "Employers tell you to work faster, or they will send you back."

The threat of forced return is at the heart of the Mexican workers' relationship with the greenhouse farmers. Tanya Basok, a sociologist at the University of Windsor, one of the few academics to study migrant workers, concluded that the Mexican workers weren't cheap labour, once the cost of housing was factored in, but they were docile. "Their loyalty is ensured mostly through their fear of being expelled from the program," she wrote in her book *Tomatoes and Tortillas.* "Their patrons [employers] have the power to decide not only whether they will come back to the same farm next year but also whether they will even stay in the program."

Being fired means more than losing a job. It means losing a chance at any job. So the workers are reluctant to say anything about injuries, illness, or pesticides. When the Mexican consulate came to inspect the greenhouses, as required under the Canada–Mexico agreement, the workers stayed quiet. "It's better to just put up with it," one worker told Basok.

When they go home, the workers take with them a sealed envelope containing a letter evaluating their work habits in Canada. The letters, written by their employers, have to be handed over to the Mexican Ministry of Labour, which picks workers to go to Canada each year. A bad evaluation bars a worker from the program for at least a year, a hardship few migrant workers could endure. "The fear of not having their contracts renewed forces many Mexican workers to return to work even when they are sick," Basok found. "Most consider these losses relatively minor compared to what they might lose if they were to confront their employers. They are willing to accept some abuse in exchange for positive letters of evaluation, since without them, their chances of getting their contracts for work in Canada renewed would be very slim."

With no obligations outside their job, Mexican workers are able to work whenever needed. And, unlike Canadians, they cannot leave the farm for better jobs elsewhere. Letting them become immigrants would make them less attractive as farm workers. "The disadvantage in legalizing the Mexicans would be that they would be free to leave the greenhouse," a greenhouse owner told Basok.

Didychuk says the greenhouse industry could not exist without the Mexican workers. "If the government were to take it away, we would be in very serious trouble." The greenhouse farmers would have to pay local residents a lot more than they pay the Mexicans. "Our cost would go up. There would be so much demand and the supply is so thin," he says. It's cheaper and easier to hire Mexicans.

Leamington's Mexican workers are part of a wider trend in the Canadian food industry. From the market gardens in the Holland Marsh, north of Toronto, to the wineries and tender-fruit farms of Niagara, to the slaughterhouses of the prairies, the Canadian food industry is increasingly being propped up by Mexican workers. We have also drawn workers from Caribbean countries such as Jamaica and Trinidad. Such practices have been more a feature of the American food industry, where Mexican workers, many of them in the country illegally, form the backbone of the industry. On each of the big Pennsylvania dairy farms I toured in March 2000, rows of dilapidated trailers housed Mexican workers. And in December 2001, Tyson was indicted by a U.S. federal grand jury on thirty-six counts of smuggling illegal aliens across the border from Mexico to work in its slaughterhouses.

Agriculture was not the first industry to rely on migrant labour. The steel industry, at one time, also relied on workers who came to Canada, worked for a few months, and then went home. Mostly peasants from Italy, these workers were not interested in spending their lives in Canada's steel mills. They saw the work as a way to help them pay their bills at home. For the first two decades of the twentieth century, they formed the backbone of the steel industry in Canada, working in mills in Hamilton and Sault Ste. Marie. As with modern farm work, the steel plants relied on migrant labour because they had trouble attracting Canadians to the jobs, and those doing the work in part defined the nature of the job. Migrant labourers cut off from the rest of the community tended to prefer working long hours six or seven days a week so they could get home sooner. But increasingly, the migrant workers decided to stay in Canada. They soon demanded better working conditions and by the mid-1940s formed strong unions to back their demands. Now, workers line up for the well-paid jobs inside the mills.

Just as desperate conditions elsewhere drove men from Italy to seek work in Canadian steel mills, tough times in Mexico drive its men to seek work in Canada and the United States. And just as the migrant labour was essential to the early steel industry in Hamilton and Sault Ste. Marie, migrant labour is essential in Leamington's greenhouses. "It's come to the point where it's totally impossible to do this without this offshore labour. I don't know anybody that does," one greenhouse owner told Basok. The Mexicans have become, Basok says, a "structural necessity" in the industry. As one greenhouse owner told Basok: "Without the offshore labour, we wouldn't be the size we are now."

Bill Heffernan was not a welcome guest at the 2000 meeting of the Ontario Federation of Agriculture. A group of farmers led by Tony Beernink of Forest, Ontario, tried to get him added to the agenda, but the conference organizers said they couldn't find time for him. Beernink suspected that the OFA did not want to offend the food companies by putting Heffernan, a leading critic of big food companies from his post in the rural sociology department of the University of Missouri, on the agenda. The federation rejected the claim, saying it was just a matter of scheduling.

Still, the farmers were anxious to hear Heffernan's message and pooled their money to bring him to the meeting. The best they could do was arrange a session the night before the conference began. More than two hundred farmers came to hear Heffernan talk about consolidation in the food industry and the effect it was having on farmers across North America. They paid for an extra night's accommodation to hear his talk, and a hat was passed around to pay Heffernan's expenses. Tapes of his presentation sold for $2 each, and more than half the farmers bought a copy. The farmers had good reason to be worried about the power of the companies they deal with and nothing Heffernan said that night made them feel any better.

Heffernan has spent more than thirty years researching and documenting corporate concentration in the food industry from his post at a school local farmers derisively call the University of Monsanto because of the industry funding it receives. A team of researchers –

students, fellow faculty members, and his wife, Judy – comb through company reports, industry publications, and newspaper clippings for clues on how companies are merging and the empires they are building. "The real freight train, folks, is what is happening globally," Heffernan told the Ontario farmers. Globally, food companies are getting bigger and controlling more and more of the market, to the point that a free market no longer exists, Heffernan said. A free market, with prices determined through competitive pressure, could be beneficial. But corporate concentration is becoming so great that such competition has become a thing of the past.

To illustrate the point, Heffernan told the farmers to think of the food system as an hourglass. Farmers were at the top of the hourglass, and consumers at the bottom. For the food to get from the farmers to the consumers, it has to pass through the narrow part of the hourglass – the companies that control the industry.

Heffernan said that in the U.S. meat industry four companies control 55 per cent of the chicken industry, 79 per cent of the beef industry, and more than 60 per cent of the pork industry. In each category, the same four names keep popping up – Tyson, IBP, ConAgra, and Smithfield. "Economists say that when four firms have more than 40 per cent of the market, you basically no longer have a competitive system," Heffernan said.

Big companies can pit farmers against each other, since they control so much of the industry and thus farmers' access to the market. With their global reach, they can also pit countries against each other. Cargill, for instance, has operations in more than seventy countries and controls about 45 per cent of the world grain export market – about twice as much as the entire Canadian industry. A company of that scale can pick and choose which countries to deal with and buy its produce wherever it gets the best price.

In Washington, Brian Halweil of the Worldwatch Institute likes to use the example of food giants Archer Daniels Midland and Cargill lobbying the U.S. government to dredge the Mississippi River to make it cheaper to move American soybeans to market, arguing it would give Midwest farmers a competitive advantage on the world market. At the same time, the companies were lobbying the governments of Brazil, Bolivia, Paraguay, and Argentina to dredge the Paraguay-Paraná River to give Latin American farmers a competitive advantage. The result, after both projects were approved at public expense (with the Paraguay-Paraná project split into several smaller projects to sidestep environmental objections), was that neither group of farmers gained a competitive edge. The companies managed to shave millions off their shipping bills, with taxpayers picking up the tab.

This was not unique. Subsidies paid to farmers to help them through tough times brought on by bad weather or bad prices (or both) have been roundly criticized by both farmers and governments for keeping prices low by encouraging farmers to overproduce. In the United States, for instance, up to half of a farmer's income can come from the government, according to U.S. Department of Agriculture figures. Keith Collins, the chief economist for the USDA, says that if a farmer gets $2.50 a bushel for corn, only $1.25 comes from the market; the rest comes from the government. With production costs at $1.40 a bushel, Collins said farmers would be selling at a loss if it weren't for government help. Under normal market conditions, farmers selling at a loss would either switch to other crops or cut production. But while such moves would force commodity prices back up, farmers see no reason to change as long as the government bails them out, Collins says. "Farm incomes are pretty good (with government help), so why would a farmer cut back?" he asked. "There's no risk." In the early 1990s, subsidies accounted for only about a third of U.S. farmers' total incomes.

As long as subsidies suppress the prices paid to farmers, food companies can buy cheap raw food. It is little wonder, then, that food companies advocate for more government help for farmers. At his company's 2000 annual meeting, for example, Maple Leaf Foods head Michael McCain made a public plea for more help for Canadian farmers, saying they could not compete with the heavily subsidized Americans. "The Canadian food and agricultural supply chains can compete and succeed against anyone in the world – except perhaps Washington," he said. Speaking to reporters later, he called on Ottawa to match U.S. subsidies "line item by line item."

Cutting costs and maximizing profits are the underlying principles of any business. They are meant to spur innovation and efficiency in all markets, but as companies get big, they become the ones deciding what is best – which they define as being best for them and their shareholders. The result was dredged rivers that didn't help the taxpayers who paid for them, and farm subsidies that went straight to the bottom lines of the companies that lobbied for them. Such power, Heffernan said, is the real driving force behind consolidation in the food industry. "When you get that big, you've got economic power, and that was more important than any little increase in efficiency."

A few years back, Heffernan and his team began to notice a new trend. Companies were no longer just buying each other out; they were striking strategic alliances across industry sectors, tying together the food chain in ways that had never before been imagined. In such "clusters," as Heffernan calls them, the companies continue to operate as separate entities, but work together on specific projects. "You don't have to own everything to control it," says Heffernan.

Monsanto and Cargill set up one such joint venture in 1998 just as Cargill was selling its seeds business to Monsanto for $1.4 billion. Renessen, a play on the word Renaissance, was set up to develop seeds to meet both companies' needs. The seeds are genetically modified to grow best with Monsanto's weed killers and grown under contract for Cargill. Farmers wanting such contracts buy Monsanto seeds at Cargill outlets, use Monsanto chemicals and Cargill fertilizers to help grow them, and then sell the crops to Cargill elevators – from where they are sent to Cargill's processing plants, to livestock farmers working under contract to Cargill, or to the company's export terminals. "The 50-50 joint venture draws on Monsanto's capabilities in genomics, biotechnology, and seeds and on Cargill's global agricultural input, processing, and marketing infrastructure to develop and market new products with traits aimed at improving the processing efficiencies and animal nutrition qualities of major crops," Cargill said in press release. The arrangement gives the Monsanto–Cargill cluster effective control of food production from the seed to the supermarket shelf. Halweil calls such arrangements "OPEC-like food cartels" that pass control of food to a very few hands.

In such an arrangement the free market no longer exists. Decisions that were once made at each stage of production by buyers and sellers working in an open market are now pre-arranged and negotiated from the top down. Cargill's head office, for instance, establishes the price the company will pay for grain and transmits that price to its elevators across North America. Local managers can buy grain only at the centrally determined price, not at a price determined by the local market. Cargill made the move saying its contractual arrangements created efficiencies in the system to ensure the lowest-cost and safest food supply possible.

Back on Wall Street, analysts applauded the centralized planning that came with consolidation of the food industry. "This is the reason we have the most productive and efficient food system in the world," said David Nelson at Credit Suisse. Wall Street used to say the same thing about competition. "This whole system is backed up by neoclassical business theory, but none of those theories hold any more," Heffernan told the Ontario farmers.

Once the Tyson model takes over, free markets are replaced by planned economies. The free market lasts only long enough to force a restructuring of the industry. Pro-business commentators like Owen Lippert of the Fraser Institute decry the softening of market forces under supply management, but fail to see that top-down management of supply lies at the very heart of vertical integration. Both supply management and vertical integration attempt to predetermine the needs of the market. Either way, the result is a planned economy. The only question is, who is doing the planning, and to whose benefit – society's or the companies'?

When he's feeling mischievous, Heffernan compares such corporate food giants to the old Soviet Union, which also replaced the free market with a planned economy. When power becomes centralized, as it did in the Soviet Union, a bureaucracy is needed to keep the system running and to do the work once performed by the invisible hand of the market – such as setting prices, determining what will be produced, and where it will be sold. Bureaucracies, however, create inefficiencies, as individual advancement becomes paramount and the efficiency of the system as a whole secondary. With no personal stake at play, as would be the case in a free market of entrepreneurs, employees are more likely to paper over problems for fear that bad results will be blamed on them or that any criticisms of the company's strategy could brand them as not being a team player and hurt their career aspirations.

Employees also tend to take fewer risks than entrepreneurs, depriving the food system of one of the great advantages of capitalist markets. As Heffernan wrote in a 1999 study: "The vulnerability of the emerging food system is called into question when one remembers the former Soviet Union. Large centralized organizations have problems adapting to change. They commonly have problems with management, with co-ordination, and with worker satisfaction. These are good reasons to believe that the evolving system is vulnerable."

Maple Leaf's enthusiastic adoption of Tyson's industrial model shows that the trends that drive the U.S. food industry also drive it here, especially in this era of free trade. The George Morris Centre in Guelph summed it up best in a 1994–95 paper of what the twenty-first century might hold for Canadian agriculture: "As the world market becomes easier to access, we increasingly find that Canada has to compete with companies that are extraordinarily focused, efficient and coordinated. The major competitors are in the United

States. They have names like Tyson, Murphy Farms, Larson, Hunt
and so forth. . . . All of them will be Canada's competitors in the U.S.
market, overseas and even in our domestic market. Strategically,
Canada needs to decide whether to challenge the U.S. competitors at
the game they play well or to invest in a new game."

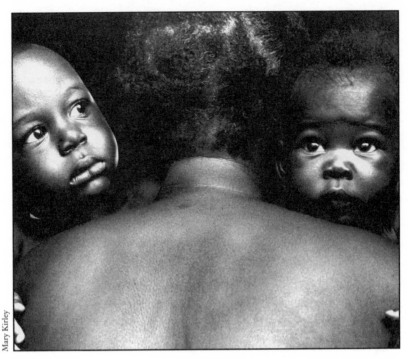

Mary Kirley

Babies orphaned by AIDS, Uganda, 1991

"The world at large is witnessing that hundreds of millions of people are still exposed to famine, poverty, malnutrition and food insecurity. As people we have no moral to tolerate this situation. As governments, I think, we are obliged to improve such conditions."

Ghebre-Medhin Belay,
Ethiopia's vice minister of agriculture

CHAPTER NINE

NO PLACE AT THE TABLE

O n November 7, 2001, Ghebre-Medhin Belay, Ethiopia's vice minister of agriculture, rose to speak in the buildings where his country's fate had been discussed, debated, and dictated for more than seventy years. Benito Mussolini built the plain structures that are sandwiched between Rome's Circus Maximus and the Caracalla Baths to house his colonial offices. Ethiopia was one of those colonies. After the Second World War, once fascism was defeated in Italy and Ethiopia was again under the rule of Haile Selassie, the buildings were made the home of the United Nations Food and Agriculture Organization – and, later, the World Food Program – to help developing countries feed their hungry. Ethiopia is one of those countries.

Belay, speaking to the thirty-first gathering of world agriculture ministers since the FAO was set up, reminded the delegates of just how much work was left to be done to fight "the long-lasting enemies of the people – hunger and poverty."

Ethiopians know about hunger. "Food insecurity covers a wide range of areas and affects a large number of people," Belay said. "Adverse climate changes, severe land degradation, wide use of backward agricultural production systems, inappropriate policies, protracted civil strife, and a widening gap between food production and population growth all had colluded to bring about this situation." Most of Belay's audience had plans to attend, a few days later, a pivotal meeting of the World Trade Organization in Qatar to launch a new round of trade talks. He pleaded with them not to forget the poor and hungry. "The world at large is witnessing that hundreds of millions of people are still exposed to famine, poverty, malnutrition, and food insecurity. As people we have no moral to tolerate this situation. As governments, I think, we are obliged to improve such conditions."

The same pleading statements had been made in the same building five years earlier. In 1996, just as the first genetically engineered crops were silently slipping into the food system, senior representatives of 185 countries gathered for the World Food Summit. For the first time, the FAO had called heads of state to Rome to find ways to fight hunger. Tellingly, only developing countries heeded the call for national leaders to attend. The issue was that important to them. Other countries, including Canada, sent their agriculture ministers.

Through more than a week of meetings, the group had only one item on the agenda: fighting hunger. There were more than 840 million hungry people in the world, and the delegates committed themselves to cutting that number in half by 2015. It was an ambitious goal, but they left Rome sure they could meet it. They made plans to convene again in ten years to chart their progress.

Instead, the FAO summoned them back to Rome just five years later. It had determined that by 2001, 800 million people were still going hungry. Progress had been made, but it was painfully slow. At the current rate, the FAO concluded, the Food Summit goal would not be reached until 2030 – fifteen years late. In reports and studies prepared by the FAO both in Rome and in developing countries, the conclusion was the same: the world had not done enough to fight hunger, and the efforts that had been made were often misguided. The FAO argued against the prevailing theory that increased trade would bring prosperity to poor countries – giving hungry people the money to buy food. A hungry person, it said, could not work. A person who cannot work would remain poor and hungry. Hunger, then, wasn't just a *result* of poverty, but it was also a *cause* of poverty. The theory that prosperity would end hunger failed, the FAO said, because a hungry country could not prosper. Hunger and poverty must be fought together.

That was the message Mallam Adamu Bello, Nigeria's agriculture minister, brought to Rome in November 2001. He said rich countries pushed free trade as an answer to the developing world's problems, and then flooded his country and others with food kept cheap by huge subsidies. Globalization, he said, must mean more than rich countries using their power to drive farmers in poor countries out of business. "The international community is continually paying lip-service to an issue of fundamental importance to the survival of humanity. The time to take concrete steps to match our rhetoric with concrete action is now." African countries were too poor to match the subsidies in rich countries that encouraged overproduction and cheap prices, he said. "These countries have continued to suffer some of the unpalatable and unintended consequences of trade liberalization."

Geetapersad Gangaram Panday, Surinam's minister of agriculture, echoed Bello's concerns about free trade, saying farmers in his country could not compete with cheap imports. "Some countries are selling their products at lower prices because they are able to subsidize their exports, which endangers our own products in our domestic market."

The worst fears of the African delegates were confirmed, it seemed, just six months later when George W. Bush signed the Farm Bill. Across Africa, farm ministers denounced the bill as providing protection for American farmers while Washington was demanding that poor countries open their doors to free trade. "This is terrible and it is scaring us," Zambian agriculture minister Mundia Sikatana said. "They are the same people who tell us not to subsidize production but are doing it themselves."

Moses Ikiara, a policy analyst in Kenya, called the bill a "slap in the face for African countries" that could turn them against the free trade talks at the WTO and derail the entire Doha round of negotiations. It was, after all, the refusal by developing countries to sign on to a backroom deal made by rich countries that had derailed the talks in Seattle in 1999. "The world is teetering on the edge of a trade war," said an editorial in Uganda's state-owned *New Vision Daily*. Even the American-controlled World Bank decried the bill, with one unidentified official telling the *Washington Post*, "A few American farmers will benefit, but at the expense of a large number of poor people in developing countries."

These people were already suffering enough. At the meeting in Rome in November 2001, the FAO's assistant director general, Hartwig de Haen, unveiled the agency's annual *State of Food Insecurity in the World* report. The report's details were no surprise to delegates from the developing world but were a sharp rebuke of the trade-based response to hunger by the world's richest countries.

Instead of reducing the number of hungry people in the world by 20 million a year, as was needed to meet the original goal, only 6 million had been cut each year since the 1996 summit. "Continuing at the recent rate, it would take more than sixty years to achieve the World Food Summit target, rather than the twenty years envisaged by the Rome Declaration," de Haen said. Through a series of charts and graphs flashed on the screen in the FAO's plenary hall, de Haen showed that countries able to invest in their farm sector – developed countries, in particular – were able to boost the food output. Poor countries forced to cut spending to service their debts saw dramatic reductions in food production. This left people in these countries hungry, he said, hurting the ability of children to benefit from their already limited schooling, and leaving people more susceptible to illness. "All of which translates into lower economic growth," he said, repeating the FAO's mantra for the week-long meeting: "Hunger is both a consequence and a cause of poverty. Investments are required to break this cycle."

Since the 1996 summit, however, in rich nations hunger in the Third World had become more of a public relations tool than a cause requiring serious work. It became a justification for every unsavoury practice in agriculture, from the use of chemicals, to animal welfare problems to genetic modification. Patrick Moore, a founding member of Greenpeace and now a favoured biotechnology spokesman for his criticism of his former friends, opened the BIO 2002 conference in Toronto in June 2002 with a call for more GM crops. There were 800 million hungry people in the world, he said, and without GM foods, forests would have to be cleared to grow enough food. "It's simple arithmetic," he said, rejecting studies that showed GM foods do not boost overall yield. "Low intensity and organic agriculture are proven to produce less food per acre." He was especially critical of Greenpeace for opposing golden rice. "Their approach is anti-humanitarian, and I can't stand that the organization I founded is trying to discredit the scientific community." Greenpeace has said that a balanced diet would be better than a vitamin-fortified rice. A person would have to eat fifteen pounds of golden rice a day to get the recommended daily intake of Vitamin A.

Later in the week, Robert Horsch, a Monsanto vice-president, used a BIO 2002 seminar on biotechnology and hunger to showcase his company's three-pronged strategy to sell its products in the developing world. The first tactic was to sell GM seeds. "It's just good business," Horsch said. The second was to pay for research programs in developing countries to produce seeds tailored to the needs of those countries and to set up educational programs to teach farmers how to grow GM crops – much as Monsanto had done in North America. This included such projects as Monsanto's work with the Kenyan Agricultural Research Institute in Nairobi to develop genetically modified corn, cassava, and bananas. The third approach was what Horsch called "non-commercial." This included distributing pest-resistant seed potatoes to farmers who needed them, developing golden rice, and making public the rice genome to further research. "These are not profitable now, but they could be in the future," he said.

After he spoke, several men in suits left before the presentation by Vibha Dhawan, a researcher from India who told those remaining that the mistakes of the Green Revolution must not be repeated.

"The excessive use of Green Revolution pesticides and fertilizers rendered much of the land unusable for agriculture," said Dhawan, director of biotechnology at the Tata Energy and Resources Institute, a sustainable development think-tank with offices in Washington, Europe, and the developing world, including India. While acknowledging that the Green Revolution had boosted cereal production in her country, she said it had also caused great turmoil that would be repeated if the biotech industry did not learn from past mistakes. She warned that the cost of patented seeds would exclude poor farmers from any benefits that growing GM crops might offer – marginalizing them, just as the Green Revolution had done a generation before. "The Green Revolution concentrated on a few crops and heavy inputs of purchased pesticides and fertilizers," she said. "It helped the rich farmers much more than it helped the marginal farmers."

Sakiko Fukuda-Parr from the United Nations Development Office, who chaired the seminar, made much the same point, saying poverty in rural areas must be addressed if farmers are to benefit from GM crops. "People making less than a dollar a day don't make much of a market."

At a counter-conference the weekend before, Tina Conlon of Oxfam Canada talked about going on a field trip as a Grade 3 student in 1963 to see the first ceremonial planting of high-yield Green Revolution rice in her native Philippines. There were busloads of schoolchildren, bands, and photographers on hand for the historic planting in Los Baños, Laguna, just outside Manila. The kids were told that this new rice would help feed all the hungry people in the country. "One of the things we were not told was what those higher yields needed to survive," she said, referring to the pesticides, fertilizers, and irrigation programs on which the new variety of rice depended. Their cost drove small farmers from the land and into the cities to work in factories. Even the big farms, the only ones that could afford the new technology and were able to get the loans needed to buy the chemicals and install the irrigation systems, "are one emergency away from being wiped out" under their debt, said

Conlon. "When I was a little girl, we prided ourselves that the Philippines was the rice bowl of Asia. Now, we are a net importer of rice from California," she said. "The Green Revolution has not done what it was intended to do."

Gene Grabowski couldn't accept arguments like that. He is vice-president of communications for the Grocery Manufacturers of America, and the food industry's chief spokesperson on GM foods. He defends GM technology and dismisses its critics. The average person, he said, really isn't concerned about GM foods. "In North America, we think of food as fuel," he said. In my interview with him, Grabowski had a lot to say and was determined to say it all. He spoke fast and loud, cutting me off when he had a point to make. He made few concessions to GM's critics, except to allow that biotechnology had yet to offer anything consumers might see as a benefit. That would soon change, he said, when vaccines and drugs and enhanced taste and nutrition were embedded in food. "You know everyone says food has no taste any more? Well, we can put that back in."

He was optimistic that biotechnology would one day be accepted in Europe, where major grocery store chains removed GM products from their shelves. Such voluntary moves, he said, have left the door open to the stores putting GM products back on the shelves once the controversy dies down – something that would be impossible should the EU ban GM foods. He could not contain his frustration at Europe's refusal so far to accept genetically modified crops from the United States. "Europe should be down on its knees to the U.S. thanking God that we were there for them" during the Second World War, he said.

GM's critics, Grabowski said without being asked, are not really interested in agriculture or even in the food we eat. They are interested, instead, in undermining the entire capitalist system and the American way of life. "America is about progress. Progress and profit," he said. "It may sound jingoistic, but I love America," he added, referring to the fight over GM food as "a global struggle that puts companies at risk." In their zeal to slow the development of GM food, critics make victims of African farmers who might be able to use GM crops to grow more food for their families and maybe even develop export markets that would enable them to join the world's richer nations, he said. "What are we supposed to do, leave them in the dark ages?"

The first attempt to hold a follow-up to the 1996 Food Summit failed. In the spring of 2001, the FAO called world leaders to come to Rome the following November. Then in July of that year, the heads of the G-8 group of industrialized countries met in Genoa, Italy. Massive street protests greeted the delegates. A member of the Carabinieri paramilitary police was cornered in his Jeep by a crowd when he shot one protester, twenty-three-year-old Carlo Giuliani, in the head, killing him. The protest by eighty thousand resulted in 184 injuries and 70 arrests.

Italian prime minister Silvio Berlusconi was outraged and declared that "sacred" Rome was off limits for the Food Summit for fear that protesters might damage the city's ancient ruins. He suggested that the FAO shift the summit to an African country. The FAO resisted, saying it was too late to move the summit out of the country and suggesting that if the summit moved, so might the entire FAO. Several alternative Italian sites were then considered, and the Italian government and the FAO finally agreed on Rimini, a resort town on the Adriatic Coast. The changed venue made planning for the summit difficult, but possible, until September 11. After the terrorist attacks in New York and Washington, and the subsequent war in Afghanistan, support for the summit dropped off dramatically, and it was eventually postponed until June 2002.

Despite this development, a meeting of agricultural ministers and deputy ministers went ahead as planned in November 2001. Several non-governmental organizations from around the world also sent delegates to plan for the full summit the following June. A few reporters showed up, including Barry Wilson from *The Western Producer* and me. Wilson would go on to Qatar the following week for the WTO meeting, which was going ahead as planned despite September 11. After a week of meeting with FAO staff and NGO representatives, and sitting in on the ministers' many meetings, one thing became very clear: hunger is too complex an issue to be fought with simple solutions, and the solutions preferred by industrialized countries – trade and industrial agriculture – could actually make the situation worse.

Wilberforce Kisamba-Mugerwa of Uganda told the meeting that even while his country's economy had grown twice as quickly as the population as a whole between 1997 and 2000, 36 per cent of the people – some 8 million – earned less than $1 (U.S.) a day. Most of the poor lived in rural areas and were unable to get enough food despite the abundance around them. "We are currently experiencing a surplus of food production, especially bananas, maize, and beans," he said, but this food was destined for the export market and Uganda's capital city, Kampala. The surplus had driven down food prices. That was good for the people in Uganda's cities and in the countries that imported the food, but bad for Uganda's farmers. "Uganda is not proud to be counted among countries where people are experiencing hunger and malnourishment."

Solving world hunger means more than providing lots of cheap food. It means addressing the needs of rural people. "The problems of food insecurity cannot be addressed in isolation. Parallel investments in water, land, capacity building, health, education, and infrastructure is needed to utilize Uganda's potential," Kisamba-Mugerwa said. "This requires national and international support."

At the June summit, which took place the same week as the BIO 2002 conference in Toronto, Third World countries stepped up their attacks on the richer countries, especially the United States. Just as she had the previous November, U.S. Secretary of Agriculture Ann Veneman went to Rome stressing the virtues of open trade and continuing to push GM foods as the best way to solve Third World hunger. "Biotechnology has tremendous potential to develop products that can be more suited to areas of the world where there is persistent hunger," she said. But the developing countries were having none of it. "Let us stop beating around the bush," Ugandan president Yoweri Museveni said. "The most fundamental problems are not the weather, are not lack of approved seeds. The main causes of food shortages in the world are really three: wars, protectionism in agricultural products in Europe, the U.S.A., China, India, and Japan, and protectionism in value-added products on the part of the same countries."

Between the November meeting and the June summit, the United States passed into law its $190-billion (U.S.) farm subsidy bill. In November, delegates to Rome could speak only about general trade policies. By June, they had a clear target to focus on and went on the attack. "We are poor. You are rich. Level the playing field," Teofisto Guingona, the foreign minister of the Philippines, said in a passionate speech calling on developed countries to cut their subsidies.

The week ended with a renewed commitment to end hunger, but no new plans to reach the goal. The United States still refused to recognize food as a basic right (fearing that would expose it to lawsuits from countries facing famine), and Europe blocked a United Nations plan to boost aid to Africa by $24 billion (U.S.) a year, saying that political turmoil was at the heart of much of the hunger problem in sub-Saharan Africa. The United States did, however, manage to push through an endorsement of GM foods as a way to fight hunger.

Within weeks, Africa was thrown into another food crisis, and the abstract debates and anecdotes of Rome bumped up against reality. The FAO and the World Food Program warned that 13 million people in the southern African countries of Malawi, Lesotho, Swaziland, Zambia, and Zimbabwe were at risk of starvation due to drought. In Mozambique, where flooding had devastated food production for two years, farmers were suddenly dealing with drought. The FAO put out an immediate appeal for $500 million (U.S.) in aid, asking for food donations and seed and fertilizer so the crisis might be stemmed.

A week after the appeal was made, Zimbabwe turned back a shipment of corn from the United States, saying it could not be sure the corn was GM-free. Zambia also refused the corn, saying it saw no reason to accept American assurances the food was safe. "If it is not fit, then we would rather starve," said Zambian president Levy Mwanawasa. Because most of its food exports were to Europe, Zambia worried that GM corn might contaminate its own produce and cut it off from its main market. "We must not put our markets at risk," said Nico Hawkins, an economist with Grains South Africa in Johannesburg. Some in Africa feared the United States was using the crisis to circumvent the African countries' debates over the future of GM food on the continent. "The American government wants to force us into accepting this," said Lovemore Simwanda, of the Zambian Farmers Union. "They think we've got hunger and we're going to be forced into accepting their food and ultimately GM."

Milling the corn – at a cost of $25 a tonne – would alleviate the problem by ensuring no one planted any corn kernels, but a United Nations official told the *Christian Science Monitor* privately that the United States rejected this idea because it might be seen as implicit acknowledgement of a problem with the food. In the slums of Lusaka, the hungry echoed their president's sentiments. "I would rather starve than eat that food," George Chilumbo told the *Christian Science Monitor*. In the midst of the controversy, the *Zambian Post* editorialized that "even the beggars deserve some dignity."

The World Bank also came under attack during the food crisis for refusing to consider a moratorium on debt payments. The six affected countries paid a total of $150 million (U.S.) a year on debts of more than $23 billion. Malawi alone paid $36 million (U.S.) a year in debt payments, one-third as interest charges. The food crisis in southern Africa was years in the making, with floods in 2001 wiping out crops, followed by droughts. It was much the same weather pattern as has hit the Canadian prairies in recent years, but the effects were far more devastating. In the months before the floods that began the crisis, Malawi exported virtually all of its 167,000 tonnes of corn stockpiles to raise money to cover its debt payments. That left it with nothing to offer its people when successive crop failures pushed three of its eleven million people to the brink of starvation in 2002. The IMF denied it had pressed Malawi to sell the corn, saying it had merely suggested the move. President Bakili Maluzi told the Reuters news agency it seemed like more than a suggestion to him. "The IMF cannot refute this. I myself argued with them over this issue of selling government reserves, and they insisted. It was their decision imposed on us," he said at the World Economic Forum's Africa summit in Durban in June 2002. "If the IMF policies had not failed, we would not be where we are." To feed its people, Malawi later accepted milled GM corn donated by the U.S. government.

A study by the International Food Policy Research Institute, which is funded by the World Bank, found that World Bank and International Monetary Fund policies in Malawi had left the country unable to help its people in time of crisis. To qualify for World Bank and IMF help, the country was told by both agencies to cut back on aid to farmers. This aid included commodity boards that helped farmers sell their produce, rural offices that aided farmers and other rural people through droughts and advised them on water-saving farming techniques, and direct aid programs in which the state grew food and distributed it to the needy.

Just as they had in Mexico in 1982, the World Bank and IMF assumed that the market would replace these services, but that didn't happen. "You now have a situation in which neither the government nor the private sector is in place to provide what is necessary," the report said. "The majority of farmers feel worse off since the reforms." The World Bank's commitment to agriculture shrank from 40 per cent of its expenditures in the 1980s to just 7 per cent by the end of the century. That left developing countries struggling to meet the needs of their rural majorities. "There has to be a greater focus on rural areas, because that is where the poor reside," the institute's Per Pinstrup-Andersen said in the report.

As the crisis in southern Africa deepened, world leaders and activists gathered in Johannesburg in the summer of 2002 to discuss sustainable development. In a surprise move, one of the Indian scientists who helped Borlaug introduce the Green Revolution to his country lamented his life's work in a speech to the summit. M.S. Swaminathan said the key to fighting hunger was not biotechnology or more industrial agriculture, but small-scale projects that let people feed themselves. "It's production by the masses versus mass-production farming systems," he explained.

The FAO marked 2002's World Food Day, on October 16, by releasing an updated *State of Food Insecurity* report. Once again it scolded the developed world for its inability to meet the needs of the hungry in the Third World. In the year since the 2001 report was released, the situation had worsened dramatically – largely because of hunger in Africa – all but wiping out the modest gains that had been made since the 1996 World Food Summit. "Progress has ground virtually to a halt," FAO director-general Jacques Diouf said in the report. The report found that there were barely 2.5 million fewer hungry people than were reported at the 1996 summit – enough to throw the summit's goals into shambles. Where de Haen had warned a year earlier that it could take sixty years to reach the summit goal of cutting hunger in half, Diouf said that at the current pace it would now take more than a century. "That is simply unacceptable."

AIDS adds yet another level of instability to Africa. To cite one example, the village of Gwanda, near the shore of Lake Victoria in Uganda, was a healthy community before AIDS began its deadly spread around the world in the 1980s. For generations, Gwanda's families grew beans and groundnuts, bananas, mangoes, maize, cassava, and sweet potatoes on farms of just a few hectares each, the FAO said in a study of the area. Most families also kept a few chickens, goats, and pigs to provide eggs, milk, and meat. Some fished in Lake Victoria, and until the 1970s, when prices declined, coffee provided them with a cash crop.

Life was far from easy, but generations of tilling the same land had taught people a few tricks for growing the most food on their small plots. They knew when to plant to take best advantage of the seasonal rains. They had developed a system of mulching and recycling cuttings from the banana plantations to keep other fields fertile. They also knew to take cut grass from open fields and use it to mulch the banana plantations. They saved their best seeds from year to year and used plant and animal waste on their farms as fertilizer. They weeded their fields by hand and as a community picked insects and drove other pests from their crops. The people ate well and regularly, their farms providing the fruits, vegetables, and protein they needed. In Africa, that was enough to make Gwanda a relatively wealthy village.

But those days are gone. The practices that had fed the village for generations were labour intensive, and labour was in short supply since AIDS came to the village in the late 1980s. One farmer in the village, Martin, lost three of his nine children to AIDS, and one son was murdered. Three more children and his wife left the village because of the strain. The seventy-year-old struggled to keep his one-hectare farm productive, but it was a losing battle. Twenty years ago, it took the entire family to keep the fields clear of weeds and insects, but they lived well. Their small chicken flock provided protein year-round. The money Martin made selling coffee, fish, and bananas in nearby cities paid for any food he could not grow, as it did for most men in the village. It was probably during one of those trips that someone from the village picked up the AIDS virus and brought it back to the village.

Since then, Martin had lost more than half his family to death or migration, and with them the labour to keep his farm operating. His 0.6-hectare banana plantation was weedy and dying. Weevils ate what few bananas were growing. The soil became depleted without the labour available to work compost and manure into the soil. As the family slipped into poverty, Martin sold his livestock, leaving the farm without manure to fertilize the land. He could not afford the chemical fertilizers that would make up for the loss, so the farm could no longer provide enough cassava and sweet potatoes to last the year. Martin no longer grew corn because he could not afford the seed. He could not even turn to the country's agriculture ministry for help. The head of the region's farm outreach office told the FAO that he had lost half his staff to AIDS and could not find people to replace them. In Gwanda, ten to fifteen people died of AIDS every month.

Crop diversity diminished as farmers scaled back their operations. Livestock herds dropped as farmers sold animals to pay for medicines and funerals. Weeds, insects, and disease infested both the banana plantations and the farm fields. Few farmers had the time to go to Lake Victoria to find fish. Others, sick with AIDS, hadn't the strength. And, as banana plantations became overgrown, the population of wild cats grew and preyed on the few chickens, goats, and pigs that had been kept.

Gwanda's story is a sadly typical story of the devastation AIDS is wreaking on a farming community. Once considered a wealthy village, now half the people there are counted among Uganda's chronically poor – with 45 per cent earning less than $1 (U.S.) a day, the World Bank's threshold for "absolute poverty."

Across Africa most people infected with AIDS are those between the ages of fifteen and forty-nine. These are people of prime working age, many the heads of their families. When they die, they leave behind children on depleted and declining farms – and debt. The FAO calculates that once AIDS takes hold in a farming village like Gwanda, food consumption drops by 41 per cent, while spending on health care jumps by more than 400 per cent. In sub-Saharan Africa, 7 million farmers have died of AIDS since 1985, with another 16 million expected to die in the next twenty years. The FAO predicted that one-quarter of the farm labour force would be lost by 2020, and children would not have their parents with them long enough to learn farming skills. A study in Kenya found that only 7 per cent of the farm households headed by orphans had adequate knowledge of farming methods. Once such skills are gone, they are lost forever.

A study by the United Nations in 2002 found there were 29.4 million people with HIV/AIDS in sub-Saharan Africa. With 3.5 million infections in 2002, the worst of the epidemic, already claiming more than a third of the population in Zimbabwe, Swaziland, and Botswana, has not yet been seen, according to the UN. Stalled efforts to bring cheap drugs to Africa to deal with the crisis have left millions without the antiretroviral treatments they need. "In the absence of massively expanded prevention, treatment and care efforts, the AIDS death toll on the continent is expected to continue rising before peaking around the end of this decade," the UN said in its report, *AIDS Epidemic Update*. Stephen Lewis, the UN special envoy for AIDS in Africa, said the growing death rate due to AIDS will cripple the continent's ability to recover from famine. "Everything breaks down in the face of AIDS," he told a press conference. "You can't decimate your agricultural workers and expect to produce the same kind of food you had before."

Unless AIDS can be curbed in Africa, the continent may have no choice but to adopt low-skilled industrial agriculture. As it has else-where, this would force thousands, perhaps millions, of farmers off the land and into the cities – where they might find work in the fac-tories that are now proliferating throughout the Third World in search of cheap labour.

That trend would be exacerbated by the devastation of Africa's already shaky educational networks by AIDS as it kills teachers and obliges children to leave school to become the new heads of their families. In Africa, more teachers die of AIDS than retire. In Zambia alone, AIDS killed 1,300 teachers in the first ten months of 1998. The World Bank estimates that Africa needs between $450 and $550 million (U.S.) each year to recruit and train new teachers. It also estimates that schooling costs could be cut by up to 66 per cent if students left their villages to be educated in larger centres. But taking children out of their villages after they lost their parents would do much more than just save money. It would ravage the culture and traditions of rural Africa by removing a whole generation of farmers from the land.

Protest outside Loblaws annual meeting, April 2002

"You can go out of business waiting for the government to help."

Peter Cumming,

soybean farmer

CHAPTER TEN

CHANGING THE MENU

D an Weins's proudest possession is a 1949 Massey Pony tractor
he bought used. It is small by today's standards – about the
length and width of a mid-sized car. It is perhaps one of the earliest
tractors to make its way to the Canadian prairies, ushering in a new
era of efficient farming after the Second World War. Weins keeps it
in a shed at the edge of his garden plot on the banks of the Red River
just south of Winnipeg. "We still use it," Weins says proudly. "It's all
we need." Like his tractor, Weins's farm is tiny by modern prairie
standards at just fifty acres spread over two plots. Not far away,
farmers work long hours, struggling to get by on farms of five thousand acres or more with machinery many times the size and price of
Weins's Massey Pony. Weins, like a lot of farmers trying to keep his
costs down, bought all his machinery used. But he took it one step
further by buying tractors, tillers, and other machinery most farmers
would regard as museum pieces. "The combined age of all our
machinery is about two hundred years," he says.

I first met Weins at a conference on farming in Brandon,
Manitoba, in October 2001. I had been asked to speak about the gap
between farmers and consumers, and some of the efforts underway
to bring the two together. In my speech, I outlined some ways that
ties between shoppers and the people who grow their food were
being re-established, including community supported agriculture –

or CSAs. These are small farms that contract directly with urban shoppers to provide fresh produce. For a set fee per week, the shoppers get a bin of fruits and vegetables grown on the farm. How much they get depends on the growing conditions and the season. In effect, they share in the ups and downs of the farm. In a good year, they get lots of good food. In a bad year, they get less. Whatever they receive, they know where their food comes from and how it is grown, and the farmers get a stable source of income. While the farmers can't benefit from a bumper crop as much as they might otherwise, a bad crop doesn't wipe them out, either.

Weins runs just such an operation. He has contracts with sixty-five families in Winnipeg, some of whom like to help with the planting, weeding, and harvesting. "Our sharers are much more than just customers," Weins says. "Our farm is their farm. Our dog is their dog." The sharers, as Weins calls his customers, get first crack at the produce from the farm's vegetable gardens and apple orchard, and the rest goes to organic stores in Winnipeg. During the fall and winter, Weins meets with the sharers to find out what they liked and didn't like from the previous season, and what they would like to see grown the following year. A regular newsletter keeps them informed of growing conditions on the farm so they are not surprised if they receive too much food (or too little) one week.

When we spoke, Weins was making plans to buy a herd of sheep so he would have fresh manure for his fields and perhaps some meat to sell. He encouraged sharers to start their own gardens at home, and a few became good enough that they dropped out of his CSA. "We consider that a success," Weins says. With hundreds of inquiries a year from people wanting to join, Weins wasn't worried about not having enough city people to share his harvest. "We could have hundreds of farms like this, just for Winnipeg," he said.

There are more than a thousand farms like Weins's across North America, and many variations on the plan. Some deliver the food to customers' houses, some require the customer to go to the farm. There are monthly, weekly, and biweekly deliveries and payment plans ranging from up-front payments to payments with each delivery. But one thing is the same about all CSAs: they are a direct link between city dwellers and the people who produce the food.

What brought Weins and me together was a comment I made in my speech that such programs are great, as far as they go, but they are not the answer to what ails agriculture, and they are not capable of bridging the gap between the farmers and the majority of city people.

The argument of CSAs, organic food stores, and others who have adopted alternative sources of food is that if enough people voted with their consumer dollars to choose this food supply or that, the large corporations running our food system would have no choice but to listen. I admire the efforts of people like Weins in setting up alternative food systems, but their efforts do little to ensure that the vast majority of people get the food they want from Sobeys or Loblaws. Most of us dash off to the supermarket when we get a chance, fill our carts as fast as possible, and hope the lineup at the checkout is not too long. We presume that the store will continue to stock the items we routinely buy and will stop stocking the ones we don't. But we make our buying decisions within the parameters of the store or chain's buying decisions and hope that someone in government is making sure the food is safe.

Dropping out of this system, I told the conference, is a solution that makes one person, or a small group of people, feel better about the food they eat. But by creating an oasis for themselves, these people lose any influence over the dominant food system. Worse, it lets the corporations and government off the hook for bringing about any real change. It tells them they don't have to do anything because their core constituency is voting with its dollars to keep buying conventional food. The food companies know that too many of us are too busy, or have too many other priorities, to put as much effort into buying and preparing food as those who drop out. Worse, the companies can say that there is no need for change since consumers can always shop elsewhere if food matters so much to them.

As well, CSAs are limited in how much they can do. Fresh produce is one thing, but I still need someone to slaughter and prepare the meat I eat or to grind wheat into flour.

Weins didn't like those comments and approached me in the hallway afterwards to tell me so. He invited me to his farm to see his operation and to talk about what brought it about. Weins, who grew up in the city, attended a farm rally on the lawn of the Manitoba legislature in 1990 and came away thinking that the answer to what ails farms is not the increased aid they were demanding, but getting off the treadmill of industrial agriculture and mounting debt that had got them into trouble. "For the government to put more money into the current paradigm didn't make much sense to me since the current paradigm isn't working," he said. "I remember standing on that grass and thinking there must be a better way."

What he came up with was a system of farming and selling produce he had seen during his work in Swaziland a few years earlier helping that country's schools develop a new curriculum. He had not heard of the CSA movement, then only in its infancy in North America, but knew of farms in Swaziland that sold their produce to the same city people every week. He decided to try it in Canada and bought a patch of land about a ten-minute drive from Winnipeg's southern boundaries. The location was ideal for a CSA. Because it is part of a floodplain, it could not be developed, so it sold for only $2,000 an acre – about the going rate for farmland in Manitoba – despite its proximity to the city, which made it easy for Weins to find city people interested in joining a CSA. Over the winter, he met with small groups in church basements and school gyms to talk about his ideas. The meetings got the attention of the *Winnipeg Free Press*, which did a story on his plans. In the following days he received more than three hundred calls from people wanting to join. "I was trying to talk people out of it," said Weins, who studied plant science at university. He interviewed everyone who wanted to join and accepted only those who seemed most committed to its ideals.

The plan worked. While most farmers operate on razor-thin

margins, and often lose money, Weins makes money. He benefits both from the free labour he gets from CSA members who want the experience of working on a farm and from the higher prices he is able to charge. While both he and his wife, Wilma, also work off the farm – he is a program director at the Canada Foodgrains Bank, a Winnipeg-based aid agency, and Wilma is a supply teacher – he was quick to point out that most farmers and their spouses work off the farm just to maintain debt-laden farms that don't make money. He has no debt.

We spoke for almost two hours about how the farm evolved, and how he keeps members involved through harvest parties and salsa-making and pickling parties so they can use the farm's produce through the winter. Rather than demanding solutions within the current model of industrial farming as others were doing that day in 1990 on the lawn of the legislature, he had looked for ways to break out of that model. And he did that by looking to a society that many in the industrial farm world think of as backwards and in desperate need of the Green Revolution's tools – Africa. "CSAs are not the answer to the crisis in agriculture, but the kind of thinking that led to it is," he said.

The conventional wisdom in the food industry is that consumers will not pay more for food, even if they believe it is better tasting or better for them. Premium products might be able to find niche markets, but the majority of people want the cheapest food possible. This assumption has been the basis of farm and food policy in Canada since the beginning of the Green Revolution and has been used to justify the industrialization of agriculture. Those who argue against it are dismissed as dreamers.

But big food companies like Maple Leaf are now turning that assumption on its head with products such as Prime Naturally chicken and Medallion Naturally pork. Cargill did the same with its Sterling Silver beef sold in Canada at Sobeys grocery stores. These are brand-name products in a part of the store once dominated by generic products in plain packaging. On their new branded products, the lettering is big and full of corporate logos, often with succulent photos of the meal you can make with the meat inside.

But there is a broader issue at play here. By moving to grain-fed chicken and pork, and marketing them as premium products, Maple Leaf showed that there is a mass market for high-quality foods if they are marketed well and produced on a large enough scale to keep costs down. Maple Leaf demonstrated that companies could build a successful business around products that address consumer concerns. The mad cow crisis awoke people to the cannibalistic feeding practices of modern farms – a production standard that made sense for the industry at the time, but which consumers instinctively rejected as unnatural. Prime Naturally chicken and Medallion Naturally pork, which boast a vegetarian diet for its animals, turned what was modern agriculture's darkest hour into a marketing opportunity.

In a speech to the Empire Club in September 2002, Michael McCain said his company's vertical integration model would one day allow consumers to trace the origin of their food from DNA to dinner table to ensure its safety. "Consumers around the world care about this subject," he said. "They are willing to pay a premium."

Other big food companies are also turning consumer worries into marketing opportunities. Tyson, Perdue, and Foster Farms – which together produce about one-third of the chickens in the United States – have cut almost all the antibiotics from the feed of their chickens in response to concerns that the constant medication was helping speed the development of antibiotic-resistant viruses. Loblaws has put dozens of products on its shelves under the President's Choice Organics brand, a clear signal from Canada's largest grocery store chain that it makes good business sense to listen to consumers' concerns about modern farm practices. At A&P, a line of vegetable-fed chicken was launched under the chain's Master Choice brand. And in the summer of 2002, Heinz announced that it would start offering organic ketchup.

Branding food products can be a very good thing if the added value it brings to food works its way through the entire food chain, improving operations along every step in the process by keeping family farmers on the land, addressing animal welfare issues, and tackling environmental problems caused by factory farms. To date, however, branding's insistence on quality and consistency has had the opposite effect – just as high-priced brand-name sneakers have done little to improve the lives of the Third World women and children who put them together, or the North American workers left jobless when their shoe factories moved offshore.

At the conference where I met Weins, I told the farmers they had better figure out a way to get ahead of the move to branding premium products or corporations like Maple Leaf and Loblaws would beat them to it and extract all the benefit for themselves. If farmers want to seize their share of branding's added value, they need to stand together and say so. The supply-managed farmers proved that they can supply standardized products on a large scale while providing a good living to family farmers.

The experience of chicken farmers in the United States shows just how little power farmers have negotiating on their own. In just one generation, they have been transformed from being independent farmers into contract employees of huge corporations with little or no say on how their farms operate. In Canada, poultry farmers resisted a similar fate through the negotiating strength of their marketing boards. The same is true for Canadian dairy farmers, who have kept the family farm alive through their ability to negotiate a decent price for raw milk.

Farmers, however, can be fiercely independent. The old spirit of cooperation that gave us the prairie pool elevators and the cooperative supply stores across the country fell by the wayside in the modern era of competition. Farmers no longer hold penny auctions when their neighbours go under. Today's large-scale farmers believe in the cutthroat, high-efficiency approaches of the big companies that supply them. Their attempts at unity are ad hoc and centred on immediate crises, such as the floods of 1999 in the west or the droughts of 2002. Once the crisis passes, so too does their solidarity.

Brewster Kneen, in his book *The Rape of Canola*, laments the rise of the commodity-based farm group that has accompanied the monocultures of the Green Revolution. As farmers focused on a single crop, the groups organized around that crop became their voice. The groups have their own constituencies and their own priorities. They serve the needs of corporations well by perpetuating monoculture farming. They put most of their efforts into researching ways for farmers to boost their yields in that crop and soon found themselves working closely with industry to do that.

Governments benefit from the segregation of farmers into commodity groups by using the lack of unity of farm organizations as an excuse for doing nothing. If farmers cannot agree among themselves what is needed, how can government know what to do? When floods hit Ontario in the summer of 2000, for instance, Terry Daynard of the Ontario Corn Producers Association organized a series of meetings across the province to demand relief. A year earlier, he had been critical of any talk about helping western farmers. In Ottawa, Vanclief was able to get away with doing very little for either group.

The situation is not the same in Quebec. There, farmers also belong to commodity groups, but all those groups are affiliated with an umbrella organization called l'Union des Producteurs Agricoles, or UPA. The UPA was established in 1972 as a farmers' union, with Quebec as a closed shop. All of Quebec's fifty thousand farmers pay dues to the UPA of about $250 a year. It operates like the Rand formula used with industrial unions, which stipulates that all workers in a unionized shop must pay union dues, even if they do not want to be in the union. The idea is that if all workers benefit from the union contract, they should all pay dues to the union that negotiated it. The UPA works on the same principle. "Everybody must pay their dues," Hugh Maynard, editor of the *Quebec Farmers Advocate*, told the Brandon conference at which I spoke. "You don't have to be a member, but you have to pay your dues."

Maynard's group, the Quebec Farmers Association, held a vote a month after the conference to join the UPA, making it the last major farm group in Quebec to join. The result, he said, is that in Quebec, unlike the rest of the country, "there is only one official farm organization." The UPA is the only group that meets with government to discuss aid packages, environmental legislation, or anything else that might affect Quebec farmers. While farmers across Canada struggle to keep up with ad hoc programs tossed together in response to the crises of the day, Quebec farmers negotiate long-term plans that set out the sort of government help farmers could expect. "There is some predictability and there is some stability so farmers know how much is going to be there for farm financing," Maynard told the conference. "How much is going to be there for income stabilization. How much is going to be there for extension services, and so on."

The UPA has an office in Quebec City, where staff researchers prepare reports on whatever issues come up at the legislature. As well, commodity groups meet to hash out their differences in private before presenting a unified face to government or industry. Farmers, Maynard said, have had to give up some of their individuality, but have gained a strong, unified voice – with a budget of $8 million a year. "If you don't have those resources, you don't get your voice across."

Across Canada, the farm groups that have been most successful at speaking for their members are those given government authority to speak and act on behalf of farmers – the Canadian Wheat Board and the provincial marketing boards for milk, poultry, and eggs. Without that authority, farmers have very little bargaining power. It's a message the marketing boards have pushed to their members at annual meetings over the last few years as the United States and others challenge their existence at the WTO. "When producers have no power in the marketplace, the market usually works at their expense," Leo Bertoia of the Dairy Farmers of Canada told Ontario dairy farmers in January 2002. "This market power must be legislated and it must be anchored in legislation."

That's something that Ontario potato farmer Wayne Dorsey knows all too well. As head of the Ontario Potato Marketing Board, he bargained with the province's potato chip makers to get a better deal for farmers, but the chip makers proved tough negotiators. The talks ended in arbitration, with the arbitration board siding with the farmers' demand for an immediate hike in the price of potatoes from $7.10 per hundredweight to about $8.85, depending on the quality of the potatoes. Dorsey estimated the raise, while significant for farmers, would add about three or four cents to the cost of a bag of potato chips. Then the chip makers appealed. The case dragged on in the courts through the spring, summer, and fall of 2001. "A crop went into the ground and out again, and this thing still wasn't settled," Dorsey said. Finally, with winter setting in and farmers beginning to think about what to grow the coming year, Dorsey's board settled one by one with the chip makers to spread the $1.75 price hike over three years. The farmers had no choice but to take a deal giving them in three years what the arbitration board had ruled they deserved in one. The companies were just too big for farmers to fight, Dorsey said. "Those who have the deepest pockets can go the furthest in this world."

All farm groups advocate on behalf of the "family farm," but there is no single definition of what a family farm is. A Supreme Court judgment in 2001 ruled that a ban on farm workers unionizing made sense for family farms, but not for factory farms. It did not, however, spell out a difference between the two. And the Ontario government, in legislating manure handling on farms, chose to apply new rules to large farms first, with plans for less stringent rules for smaller farms to follow. Across Canada, rural municipalities charge higher property taxes for large livestock farms, saying they no longer qualify for the break in taxes given to family farms. Saskatchewan has brought in new rules requiring hog farms with six or more workers to pay their staff extra for overtime or weekend work, denying factory farms the labour law exemptions granted to family farms.

But such efforts are spotty and uncoordinated. Factories need to be treated as factories, whether the machines inside are mechanical or biological. If factory farms had to live by the same environmental, labour, and health and safety laws as manufacturers, their economies of scale would be diminished, offering family farms a better chance to compete. Large farms would not be wiped out, but some of their less desirable attributes would be eliminated, as would their threat to the profitability of smaller farms. This would not lead to a big jump in food prices. More likely, it would keep them from falling even further. But as we have seen with Maple Leaf's Prime Naturally chicken and Medallion Naturally pork, the food industry has no intention of letting food get cheaper, anyway. The talk at grocery conferences the last few years, in fact, has been about ways to raise prices, not how to keep them down. Besides, farmers get so little of the food dollar that any increase in the money they receive should have little effect on retail food prices.

None of this is to say that big farms are always bad and small farms are always good. Big farms can do things that small farms simply cannot. The methane-powered generator at the Mason Dixon Farm in Pennsylvania is a good example. "By the time it comes out of there, it smells just like soil," said Richard Waybright, owner of Mason Dixon, of the leftover manure. None of the Ontario farmers on that tour had a farm big enough, or producing enough manure, to do the same thing. And none produced enough manure to put in place a program like the one Cliff Hawbaker has established with the neighbouring town of Chambersburg, Pennsylvania. Hawbaker takes delivery of the town's grass clippings, garden waste, and tree trimmings, mixes it with manure from his 375-cow farm, and composts it all in huge piles behind his barn. In the spring, he sells the composted manure to gardeners and landscapers in town. It is a good example of urban and rural people working together that would be more difficult to implement on Canada's much smaller dairy farms.

Big farms are also better able to afford the latest technology or machinery needed to keep their farms environmentally safe. Allan Mussell at the George Morris Centre in Guelph says that strict environmental controls on livestock operations would be difficult for small farms to afford. Of course, big farms need to have tougher plans in place, since they produce more manure. A farm like Mason Dixon deals with as much manure as forty-six Ontario farms. So while its ability to safeguard against problems and to handle manure responsibly is increased, so too is its potential threat to the environment. Despite the methane-driven power plant, Mason Dixon still needs a massive lagoon for liquid waste, as does Hawbaker's Hamilton Heights farm.

Both farms have to find innovative ways to deal with manure because they do not have enough land on which to spread it safely. Canadian dairy farms are, in many ways, an ideal mix of crop and livestock farming. The farmers grow feed crops for the cows, and their manure is spread on the fields as fertilizer. The typical Canadian dairy farm has about four or five acres per cow on which to spread manure. Mason Dixon has a little over one acre per cow, while Hawbaker has only half an acre per cow. That is too little soil to absorb so much manure, so other solutions had to be found. Because these farms focus on dairy, they do not grow all their own feed – buying it instead from farmers who specialize in feed crops, and who use chemical fertilizers because they do not have livestock operations to provide them with manure. This is the logic of specialization.

The Europeans had this sort of scenario in mind when they coined the term "multifunctionality." In justifying its massive subsidies to farmers, the European Union argues that farms play a much larger role than just providing food. Farms also protect the environment and take proper care of their livestock. Left to deal with strict market forces, farmers might be tempted to scrimp on these roles, threatening the environment and harming the animals. Paying subsidies is a way of contracting with farmers to perform their roles as stewards of their land and animals. Subsidies to farmers would also help maintain the viability of rural communities threatened by the depopulation of the countryside.

This arrangement is not unique to Europe. The city of New

York draws much of its drinking water from the Hudson River, which flows into the city from the Catskill Mountains. The city has an obvious interest in keeping the water clean and pays farmers in the Catskills to help them do just that. Each year, the city hands $5 million over to the Watershed Management Committee to be distributed to farmers who maintain a thirty-metre buffer along the Hudson River – three times the size of buffers on P.E.I. This is land kept out of farm production so that it can filter runoff from the farms before it reaches the river. The $5 million – rather than being used to pay for new filtration equipment in the city, which would just create sludge that would have to be dumped somewhere – was used to help farmers deal with the problem in an ecologically sound way. The farmers are not subsidized for taking land out of production, they are paid for providing a service to the city.

So far, however, multifunctionality has been dismissed by both the Canadian and U.S. governments as little more than an excuse by Europe to keep subsidizing farmers. The example most often cited is subsidies provided to farmers in the Alps to maintain small dairy operations with cows pasturing on mountainsides. The European Union decided that such farms were worth subsidizing because they attract tourists. Again, this approach to government spending is not unique. The city of Toronto gave a $6,500 property tax break to the Zanzibar strip club on Yonge Street to help beautify its front façade. The move was made as part of a wider program to improve the often-tawdry look of the city's most famous street in hopes of improving tourism.

So it seems that North American governments are not completely opposed to multifunctionality, although they would never use the word to describe their programs. The most recent plan to revitalize the farm aid programs in Canada contains some elements of multifunctionality in all but name. About $53 million a year, for five years, will be spent to help farmers set up environmental plans, take marginal farmland out of production, and improve water supplies.

Farmers welcomed parts of the new plan, glad to at least have some predictability added to the system. They were, however, disappointed that more was not done to offset American subsidies. In outlining the plan in December 2001, Vanclief said Canada had a reputation for providing high-quality and safe food. Around the world, the name "Canada" evokes images of purity and virtue that help sell food. In Britain, for instance, grocery stores hold "Canada Days" from time to time to promote Canadian products. Hilary Ross, a London-based trade lawyer, told a group of Ontario farmers and food exporters gathered in Toronto in February 2000 that grocery stores know their traffic will increase when they have a Canada promotion, because consumers there believe Canadian food is of higher quality than American. It is this belief that Vanclief hopes to capitalize on in his new program, which puts $150 million into boosting food exports.

As part of the environmental provisions of the federal aid package, farmers may be able to start setting up Integrated Pest Management programs. IPM is something many farmers like to say they do, but which few actually practise. Growing GM foods may discourage it. Under IPM, a farmer decides whether to spray herbicides and insecticides by comparing the cost of the chemicals with the increase in yield to be gained by spraying. If it costs more to spray than would be gained in increased yield, it does not make business sense for the farmer to spray. But once a farmer has paid the technology fee to grow a crop that's been genetically modified to resist weed killer, he is almost certainly going to spray for weeds – even if he does not have a significant weed problem that year. In fact, farmers growing GM crops spray for weeds more often than they did on conventional crops. Most of the cost of controlling weeds is tied up in the technology fee, so farmers figure they should get their money's worth by spraying more often.

Terry Daynard, who set up the Ontario Corn Producers Association in 1985, is a strong proponent of genetically modified crops. Biotechnology, he says, is just one of many "tools" farmers need to have at their disposal to fight pests. But the heavy use of GM crops shows that the technology quickly becomes the dominant tool used by farmers, not just one of many. A farmer growing conventional corn under an IPM system assesses how many cobs would be lost to worms if he does not spray insecticide. If the worm infestation is bad, he is more likely to spray. If the infection is not too bad, however, the farmer might, instead, use other methods to control bugs and weeds, such as crop rotations or intercropping, and spray less often. The farmer could even choose to grow something else one year to break pests' life cycles. But a farmer growing corn that's been modified to kills bugs has decided long before any bugs have threatened his field how he will handle them. By growing Bt corn, he has ruled out IPM as a management tool on his farm. With almost all the soybean crop and half the Canadian corn and canola crops now genetically modified, it would seem that most Canadian crop farmers are not looking for ways to integrate their pest management strategies.

Heavy use of any pest control measure, whether chemicals or genetic modification, enables pests to build up a resistance. Odd as it may sound, pests building resistance to Bt corn could be good for biotechnology companies, as farmers would have to switch to new strains of GM corn to kill the new superbugs. Charles Benbrook says it would be to Monsanto's advantage, as well, if heavy use of Roundup Ready crops makes Roundup useless because weeds developed a resistance. The company could then go to market with a new chemical protected by a separate patent and costing more. After the patent expired on Roundup in the 1990s, the price dropped by half. "These companies are duty-bound under law to maximize their returns to shareholders," he says. "Unfortunately, for Monsanto, burning up Roundup is what's best for shareholders." Already, ryegrass in Australia has been found to be resistant to Roundup, as has horseweed in New Jersey and Maryland and waterhemp in Missouri, Illinois, and Iowa.

But by encouraging IPM programs, the government could help extend the useful life of such products as Bt corn and Roundup Ready crops. Under IPM, genetically modified crops would be used only as a backup, when less intrusive and less controversial measures failed. As it is, genetically modified crops are pushing out all others, and in the process rendering themselves useless.

In the meantime, Ottawa risks allowing a citizen backlash to kill biotechnology. Turning the tide means more than public relations on the industry's behalf, as has been the past practice. It means breaking the conflict of interest at the Canadian Food Inspection Agency, which was charged with both ensuring the safety of genetically modified foods and promoting them. It may be able to perform both duties, but its role as a promoter tends to undermine its assertion that GM foods are safe. Consumers can't be sure whether the safety assurances are coming from the CFIA's promotional arm or its regulatory arm. In its report in August 2002, the federal government's Canadian Biotechnology Advisory Committee said the perceived conflict of interest had hampered the public's acceptance of GM foods and called for "effective independence of regulatory functions."

Barry Commoner's article in *Harper's* is a good reminder of just how little we know about the changes being made to the earth's organisms through genetic modification, changes that are irreversible. Once a company has inserted a new gene into a plant or animal, that gene begins to spread throughout the species. We have seen this already in Mexico's corn and the canola grown on the Canadian prairies. Making a small change to one variety of plant or animal will eventually alter the genome of the entire species. That is part of the wonder of nature and the danger of pursuing biotechnology without considering properly where we are going. The stakes are simply too high for us to blunder ahead out of fear for the profit margins of a few companies.

At the BIO 2002 conference, Greenpeace founder Patrick Moore ridiculed the notion that we should take a cautious approach to new technology. "If you took the precautionary principle to the extreme, you would never cross the street for fear of being hit by a car," he said. Well, nobody is talking about taking this to an extreme. The idea is to just look both ways before crossing the street. Canadian taxpayers paid to get the biotechnology revolution started here through government grants to the companies to conduct research, and continue to do so through matching grants to universities that work with industry in developing new products. As well, generous patent laws have allowed the industry to flourish here. These laws have added millions of dollars to the cost of drugs, crippling the medicare system cherished by Canadians. For all this, Canadians deserve a stronger and direct say in the future of biotechnology.

Research at publicly funded universities is dominated by industry. Even government-funded research is tied to industry-backed projects. This undermines the credibility of university research. Just as the CFIA is in a conflict of interest by both promoting GM foods and ensuring their safety, universities are in a conflict by serving both industry and taxpayers. In Britain, a survey published by the *Times Higher Education Supplement* in 2000 found that one-third of scientists in government or recently privatized labs had been asked to change research findings to suit their sponsoring company's desires, and 10 per cent were pressured to bend results to secure research contracts.

In September 2001, frustrated editors of the world's leading medical journals – *Canadian Medical Association Journal*, the *New England Journal of Medicine*, *The Lancet*, the *British Medical Journal*, and the *Journal of the American Medical Association* – published a joint editorial declaring that they would no longer publish papers based on corporate-sponsored research without guarantees of scientific independence by the researchers and full access to all data. "I've had it up to here, had it up the wazoo, had it up the eyebrows with the tricks people have played," Drummond Rennie, deputy editor of the *Journal of the American Medical Association*, told reporters. The "tricks" included suppressing unfavourable results and rewriting already published favourable studies and then resubmitting them for publication to multiply their effect.

Science that comes primarily from companies with a vested interest will never be fully trusted, especially when industry treats science as a public relations tool. Such practices risk undermining the reputation of science in general, a chancy proposition as we develop from an industrial economy to a knowledge-based economy founded in science. For Canadians to embrace that evolution, they need to be able to trust both the scientists and their science.

Peter Cumming, who grows soybeans near Blenheim, Ontario, has found a way to keep his farm small and manageable, much like Dan Weins has. But instead of selling to customers in the nearest city, Cumming sells to a company on the other side of the world. He grows soybeans under contract for a Japanese food company and has weaned himself off government aid. He has his own equipment for cleaning his machinery, as well as a small machine for cleaning the soybeans before delivering them to market, boosting their value. He has turned his entire farm over to growing crops under strict contracts called identity preservation, or IP, and hasn't collected a government subsidy in years. "You can go out of business waiting for the government to help," says Cumming.

Cumming grows a variety of soybeans that's made into snacks in Japan. They have to be perfect, since the snack is sold in clear plastic bags, so Cumming's IP contract is especially strict. All it takes is one weed in his harvest for the entire thirty-acre crop to be rejected at the elevator. If that happened, Cumming would have put in all the extra work required under his contract, but be forced to take the much lower commodity price for his crop. He has to weed by hand to make sure he gets everything. He also has to clean his machinery very carefully to ensure the purity of the crop until delivery and keep a paper trail of all his work to prove that he has preserved the identity of the crop. "The risks can be pretty high," he says.

But the results are worth it. The crop sells for more than double the going price at the Chicago Board of Trade. Cumming figures that once he factors in all the extra care the IP contract stipulates – including the hand weeding, the paper work, the slower harvest, the cleaning, and the lower yield – he makes about 20 per cent more than if he had grown regular soybeans. Cumming is happy. "No farmer should be unhappy with 20 per cent more money," he says. "In fact, these days, that's pretty damn good."

Any financial assistance to farmers to explore such niche markets would be more of an investment than an expense. It would help farmers find ways to make their money from the market instead of government aid programs. The same holds true for helping farmers switch to organic production. To be certified organic, farms must grow under organic's strict production rules for three years before they can sell their produce at the higher price available to organic farmers. The three-year transition is meant to cleanse the farm's soil of all the chemicals and artificial fertilizers used before the organic farming began. During those years, however, productivity on the farms drops off dramatically while the soil replenishes itself.

Farmers operating on very tight margins can rarely afford three years of diminished yield, even if the future holds the promise of higher and more stable prices. Strict new government standards are now in place for organic products in the United States, and Canada could help farmers here adjust their production methods to meet those standards. The organics market is expanding at 20 per cent a year, according to most estimates. Since the only hurdle to fulfilling that demand is the onerous transition period for farmers, it makes long-term financial sense for the government to help farmers tap into that market.

Taxpayers' money need not be used to prop up an unsustainable system of industrial agriculture. Bailing out farmers has only driven down the price of commodities, which has hurt them down the line. The only ones to benefit from the drop in prices are the companies buying the produce. Rather than continuing with a system of subsidies that ends up fattening the bottom line of the big food companies, taxpayers' money might be better invested in finding new, more profitable, ways for farmers to make their money from the land.

But there would be cultural hurdles to overcome. Nettie Weibe, another organic farmer in Saskatchewan and past president of the

National Farmers Union, says farm kids are raised to respect their parents, and for them to convert their farms to organic is seen as rejecting their elders' knowledge and skill. It's insulting. For older farmers to convert their farms to organic would mean turning their backs on a lifetime's work. "When they took over their farms, they came in with new ideas and new ways of doing things," Weibe says. "To change things now would be like admitting that they were wrong." With decades of Green Revolution statistics to back them up, few in today's generation of farmers are likely to follow Barry Hamilton's organic lead and change how they operate, however much he may be turning a few heads in Rose Valley. That's why the emphasis must be on the next generation, who have grown up more with the Green Revolution's disappointments than its early stellar successes. They can more readily grasp that just as the world changed when their parents took over the farms – requiring new ways of farming – the world is again changing and new ways of farming are once more needed. And just as the Green Revolution got much of its seed money from government, so too should this one.

According to the agricultural census released in November 2002, 20 per cent of Canada's farmers are expected to retire by 2011 and will be replaced by young farmers taking over not only their parents' farm, but also those of their neighbours. According to the census, farmers under thirty-five are twice as likely to run a big farm – with annual receipts of $250,000 or more – than are farmers fifty-five or older. As older farmers retire, with fewer young farmers to replace them, the trend to bigger farms will continue without efforts to stem their development.

When the Dairy Farmers of Canada began its lobbying effort to overturn a WTO ruling against supply management, it sent delegates to Europe to discuss the issue with farm groups, trade experts, and government officials there. They also met with the editorial boards of trade journals, but not with mainstream newspapers. I asked

Richard Doyle, the DFC's executive director, why they went all that way to meet with editors and writers from publications with such limited readership, but stayed away from those with a broad readership. "Isn't it public opinion you're trying to change?" I asked. No, he said, public opinion didn't need changing. It was the opinion of those involved in international trade that needed changing. "The people who sit on the dispute panels read these journals," he said. "That's why we're seeing them."

When those affected by the WTO's decisions see no value in getting public opinion on their side, and instead focus on the trading class, the WTO has seriously eroded the world's democracies. Breaking down the secrecy of the WTO would stem that erosion, to the benefit of farmers and city folk alike. The WTO can overrule the laws of member countries that it deems to be interfering with the free flow of goods and services. It is under this principle that the United States has challenged supply management and has taken aim at the wheat board. And as more countries turn to the WTO to settle international disputes, they legitimize the organization as a higher level of government by deferring to it on issues they once tried to resolve on their own. With each dispute the WTO settles, its legitimacy as an international government strengthens.

It's hard to blame the DFC for its tactics. It is, after all, dealing with a food system that has little to do with the food itself. It is a system based on market share, exports, and the creation of wealth. Food is just a means to these ends, and government policies that favour industrial production only perpetuate this perception of the role of food. In the same way, the solutions offered by the food companies only perpetuate the problems they seek to solve.

Home meal replacements were originally marketed as a way to get a quick meal on busy days, but soon became the norm in many families. They became less a way to gain some advantage, and more a necessity in our hectic world. And just as tractors and other farm equipment quickly moved from being time savers to being ways to allow farms to get bigger, time-saving products in the home soon moved from being mere conveniences to necessities. And the companies making them, rather than finding ways to help us simplify our lives, flood the market with products that perpetuate – even encourage – this hectic and stressful lifestyle. They are no more likely to encourage us to slow down and eat fewer of their products than Monsanto is to advise a farmer to go organic and cut his costs.

No one can blame them for that. They are in business to make money, and they make a lot of it by operating in a system based on the things they do best – gaining market share, boosting exports, and creating wealth. That was what the dairy farmers at our lunch in York, Pennsylvania, were facing as they toured those big farms south of the border. We got a rare peek at what the future held for Canada if those priorities were left unchecked.

Dan Weins says his farm south of Winnipeg is not the solution, but the thought processes that led to it are. It's a thought process more of us need to go through, from consumers to food companies to farmers. We all need to put the emphasis of the agricultural system back on food. Good food should be produced for the sake of good food, not because it can gain a company market share. Canada's image as a source of good food should stem from our desire to eat well, not from some ambition to boost exports. We should produce food that doesn't kill fish or send children running inside at recess to escape the pesticides. We should do these things not just because it's better for our wholesome image abroad to do so, or even because we believe the food on our plate would be better for us, but because it would be better for the planet.

We need to think about these things, and we need to think about them before it's too late.

SELECTED BIBLIOGRAPHY

BOOKS

Douglas Baldwin. *Land of the Red Soil: A Popular History of Prince Edward Island*. Charlottetown: Ragweed Press, 1998.

Tanya Basok. *Tortillas and Tomatoes: Transmigrant Mexican Harvesters in Canada*. Montreal & Kingston: McGill-Queen's University Press, 2002.

Wendell Berry. *The Art of the Common Place: The Agrarian Essays of Wendell Berry*. Edited and introduced by Norman Wirzba. Washington, D.C.: Counterpoint, 2002.

Wendell Berry. *What Are People For?* San Francisco: North Point Press, 1990.

Ingeborg Boyens. *Another Season's Promise: Hope and Despair in Canada's Farm Country*. Toronto: Penguin/Viking, 2001.

Ingeborg Boyens. *Unnatural Harvest: How Genetic Engineering Is Altering Our Food*. Toronto: Doubleday Canada, 1999.

Daniel Charles. *Lords of the Harvest: Biotech, Big Money, and the Future of Food*. Cambridge: Perseus Publishing, 2001.

Ann Cooper, with Lisa Holmes. *Bitter Harvest: A Chef's Perspective on the Hidden Dangers in the Food We Eat and What You Can Do About It*. London & New York: Routledge, 2000.

Roger Epp and Dave Whitson, eds. *Writing Off the Rural West: Globalization, Governments, and the Transformation of Rural Communities.* Edmonton: University of Alberta Press, 2001.

Grains and Oilseeds: Handling, Marketing and Processing. Fourth Edition. Winnipeg: Canadian International Grains Institute, 1993.

Kathleen Hart. *Eating in the Dark: America's Experiment with Genetically Engineered Food.* New York: Pantheon Books, 2002.

Craig Heron. *Working in Steel: The Early Years in Canada, 1883–1935.* Toronto: McClelland & Stewart, 1988.

Phil Jenkins. *Fields of Vision: A Journey to Canada's Family Farms.* Toronto: McClelland & Stewart, 1991.

Brewster Kneen. *Farmageddon: Food and the Culture of Biotechnology.* Gabriola Island, B.C.: New Society Publishers, 1999.

Brewster Kneen. *Invisible Giant: Cargill and Its Transnational Strategies.* Halifax: Fernwood Publishing, 1995.

Brewster Kneen. *From Land to Mouth: Understanding the Food System, Second Helping.* Toronto: NC Press, 1993.

Brewster Kneen. *The Rape of Canola.* Toronto: NC Press, 1992.

Bill Lambrecht. *Dinner at the New Gene Café: How Genetic Engineering Is Changing What We Eat, How We Live, and the Global Politics of Food.* New York: Thomas Dunne Books, 2001.

William Leiss. *In the Chamber of Risks: Understanding Risk Controversies.* Montreal & Kingston: McGill-Queen's University Press, 2001.

James Lieber. *Rats in the Grain: The Dirty Tricks and Trials of Archer Daniels Midland, the Supermarket to the World.* New York: Four Walls Eight Windows, 2000.

Ian MacLachlan. *Kill and Chill: Restructuring Canada's Beef Commodity Chain.* Toronto: University of Toronto Press, 2001.

Alan McHughen. *Pandora's Picnic Basket: The Potential and Hazards of Genetically Modified Foods.* New York: Oxford University Press, 2000.

Charlotte Montgomery. *Blood Relations: Animals, Humans, and Politics.* Toronto: Between The Lines, 2000.

William Morriss. *Chosen Instrument II: A History of the Canadian Wheat Board: New Horizons*. Winnipeg: The Canadian Wheat Board, 2000.

William Morriss. *Chosen Instrument: A History of the Canadian Wheat Board: The McIvor Years*. Winnipeg: The Canadian Wheat Board, 1987.

Marion Nestle. *Food Politics: How the Food Industry Influences Nutrition and Health*. Berkeley: University of California Press, 2002.

Gregory Pence. *Designer Food: Mutant Harvest or Breadbasket of the World?* Lanham, Maryland: Rowman and Littlefield Publishers, 2002.

Peter Phillips and Robert Wolfe, eds. *Governing Food: Science, Safety and Trade*. Montreal & Kingston: McGill-Queen's University Press, 2001.

Per Pinstrup-Andersen and Ebbe Schioler. *Seeds of Contention: World Hunger and the Global Controversy over GM Crops*. Baltimore: Johns Hopkins University Press, 2000.

Michael Pollan. *The Botany of Desire: A Plant's-Eye View of the World*. New York: Random House, 2001.

Douglas Powell and William Leiss. *Mad Cows and Mother's Milk: The Perils of Poor Risk Communication*. Montreal & Kingston: McGill-Queen's University Press, 1997.

Sheldon Rampton and John Stauber. *Trust Us, We're Experts: How Industry Manipulates Science and Gambles with Your Future*. New York: Penguin Putnam, 2002.

Jeremy Rifkin. *Beyond Beef: The Rise of the Cattle Culture*. New York: Dutton Books, 1992.

Wayne Roberts, Rod MacRae, and Lori Stahlbrand. *Real Food For a Change*. New York: Random House, 1999.

Eric Schlosser. *Fast Food Nation: The Dark Side of the All-American Meal*. New York: Houghton Mifflin Company, 2001.

Vandana Shiva. *Stolen Harvest: The Hijacking of the Global Food Supply*. Cambridge: South End Press, 2000.

Vandana Shiva. *Biopiracy: The Plunder of Nature and Knowledge.* Cambridge: South End Press, 1997.

Vandana Shiva. *The Violence of the Green Revolution: Third World Agriculture, Ecology and Politics.* London: Zed Books, 1991.

Steven Shrybman. *The World Trade Organization: A Citizen's Guide.* Toronto: The Canadian Centre for Policy Alternatives and James Lorimer & Company Ltd., 2001.

Upton Sinclair. *The Jungle.* First published 1906. London: Penguin Classics, 1986.

Adam Smith. *The Wealth of Nations: Books I-II.* First published 1776. London: Penguin Classics, 1999.

Margaret Somerville. *The Ethical Canary: Science, Society and the Human Spirit.* Toronto: Viking, 2000.

Michael J. Trebilcock and Robert Howse. *The Regulation of International Trade.* London & New York: Routledge, 1997.

Neil Tudiver. *Universities for Sale: Resisting Corporate Control over Canadian Higher Education.* Toronto: James Lorimer and Company, 1999.

Lori Wallach and Michelle Sforza. *Whose Trade Organization? Corporate Globalization and the Erosion of Democracy.* Washington, D.C.: Public Citizen, 1999.

Allen Wilford. *Farm Gate Defense: The Story of the Canadian Farmers Survival Association.* Toronto: NC Press, 1984.

Barry Wilson. *Beyond the Harvest: Canadian Grain at the Crossroads.* Saskatoon: Western Producer Prairie Books, 1981.

Anthony Winson. *The Intimate Commodity: Food and the Development of the Agro-Industrial Complex in Canada.* Toronto: Garamond Press, 1993.

REPORTS

Auditor-General of Canada. *Canadian Wheat Board, Special Audit Report.* 2002.

Charles Benbrook. *Troubled Times Amid Commercial Success for Roundup Ready Soybeans*. 2001. Northwest Science and Environmental Policy Centre.

Brandon Homelessness Steering Committee. *Community Action Plan on Homelessness*. 2002.

British Ministry of Agriculture, Fisheries and Food. *The BSE Inquiry: The Report*. 2000.

British Competition Commission. *Supermarkets: A Report on the Supply of Groceries from Multiple Stores in the United Kingdom*. 2000.

Canadian Biotechnology Advisory Committee. *Annual Report*. 1999–2000.

Canadian Biotechnology Advisory Committee. *Improving the Regulation of Genetically Modified Foods and Other Novel Foods in Canada*. 2002.

Canadian Food Inspection Agency. *Annual Report*. 2000–2001.

Canadian Food Inspection Agency. *Report on the Investigation of Commodities Imported from Europe, 1990–2000*. 2001.

Kerstin Dressel. *The Cultural Politics of Science and Decision-Making: An Anglo-German Comparison of Risk Political Cultures*. 2000. Doctoral Thesis. University of Munich.

Food and Consumer Products Manufacturers of Canada. *Member Report*. 2002.

Food and Agriculture Organization. *The State of Food Insecurity in the World, 2002*.

Food and Agriculture Organization. *World Food Summit Technical Background Papers*. 1996.

Gary Gardner and Brian Halweil. *Underfed and Overfed: The Global Epidemic of Malnutrition*. 2000. Worldwatch Institute.

Kevin Grier. *What Is the Impact of Manufacturing Consolidation on the Grocer Sector?* 2000. George Morris Centre.

William Heffernan and Mary Hendrickson. *Multi-National Concentrated Food Processing and Marketing Systems and the Farm Crisis*. 2002. University of Missouri.

International Food Policy Research Institute. *Livestock to 2020: The Next Food Revolution*. 1999.

Devlin Kuyek. *The Real Board of Directors: The Construction of Biotechnology Policy in Canada, 1980–2002*. 2002. The Ram's Horn.

Owen Lippert. *The Perfect Food in a Perfect Mess: The Cost of Milk in Canada*. 2001. Fraser Institute.

Loblaw Companies. *Annual Reports*.

Maple Leaf Foods. *Annual Reports*.

Larry Martin. *Taking the Bull by the Horns: Reinventing the Canadian Agri-food Sector for the 21st Century*. George Morris Centre.

Larry Martin, Ron Ball, and John Alexiou. *Cost Competitiveness of the Canadian Pork Processing Industry*. 1997. George Morris Centre.

Larry Martin and Kate Stiefelmeyer. *A Comparative Analysis of Productivity in Agri-Food Processing in Canada and the United States*. George Morris Centre.

Al Mussell and Larry Martin. *Firm-Level Forces Underlying Concentration in Agriculture*. 1999. George Morris Centre.

David Nelson and David Bianc. *Senate Testimony on Legislation to Impede Food Industry M&A, and Chartbook*. 2000. Credit Suisse First Boston.

Prime Minister's Caucus Task Force. *Future Opportunities in Farming*. April 2002.

Darrin Qualman. *The Farm Crisis and Corporate Power*. 2001. National Farmers Union.

Rounds and Associates. *The Socio-Economic Impact of Maple Leaf Pork in Brandon*. 2000.

Rounds and Associates. *Current and Future Needs for Housing in the City of Brandon and Surrounding Region*. 2001.

Royal Society of Canada. *Elements of Precaution: Recommendations for the Regulation of Food Biotechnology in Canada*. 2001.

David Schroeder, Sean Mason, and Eric Eng. *Branded Consumer Products*. 1999. Dominion Bond Rating Service.

David Schroeder, Alden Greenhouse, and Sean Mason. *The Grain Industry in Canada*. 2001. Dominion Bond Rating Service.

Statistics Canada. *Intensive Livestock Farming: Does Size Matter?* 2001.

John Tuxill. *Nature's Cornucopia: Our Stake in Plant Diversity.* 1999. Worldwatch Institute.

United States General Accounting Office. *Mad Cow Disease: Improvements in the Annual Feed Ban and Other Regulatory Areas Would Strengthen U.S. Prevention Efforts.* 2002.

United States International Trade Commission. *Wheat Trading Practices: Competitive Conditions Between U.S. and Canadian Wheat.* 2001.

United States Department of Agriculture. *Adoption of Bioengineered Crops. Agricultural Economic Report No. 810.* 2002.

United States Department of Agriculture. *Broiler Farms' Organization, Management and Performance. Agricultural Information Bulletin No. 748.* 1999.

United States Department of Agriculture. *Consolidation in U.S. Meatpacking.* 2000.

United States Department of Agriculture. *Economic Issues in Agricultural Biotechnology.* 2001.

United States Department of Agriculture. *Milk Pricing in the United States.* 2001.

United States Department of Agriculture. *U.S.–Canada Wheat Trade: The Intersection of Geography and Economics. Commodity Spotlight, Agricultural Outlook.* 1999.

JOURNALS, MAGAZINES, AND NEWSPAPERS

The Grower
Milk Producer
Ontario Farmer
The Western Producer
Nature

LISTSERVS AND ON-LINE MAGAZINES

agbioworld.org

agnet

businesswire.com

dairy-outlook-owner (fao.org)

datamonitor.com

foodincanada.com

iatp.com

just-food.com

meatingplace.com

prwatch.org

bivings-alert

INDEX

A&P supermarkets, 238
ACNielsen Canada, 186–87
Adam, Nadege, 142
Advancement of Sound Science
    Coalition, 112
AGCare, 116–18
Agency for International
    Development (U.S.), 71
Agent Orange, 97–98
Agricultural chemicals, 58–82,
    86–87, 97, 99, 129–30,
    140–41, 195, 220, 246–47; *see
    also* name of specific chemical
Agricultural machinery, 85–86,
    196
Agricultural policy, Canadian,
    153–54
Agricultural subsidies, *see*
    Subsidies, agricultural
Agriculture Canada, 58, 114–15,
    121, 134
AIDS, 227–31
Aldrin, 78
Allen, Shawn, 48
Allmond, Jeffery, 11
APCO Associates, 112
Archer Daniels Midland (ADM),
    161, 164, 191, 208

Artificial insemination, 29–30
Asthma, 61
Astra Pharma, 61
Atlantic Monthly, 76
Auld, Neila, 60
Australia, 171, 185
Aventis, 102, 121, 125, 127, 143
Avery, Denis, 123

Bacillus thuringiensis (Bt), 92,
    96–97, 105–9, 116, 118, 128,
    141–43, 247
Baksa, Cory, 42
Baltimore Sun, 28
Bardocz, Susan, 94–95
Basok, Tanya, 204–5, 207
Bayer, 65
Bee, David, 6–10, 15, 18–19
Beef industry, 12–14, 39–42,
    194–95
Beernink, Tony, 207
Belay, Ghebre-Medhin, 214–15
Bello, Mallam Adamu, 217
Benbrook, Charles, 109, 130,
    137–42, 247
Bennett, William, 149
Benzene hexachloride, 78
Berlusconi, Silvio, 222

263